opposite 1

12

28

35-36

FIGHTING THE FLYING CIRCUS

Capt. Eddie Rickenbacker

FIGHTING THE FLYING CIRCUS

BY

CAPT. EDWARD V. RICKENBACKER

COMMANDING OFFICER 94TH PURSUIT SQUADRON
U. S. AIR SERVICE

WITH MAPS AND A FOREWORD BY
LAURENCE LA TOURETTE DRIGGS

NEW YORK
FREDERICK A. STOKES COMPANY
PUBLISHERS

FOREWORD

Eddie Rickenbacker's stories of his air battles in France are of exciting interest, both in the narration of the thrilling adventures with enemy airmen and in the revealment to the reader of his intimate thoughts and feelings, as he went out day after day to attack the boasted champions of the German Air Service.

How do they feel — of what are they thinking — where is their fear — what emotions predominate in the minds of these boys so youthful and so daring, who are the targets for thousands of deadly projectiles every moment of their flights across the battle lines of the enemy? These questions puzzle one's mind as one follows in imagination the giddy course of the aviator through enemy skies. And here Captain Rickenbacker in his story depicts his own ordinary human emotions, with a detail and an intimacy so unreserved that we feel we are following step by step the development of character of a master air-fighter, who is preordained to success.

Eddie Rickenbacker was the idol of the automobile racing world at the moment when America entered the war. He was then in England, engaged in the production of a racing car with which to win further laurels in his profession. Burning with the desire to enter war aviation and convinced of the advantages which his racing experiences would give him in this exciting sport of the air, he returned to New York where he sought to enlist all the automobile racing men into one Squadron of fighting pilots. But official enthusiasm could not be aroused in Washington for this project, and necessary funds were lacking. What such an all-star unit might have accomplished in France fires the imagination!

Mindful of the delays which the consummation of his plan might occasion, Eddie Rickenbacker suddenly accepted General Pershing's invitation to sail with him next day. He enlisted in the infantry and became the driver of the General's automobile at the front, where he wisely foresaw he would find a quicker opportunity for entering the flying service.

In eighteen months he returned, the American Ace of Aces!

Captain Rickenbacker deserves the gratitude of the American people, not only because he is the American Ace of Aces — not only because he destroyed twenty-six German aircraft in combat — but more especially because the extraordinary inspiration of his example at the front and his ability as a Squadron leader brought very remarkable success to many other American air-fighters who were under his leadership.

After having visited some sixty-odd British flying squadrons at the front, many of the French Esca-drilles and all of the American Squadrons, I was given the pleasure of entering Germany, after the Armistice was signed, as the guest of the Hat-in-the-Ring Squadron, of which Captain Rickenbacker was and is the Commanding Officer. In no other organization in France did I find so great a loyalty to a leader, such true Squadron fraternalism, such subordination of the individual to the organization. In other words, the Commander of 94 Squadron had perfected the finest flying corps I have ever seen.

This recognition of the author's character is essential to an adequate appreciation of his story. Between the lines one is impressed with the constant desire of perfecting himself that permeates his every combat. Rickenbacker is full of the feeling of responsibility

that every true leader must know. He is frankly
scared over the additional risks that leadership must
force upon him. Yet he carries on, assuming these
additional risks, which in truth not only limit his
private successes but constantly threaten to sacrifice
his life for a companion.

If he had been a free lance, Eddie Rickenbacker
might easily have doubled his score of victories even
in the short period of America's service in the war.
Without the duty of directing the movements and
guarding the safety of his less competent pilots, he
would have had both the time and the opportunity for
brilliant successes innumerable.

Never once in all his fighting career did Captain
Rickenbacker permit an enemy pilot to injure him!

This remarkable fact at once forces the conclusion
that our American Ace of Aces was not only superior
to the enemy airmen he vanquished, but by saving himself for the continued service of his country he was
superior to all those rival expert duelists who, despite
their extraordinary ability as pilots and sharpshooters,
yet unfortunately lacked that necessary judgment to
preserve from wounds their valuable persons for
further encounters with the enemy.

The Hat-in-the-Ring Squadron ended the war with
the greatest number of victories won by any American
Squadron. It was the first to go over the enemy's
lines — it was the first to destroy an enemy machine
— it brought down the last Hun aeroplane to fall in
this war.

It contained the first American Ace, Douglas Campbell, of California, and the greatest American Ace,
Eddie Rickenbacker, of Ohio. It totalled more hours
of flying over enemy lines than any other American
Squadron can claim. And finally, 94 Squadron was
given the distinction it so richly deserved when it was
selected as the only fighting Squadron in all our forces

to move into Germany with our Army of Occupation.

To the leadership of Captain Rickenbacker this crack Squadron of American pilots owes its proud position. It will go down in history as the greatest Fighting Squadron America sent to the war.

Popular as Eddie Rickenbacker is at home, that popularity does not equal the esteem in which he is held by airmen in France. Perhaps no soldier to-day holds quite so high a position in the hearts of the American aviators and the American public as does Captain Eddie Rickenbacker. I am sure it is due him to say, none could deserve it more.

LAURENCE LA TOURETTE DRIGGS.

CONTENTS

CONTENTS

GLOSSARY OF EXPRESSIONS USED IN AVIATION

ACE. A fighting pilot who has brought down five enemy machines.

ARCHY. Anti-aircraft shells.

AERODROME. Field where aeroplanes land and live.

BANK. To tilt an aeroplane sideways in rounding a corner.

BARREL. Rolling the aeroplane over and over in air, like a barrel.

BIPLACE. Two places or seats, a two-seater aeroplane. A monoplace has but one seat. A triplace has three.

BIPLANE. Aeroplane with two sets of wings, an upper and a lower. A monoplane has but one set of wings. A triplane has three.

CEILING. Topmost level an aeroplane can reach.

CHANDELLE. To make an upward corkscrew climb.

CONTACT. To put on the spark.

COUPEZ. Cut off the spark.

DUD. Dead, or bad.

HANGAR. Garage for housing aeroplanes.

JAGSTAFFEL. German term for fighting squadron.

JOYSTICK. The aeroplane's steering and control lever.

OFFICE. The cockpit of an aeroplane, where the pilot sits.

PANNE. A forced landing caused by engine failure.

PIQUE. To dive vertically downwards, with engine either open or shut.

RENVERSEMENT. A sudden reversal of direction of flight. This is not to be confused with "bank," as the latter is a slow movement. A renversement is usually executed by suddenly zooming up, then throwing the aeroplane over onto one wing and kicking the tail around to the rear.

SAUCE. Petrol or gasoline.

STRAFING. Assailing an enemy with bullets or bombs.

VIRAGE. A bank or circle in the air.

VOLUNTARY PATROL. A voluntary flight by a pilot over the lines.

VRILLE. A tail-spin. The aeroplane falls earthward, with tail above always swinging around the nose of the machine, which acts as a pivot. The motion is similar to the rotation of a match in a whirlpool.

WIND UP. Scared, having the wind go up one's spine, causing the hair to stand on end with fear.

ZOOM. To pitch the aeroplane suddenly upwards at great speed. Usually accomplished after a dive has given the aeroplane additional momentum.

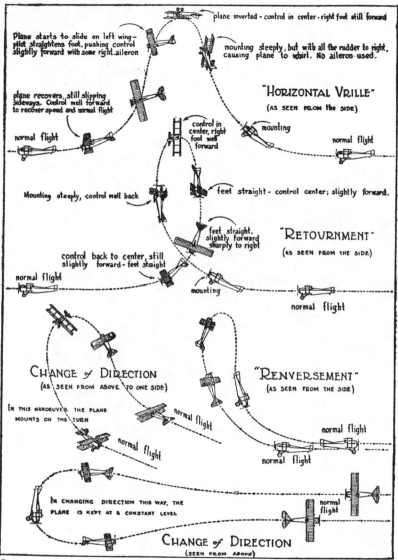

plane inverted - control in center - right foot still forward

Plane starts to slide on left wing - pilot straightens foot, pushing control slightly forward with some right aileron

mounting steeply, but with all the rudder to right, causing plane to whirl. No aileron used.

plane recovers, still slipping sideways. Control well forward to recover speed and normal flight

"HORIZONTAL VRILLE"

(AS SEEN FROM the SIDE)

normal flight

mounting

normal flight

control in center, right foot well forward

Mounting steeply, control well back

feet straight - control center; slightly forward.

feet straight. slightly forward sharply to right

"RETOURNMENT"

(AS SEEN FROM THE SIDE)

control back to center, still slightly forward - feet straight

normal flight

mounting

normal flight

CHANGE of DIRECTION

(AS SEEN FROM ABOVE TO ONE SIDE)

IN THIS MANOEUVER THE PLANE MOUNTS ON THE TURN

"RENVERSEMENT"

(AS SEEN FROM THE SIDE)

normal flight

normal flight

normal flight

normal flight

normal flight

IN CHANGING DIRECTION THIS WAY, THE PLANE IS KEPT AT A CONSTANT LEVEL

normal flight

CHANGE of DIRECTION

(SEEN FROM ABOVE)

By courtesy of the New York Evening World

FIGHTING THE FLYING CIRCUS

CHAPTER I

INTRODUCING "ARCHY"

AFTER days of schooling and nights of anticipation, I woke up one morning to find my dreams come true. Major Raoul Lufbery, the most famous of our American flyers, and the Commanding Officer of our group, announced that a flight would take off after breakfast for a look at the war across the German lines. He himself was to lead the flight. The patrol was to be over enemy territory in the Champagne sector.

"Who is to go?" was the thought in every pilot's mind, as we all stood by in more or less unconcealed eagerness. None of us had as yet caught a glimpse of our future arenas. We all had vague ideas of the several kinds of surprises in store for us over Hun lines and every one of us was keen to get into it.

Major Lufbery looked us over without saying much. Luf was very quiet in manner and very droll when he wanted to be. He had seen almost four years of service with the French Air Service and in the Lafayette Escadrille and had shot down seventeen Hun aeroplanes before the American Air Service began active work at the front. Every one of us idolized Lufbery.

"Rick!" said the Major casually, "you and Campbell be ready to leave at 8.15."

I tried to appear nonchalant as I replied, "Yes, sir."

Douglas Campbell put up a much better face than I did. The other boys crowded around and presented us with good advice, such as "Look out for Archy,

1

mind," and one thoughtful fellow kindly cautioned me to crash in our lines if the Huns got me, so that he could personally put a cross over my grave.

That memorable morning was the 6th day of March, 1918. I had joined the Hat-in-the-Ring Squadron just two days before at Villeneuve. We were then some twenty miles behind the lines and were well installed on an old aerodrome that had been used previously by several French Aero Squadrons. This expedition was to be the first essay over the lines by a made-in-America Squadron.

Sharp upon eight o'clock I walked into the 94th Squadron hangar and called my mechanics. We were flying the French single-seater Nieuport with a rotary motor, and every machine was kept in the pink of condition at all times. Nevertheless I wanted to make doubly sure that everything was right on this occasion, for Major Lufbery had a reputation for punctuality.

" Henry," I demanded, " how is my Number 1 ? "

" Best machine in the shop, sir," the mechanic replied. " She's been all tuned up since you came in last night and there's not a scratch on her."

" There will be when you see her again," I muttered. " Run her out on the field and warm her up."

I left the hangar and looked down the road for the Major. Campbell was already in his flying clothes. I wanted to be ready on the exact minute, but not too soon. So I lit a cigarette and kept an eye on the Major's door. All the boys came sauntering up, trying to look as though they were not half mad with envy over my chance to get my head blown off first. They wished me well, they said, but they would like to know what to do with my personal effects.

When Major Lufbery entered the hangar he found us ready for him. It takes about ten seconds to step into your Teddy-Bear suit, slip a flying helmet over your head and snap on the glasses. Campbell and I climbed into our Nieuports. The Major gave a few instructions to Lieutenant Campbell, then came over to me. I felt like a man in the chair when the dentist approaches. Of course I listened politely to his parting words, but the only thing that appealed to me in his discourse was the order to stick close to him and keep formation. He did not have to repeat that order. Never before did I realize how seductively cold death beckons a pilot towards his first trip over enemy lines.

Lufbery ran up his motor for a moment, then took off. Campbell followed upon his heels and then I opened up my throttle. I cast a last, longing glance at the familiar flying field as I felt my tail go up, the wheels began to skim the ground and with the wind in my teeth I pulled her up and headed after Campbell. What a devil of a hurry they were in! I knew I should never catch up with them.

The beautiful ruins of Rheims soon spread beneath my right wing. My machine was certainly not as fast as either Lufbery's or Campbell's. I continued to hang back far behind my formation. The lines of the enemy were approaching and Lufbery, my only salvation, as it appeared to me, was at least a mile ahead of me.

I shall believe to my dying day that Major Lufbery knew my thoughts at that moment. For just as I felt that he had forgotten all about me he suddenly made a virage and took up a position a few hundred feet from me, as much as to say, "Don't worry, my boy, I have an eye on you." Again and again this occurred.

It was with great difficulty that I tried to perform the same maneuvers that Major Lufbery executed with such great ease. I grew somewhat interested with my attempts to imitate his example in preserving our little flight formation, and this occupation of keeping within shouting distance of my companions made me forget entirely that old Mother Earth was some

15,000 feet underneath me and the trenches about the same distance ahead. The bitter, numbing cold which always prevails at these high altitudes was of course by this time an old and familiar experience to me.

We had been sailing along at this dizzy height for some thirty minutes between Rheims and the Argonne Woods when it occurred to me to look below at the landscape. And such a spectacle spread itself out before my eyes when I at last did look over the side of my little office!

The trenches in this sector were quite old and had remained in practically the same position for three years of warfare. To my inexperienced view there appeared to be nothing below me but old battered trenches, trench works and billions of shell holes which had dug up the whole surface of the earth for four or five miles on either side of me. Not a tree, not a fence, no sign of any familiar occupation of mankind, nothing but a chaos of ruin and desolation. The awfulness of the thing was truly appalling.

Perhaps this feeling got the best of me for a moment. I don't know of what Campbell was thinking and I suppose Major Lufbery was far too accustomed to the situation to give a thought to it.

But just when I had gained enough equilibrium of mind to keep my place in formation and at the same time take an interest in the battlefields below me, I began to feel a terrible realization that seasickness had overcome me. A stiff wind was blowing all this time and no ship upon the high seas ever rolled and pitched more than my Baby Nieuport did this 15,000 feet above No Man's Land, while I was attempting to follow Major Lufbery's evolutions and maneuvers.

I didn't want to confess even to myself that I could get sick in the air. This was what would be expected from a brand new aviator on his first trip over the lines. It would be wonderfully amusing to Lufbery and the rest of the boys in the Squadron when I got back to the field — if I ever did — to advise me to take along a bottle of medicine next time I tried to fly. I grew cold with the thought of it. Then I set my teeth and prayed that I might fight it off. I determined to look straight ahead and fly straight ahead and to concentrate my whole mind on the task of sticking it out, no matter how I felt.

I had hardly got control of myself when I was horribly startled by an explosion which seemed only a few feet in my rear. I didn't even have time to look around, for at the same instant the concussion caught my plane and I began to roll and toss much worse than I had ever realized was possible. The very terror of my situation drove away all thoughts of sickness. In the midst of it several more shocks tipped my machine and repeated sounds of nearby explosions smote my ears. No matter what happened, I must look around to see what awful fate was overtaking me.

All that I could see were four or five black puffs of smoke some distance behind and below my tail.

I knew what they were right enough. They were "Archy"! They were eighteen-pound shells of shrapnel which were being fired at me by the Germans. And the battery which was firing them was only too well known to me. We had all been told about the most accurate battery that allied aviators had met in this sector. It was situated just outside of the town of Suippe. And there was Suippe down there just under my left wing. A mile north of Suippe was the exact location of this famous shooting battery. I looked down and picked it out quite clearly. And I knew they could see me and were seeing me much more plainly than I was seeing them. And probably they had quite a few more of those shells on hand which they were contemplating popping up at me.

I shall never forget how scared I was and how enraged I felt at the old pilots at home, who pretended to like the Archies. The latter were bursting all around me again and were terribly close and I felt a vengeful desire to get home just once more in order to take it out on those blasé pilots, who had been telling us newcomers that anti-aircraft guns were a joke and never did any damage. They used to count up the cost of each shell at five or ten dollars apiece and then figure that they had cost the German Government about a million dollars for their morning's amusement in flying over the Archy batteries, with never a hit. And I had been fool enough to believe them. Any one of those shells might happen to hit me just as well as happen to burst a hundred yards away. It was due entirely to my own good luck, and not at all to those scoffers' silly advice, that one of them hadn't hit me already. I was more indignant with the boys who had been stuffing me with their criminal wit than I was with the Boche gunners who were firing at me.

Never before did I, and never again will I quite so much appreciate the comfort of having a friend near at hand. I suddenly noticed that Major Lufbery was alongside me. Almost subconsciously I followed his maneuvers and gradually I began to realize that each maneuver he made was a direct word of encouragement to me. His machine seemed to speak to me, to soothe my feelings, to prove to me that there was no danger so long as I followed its wise leadership.

Little by little my alarm passed away. I began to watch the course of the black puffs behind me. I grew accustomed to the momentary disturbance of the air after each explosion and almost mechanically I met the lift of the machine with the gentle pressure of my joystick, which righted my Nieuport and smoothed its course. And a rush of happiness came over me with the assurance that I was neither going to be sick nor

was I any longer in any terror of the bursting shells.
By Jove, I had passed through the ordeal! A feeling
of elation possessed me as I realized that my long
dreamed and long dreaded noviciate was over. At
last I knew clear down deep in my own heart that I
was all right. I could fly! I could go over enemy
lines like the other boys who had seemed so wonderful
to me! I forgot entirely my recent fear and terror.
Only a deep feeling of satisfaction and gratitude
remained that warmed me and delighted me, for
not until that moment had I dared to hope that I possessed all the requisite characteristics for a successful
war pilot. Though I had feared no enemy, yet I had
feared that I myself might be lacking.

This feeling of self-confidence that this first hour
over the Suippe battery brought to me is perhaps the
most precious memory of my life. For with the sudden banishment of that first mortal fear that had so
possessed me came a belief in my own powers that
knew no bounds. I loved flying. I had been familiar
with motors all my life. Sports of every sort had always appealed to me. The excitement of automobile
racing did not compare with what I knew must come
with aeroplane fighting in France. The pleasure of
shooting down another man was no more attractive
to me than the chance of being shot down myself.
The whole business of war was ugly to me. But the
thought of pitting my experience and confidence against
that of German aviators and beating them at their
own boasted prowess in air combats had fascinated
me. I did not forget my inexperience in shooting.
But I knew that could be learned easily enough.
What I hungered to ascertain was my ability to with-
stand the cruelties and horrors of war. If that could
be conquered, I knew I could hold my own with any
man who ever piloted an aeroplane.

This confidence in myself must have aided me con-

siderably in my learning to fly. After twelve flights
in a machine in France, I went aloft for a flight alone.
After that first solo flight, I tried several different
types of machines with never any feeling of insecurity.

I was floating along through enemy skies in ecstatic
contemplation of these thoughts when I suddenly discovered that Major Lufbery was leading us homewards. I glanced at the clock on my dashboard. It
was nearly ten o'clock. We had been out almost two
hours and our fuel supply must be running low. These
fast-flying fighting machines cannot carry a large
supply of gasoline and oil, as every pound of weight
counts against the speed and climbing powers of the
aeroplane.

Gradually we descended as we approached the vicinity of our aerodrome. This lovely section of
France, as yet undevastated by war, spread below the
wings of our little Nieuports in peaceful contrast to
the ugliness that lay behind us. Some snow still filled
the hollows as far as the eye could reach, for a severe
storm had raged over this section of the country but
a few days before.

We circled once about the field and, shutting off
motor, slid gently down into the mud which quickly
brought the machines to a full pause. Quickening the
speed of the propellers we taxied one by one towards
the door of the hangar before which every pilot and
mechanic stood awaiting us with open-armed expec-
tancy. They were eager to hear the details of our
first flight into enemy territory and to see how two
beginners, like themselves, had stood the experience.

Both Campbell and I wore satisfactory countenances
of bored indifference. We had had a little flip around
over the Hun batteries and it had been most droll seeing the gunners wasting their ammunition. We must
have cost the Kaiser a year's income by our little
jaunt into his lines. As for enemy aeroplanes, none

of them dared to venture up against us. Not a plane was in our vicinity.

Just here Major Lufbery broke into the conversation and asked us particularly what we had seen. I didn't like the sound of his customary little chuckle on this occasion. But we both repeated as easily as we could that we hadn't seen any other aeroplanes in the sky.

"Just what I expected. They are all the same!" was the Major's only comment.

We indignantly asked him what he meant by addressing two expert war pilots in such tones.

"Well," said Lufbery, "one formation of five Spads crossed under us before we passed the lines and another flight of five Spads went by about fifteen minutes later and you didn't see them, although neither one of them was more than 500 yards away. It was just as well they were not Boches!

"Then there were four German Albatros two miles ahead of us when we turned back and there was another enemy two-seater nearer us than that, at about 5,000 feet above the lines. You ought to look about a bit when you get in enemy lines."

Campbell and I stood aghast, looking at each other. Then I saw he was thinking the same thoughts as I. The Major was ragging us from a sense of duty, to take some of the conceit out of us. But it was only after weeks of experience over the front that we realized how true his statements probably were. No matter how good a flyer the scout may be and no matter how perfect his eyesight is, he must learn to see before he can distinguish objects either on the ground or in air. What is called "vision of the air" can come only from experience and no pilot ever has it upon his first arrival at the front.

Then sauntering over to my machine the Major

bucked me up very considerably by blandly inquiring, " How much of that shrapnel did you get, Rick?" I couldn't help laughing at his effort to put me in a heroic picture-frame for the benefit of the boys who were listening. Imagine my horror when he began interestedly poking his finger in one shrapnel hole in the tail; another fragment had gone through the outer edge of the wing and a third had passed directly through both wings not a foot from my body!

The boys told me afterwards that I stayed pale for a good thirty minutes and I believe them, for a week passed before the Major suggested to me that I again accompany him into the German lines.

CHAPTER II

THE AERODROME

I OFTEN wondered whether the mothers and friends of our pilots formed a true conception back home of the surroundings and daily doings of their loved ones in France. Even the term " Aerodrome," where it is known aeroplanes are landed and kept and cared for and where the pilots live and start from in their trips over the lines and where they are anxiously awaited at the end of their patrol by their comrades — even " Aerodrome " must convey a more or less uncertain picture to those who have never actually seen one.

Picture in your minds a smooth field covered with sod and occupying a situation near a town and good highway. It is on comparatively level ground and is square in shape and each of the four sides is about half a mile in length.

Such a field accommodates very nicely four squadrons of fighting machines, which means 80 or 90 aeroplanes and as many pilots. The road skirts one side of the square. Close to the road in each corner of the square are placed two large sheds, or hangars, to house the aeroplanes. Each hangar will hold comfortably ten or twelve machines of the small type. There they spend the night and each machine is carefully inspected by the mechanics who "belong to it." Each pilot has three mechanics who are responsible for his aeroplane, and it is seldom that any defect can escape their jealous attention.

Around the edges of the field, then, these eight or ten large hangars stand facing inwards, with wide open doors through which the aeroplane can pass onto the ground. A short distance away the mess and sleeping quarters for the officers of each squadron are situated. As there are but twenty pilots to each squadron, the officers of two squadrons frequently mess together. The enlisted men, including the mechanics, truck drivers, workmen and servants, occupy quarters of their own at a little distance behind the hangars. As each squadron requires almost two hundred enlisted men to take proper care of its many details it is seen that the entire personnel of the average aerodrome group numbers quite one thousand men when the Headquarters, Searchlight Company, Telephone Squad, Lighting Plant, Red Cross and Y. M. C. A. personnel are added to it. The anti-aircraft gunners who have charge of the defense of the aerodrome against enemy raids are not attached to the Air Service and are not properly part of the aerodrome membership.

Such then is the rough arrangement of the pilots' aerodrome. From the sky an aerodrome can be seen many miles away by an experienced observer and although every effort is made to camouflage hangars, huts and aeroplanes, no flying fields can long be in use by either side before they are discovered by the enemy.

We were but three weeks in the Villeneuve aerodrome and during that time the weather was so severe that comparatively little flying was undertaken by the first of our American pilots, who formed this unit. March, 1918, had snow storms, heavy rains and high winds. Our aeroplanes were not of the best and they had not yet been fully equipped.

An amusing episode occurred in this connection, which seems funnier now than it did at that time. The French authorities very kindly made arrangements to help train the new pilots of our Squadron in combat fighting over the lines. Accordingly every day or two an experienced French airman would drop down upon our field and take away with him two of our inexperienced freshmen for a trip into Germany, just as Major Lufbery had taken Campbell and myself. Naturally all of our pilots were anxious to go.

After two weeks' patrolling over enemy territory in this manner, you can imagine the consternation of these French flight leaders when they discovered that the American machines which had accompanied them carried no aeroplane guns! Our machine-guns had not yet arrived!

Fortunately the Boches didn't know it and no encounters had taken place. But the idea of this dummy fleet carrying on such a gigantic bluff over enemy lines was as comic to us as was the story of the wooden ships of the British Navy which had deterred the German fleet from leaving harbor. The Frenchmen however couldn't understand this sense of humor.

It was at this period that we lost one of my dearest friends and a commander who was respected and loved by all the pilots. Captain James Miller had left family and home and a prosperous business in New York to serve his country over the battlefields of France.

He was a light-hearted, lovable companion, but I had long ago discovered the stern, determined qualities of his character. He had often told me his greatest desire was to go into the skies and win a combat against an enemy aviator. The long delays in Paris irritated him, and his work in organizing the Aviation School at Issoudun for the training of American pilots did not satisfy him. He burned for an opportunity to get over the lines in a fighting plane.

I found Captain Miller at the Villeneuve aerodrome when I arrived there on March 4th, 1918. He had command of the fighting squadron adjoining mine, the 95th. But he had no machines and no equipment and apparently he was as remote from air combats there as he had been in Paris. Still dominated with the one idea of getting into a fight with the enemy, it was especially difficult for him to be patient.

One day towards the middle of March we received a visit from Major Johnson and Major Harmon, who were then temporarily attached to one of the French Spad Squadrons in the vicinity. I shall never forget the boyish delight with which Captain Miller came to me after their departure and confided to me what he considered the most cherished secret in his life. Major Davenport Johnson had promised him that he might call at his aerodrome the following day and take a flight over the lines in one of their machines. He was ecstatically happy over the prospect.

I never saw him again. The following evening we were notified through military channels that Captain James Miller was missing. Not until several days later did I learn the details of his disappearance. Then I learned that Major Johnson himself had accompanied Miller on his first flight and that they had passed over Rheims and proceeded towards the Argonne Forest — the very same patrol on which Lufbery had taken me but a few days before.

Two squadrons of enemy machines were discovered some distance within the enemy lines and Miller, not observing them, flew in and was attacked. The enemy aeroplanes were two-seaters, carrying machine-guns in front and behind. Major Johnson did not warn Miller, but returned to his field and landed, stating that his guns had jammed. Captain Miller was never seen again.

A month later a German official report reached us that Captain James Miller of the American Air Service had been wounded in combat and had fallen within German territory, where he died a few hours later.

Poor Jim! His was the first and most sorrowful loss that had come to our new group. Then it was I learned that I must not permit myself to cherish friendships with my pilot comrades so intimately that their going would upset the work I had to do. For every aviator's day's work included the same risks that had cost Jim Miller his life. If one permitted constant anxiety for friends to weigh down one's spirits one could not long continue work at the front.

These days of March, 1918, were trying ones for our Allies in the British and French armies. It was known that the enemy was preparing for a conclusive and tremendous push within a few days, with which to gain the Channel ports against the British, before the troops from the United States could be in position to aid them.

The Germans knew better than our own countrymen at home knew just how difficult would be our preparations for a really important force of aeroplanes. They had seen the spring months pass; and instead of viewing with alarm the huge fleet of 20,000 aeroplanes sweeping the skies clear of German Fokkers, they had complacently witnessed the Fokkers occupying the air back of our lines whenever they desired it, with never an American plane to oppose them.

On March 21st, 1918, the great German attack was launched against the British in the north. We heard serious rumors about the numbers of prisoners captured by the Huns and the rapid advances they were making in each push.

Our aerodrome at Villeneuve was at that time but 18 miles from the lines. In clear weather we could distinctly see our line of observation balloons, which stretched along the front between us and the lines. The booming of guns sounded continuously in our ears. On March 30th we were ordered to move our squadrons to another aerodrome farther away from the front. We went to Epiez that day, where we found ourselves about 30 miles from the lines and still with no machines with which we might hope to help stem the alarming advance of the enemy.

Here at Epiez the 94th Squadron was joined by Captain James Norman Hall, the author of " Kitchner's Mob " and " High Adventure "; also Captain David McK. Peterson, of Honesdale, Pa. Both of them were experienced pilots who had become celebrated for their air work in the Escadrille Lafayette and who did much to enhearten us and instruct us during this forlorn period. We had all heard of these boys and idolized them before we had seen them. I cannot adequately describe the inspiration we all received from the coming of these two veteran air-fighters to our camp.

A day or two after we had settled down in our new aerodrome we heard the buzzing of an approaching machine. All hands rushed out to see what it meant. A Nieuport bearing American colors assured us it was a friend and probably another new member of our squadron, since he was preparing to land on our field.

He shut off his motor and glided down until his wheels skimmed the ground. The next instant her nose struck the mud and in a twinkling the machine had somersaulted over onto her back and slid along towards us tail foremost. We walked out to the wreck to secure the remains of the raw pilot who hadn't learned yet how to land a machine, and some of us made rather caustic comments about the authorities sending us such unsophisticated aviators. Imagine our stupefaction when we discovered the grinning face of Captain Hall himself looking at us upside down!

Fortunately he wasn't hurt in the slightest, and I think he would be glad if he could know how much good it did all of us young pilots to discover that even the best airmen can sometimes come a cropper.

Captain Hall climbed out of his wreckage and coming over to me told me that there was another machine still at our old aerodrome which must be flown over. I was directed to get a motor car and drive back to Villeneuve and, after making certain that everything was in order with the Nieuport, fly home with it on the morrow.

I accordingly got myself ready and set out. It was late at night when we started. Shortly before midnight we entered a small village just south of Châlons on the Marne River. Suddenly we noticed people running excitedly about the streets and as they came under the glare of my headlights I saw they were absolutely stricken with terror. I stopped the car, as an old man came running up to me, and asked him what was the trouble.

" The Boches are overhead!" was his reply, pointing upwards into the night. " Please, M'sieu', put out the lights of your car!"

I snapped out the headlights and stood there for a moment, watching those poor people scurrying about for shelter. Old women whose backs were bent with age and toil were running helter-skelter through the streets for the open country, small children clinging to

their skirts. They did not know where they were
going, and many of them ran into each other as they
crossed to and fro. Their one idea was to get away
from their beds, where they imagined the bombs from
the Hun aeroplanes would be certain to find them. In
truth that would have been the safest place for them to
remain.

We proceeded through the village and a moment
later came to a rise in the ground from which we could
see the anti-aircraft shells bursting above the city of
Châlons, a few miles ahead of us. Many sweeping
searchlights were searching the heavens with yellow
fingers itching to grasp the path where the enemy
planes were pursuing their way. For almost an hour
we stood on this hill and regarded the spectacle with the
same critical interest we had often experienced in
watching an opera. Then suddenly the lights were
extinguished and the booming of exploding shells
ceased. We regretfully climbed back into our car and
continued on our way. The show was over!

It took us an hour to wake up the landlady in the
best hotel in Châlons that night. When we finally
found the night bell and kept a resolute finger upon
the button until the storage battery threatened to become
exhausted, the good woman appeared in negligée and
asked us if we wanted to come in. She apologized
most heartily when she discovered we were not Germans but Americans — her beloved Americans, she
called us — and we were soon tucked away in her
best beds, covered with mountainous eider-downs
which reached half-way to the low ceiling.

The next morning we proceeded on to the old aerodrome where I found the last of our Nieuports and
had it run out and tested. After half an hour's inspection I found everything right and climbed aboard
the little bus and waved my two mechanics good-by.
In 30 minutes I was over the Epiez field, having cov-

ered the same road which had consumed four and a
half hours by motorcar, the night before.

Up to this time — April 3rd, 1918, only my squadron (the 94th, commanded by Major John Huffer,
one of the old Lafayette flyers), and Captain James
Miller's squadron, the 95th, were at the front.   Both
squadrons had been together at Villeneuve and together had moved to Epiez.   None of the pilots of either
squadron had been able to do any fighting at the front,
owing to the lack of aeroplane guns.   In fact the
pilots of Squadron 95 had not yet been instructed in
the use of aeroplane guns, although this squadron had
been sent to the front a short time before 94 Squadron had arrived there.   We of 94 Squadron however
had been diverted to the Aerial Gunnery School at
Cazeau for a month early in the year and were now
ready to try our luck in actual combat fighting over
the lines.   But we had no guns on our machines.

Then suddenly guns arrived!   All sorts of wonderful new equipment began pouring in.   Instruments
for the aeroplanes, suits of warm clothing for the pilots, extra spares for the machines.   And at the same
moment the foolish virgins of Squadron 95 who hadn't
yet learned how to shoot in the air were sent back to
the Cazeau School, while old 94, destined to become the
greatest American squadron in France in the number
of its victories over the enemy, was ordered to vacate
the Epiez aerodrome and move on eastward and north
to Toul.   On April 10th, 1918, we took our departure, flying our Nieuports over to an old aerodrome
east of Toul which had been vacated by the French
for our use.   Supplies, beds, mess-furniture, oil and
gasoline and all the multitudinous paraphernalia of an
aviation camp followed us in lorries and trucks.   For
a day or two we had our hands full with settling ourselves in our new quarters and acquainting ourselves
with our sector of the map.   We were two miles east

of Toul, one of the most important railroad connections on our side of the front and a town that the enemy tried almost daily to demolish with aeroplane bombs. We were barely 18 miles from the lines and in a country covered with rolling hills and extensive forests.

Nancy lay fifteen miles to the east of us, Lunéville 12 miles farther east and the highway from Toul to Nancy to Lunéville lay parallel to the enemy lines and within easy shelling distance of the Hun guns. But along this highway one would not have realized that a war was on. East of this point no efforts had been made at an offensive by either side. Business went on as usual in Lunéville. Children played in the streets and traffic pursued its leisurely way. An occasional German sentry faced a French sentry along the lines from Lunéville to Switzerland, at intervals of a hundred yards or so, but it was said that these sentries messed together and slept together for the sake of companionship. This unnatural situation was considerably altered later, when the Americans came in. The country of the Vosges Mountains was thought to be too rough to permit invasion by either side.

North and west of our Toul aerodrome lay Verdun. Verdun, the *sine qua non* of German success! Under the Verdun citadel, built in 1863, lay an underground army of seventy thousand men. No use to attempt to go around Verdun and leave seventy thousand attackers in their rear. Verdun must ever be threatened, even while desperate attacks were being launched against Amiens, Ypres and the Marne. Consequently considerable aeroplane activity was indulged in by the pilots of the Huns in this sector, and here the first American fighting squadron was sent to demonstrate to the world the air ability of American flyers, in combat fighting. And 94 got that chance!

The Squadron at that time was commanded, as I

have said, by Major John Huffer. He was one of America's best pilots and finest fellows, but curiously enough, he had been born in France and had never been in America nor in any English speaking country, though he has traveled extensively abroad and speaks English like a Harvard man. Major Huffer had served in the Ambulance Division since the early days of the war, later joining the Foreign Legion with William Thaw, Victor Chapman and other American boys. When the American Escadrille was formed, he entered aviation and thus was a veteran war pilot long before America came into the war.

When he discovered that our beloved squadron was to receive the distinction of being the first actually to begin fighting for America, the question of a significant and proper squadron insignia became of prime importance to us. We were busy those first days in Toul painting our machines with the American Red, White and Blue, with our individual markings and with the last finishing touches which would prepare them for their first expedition over the lines. Then came the ideas for our insignia!

Major Huffer suggested Uncle Sam's Stovepipe Hat with the Stars-and-Stripes for a hatband. And our post Surgeon, Lieutenant Walters of Pittsburgh, Pa., raised a cheer by his inspiration of the " Hat-in-the-Ring." It was immediately adopted and the next day designs and drawings were made by Lieutenant John Wentworth of Chicago, which soon culminated in the adoption of the bold challenge painted on the sides of our fighting planes, which several scores of enemy airmen have since been unfortunate enough to dispute.

Toul then saw the launching of America's first Fighting Squadron. And it was from this aerodrome that I won my first five victories in the following 30 days.

CHAPTER III

OUR FIRST SORTIES

O N the evening of April 13th, 1918, we were indeed a happy lot of pilots, for we were reading on our new Operations Board the first war-flight order ever given by an All-American Squadron Commander to All-American pilots. It stated in simple terms that Captain Peterson, Lieutenant Reed Chambers and Lieutenant E. V. Rickenbacker would start on a patrol of the lines to-morrow morning at six o'clock. Our altitude was to be 16,000 feet; our patrol was to extend from Pont-à-Mousson to St. Mihiel and we were to return at eight o'clock — a two hours' patrol. Captain Peterson was designated as leader of the flight.

Picture the map of these French towns, as every pilot in our Squadron 94 had it indelibly pressed into his memory. While flying in the vicinity of enemy territory it is quite essential that one should know every landmark on the horizon. Every river, every railroad, highway and village must be as familiar to the airman as are the positions of first, second and third bases to the homerunner.

Toul is 18 miles almost directly south of Pont-à-Mousson, St. Mihiel is directly west of Pont-à-Mousson about the same distance. The battle lines ran straight between Pont-à-Mousson and St. Mihiel; then they turned north to run another 18 miles to the edge of Verdun. Straight north of Pont-à-Mousson some 20 miles Metz is situated. And around Metz several squadrons of Hun bombing aeroplanes and fighting machines had their lairs on a hilltop, from which they surveyed the lines which we were to patrol this 13th day of April. In short, the sector from Pont-à-

Mousson to St. Mihiel was fairly alive with air activity when weather conditions permitted the use of aeroplanes at all.

This was the beat on which Captain Peterson, Chambers and I would find ourselves to-morrow at six. Lieutenant Douglas Campbell and Lieutenant Alan Winslow were directed in the same order to stand by on the alert at the hangar from six o'clock until ten the same morning. This "alert" was provided for any sudden emergency; such as an enemy bombing raid in our direction or a sudden call for help against an enemy aeroplane within our lines.

Immediately after dinner that night Reed Chambers and I retired with Captain Peterson to his room, where we talked over the coming event. The Captain gave us some curt directions about the precautions we should take in case of an attack, instructed me particularly that I was to lead the flight if anything happened to him or his motor, and under these circumstances I was to continue our patrol until the time was up. Then he summoned an orderly and gave orders to call all five of us at 5.00 A. M. Advising Reed and me to sleep tight and try not to dream about Fokker aeroplanes, off he went to bed.

We knew very well what we would dream about. Try as I might, I could not get to sleep that night for hours. I thought over everything I had ever read or heard about aeroplane fighting. I imagined the enemies coming at me from every direction. I pictured to myself the various ways I would circumvent them and finally bring them tumbling down to their final crash. At last I dropped off to sleep and continued dreaming the same maneuvers. Just as I was shooting down the last of a good-sized number, the orderly punched my elbow and woke me up. It was five o'clock.

A wonderful morning greeted us and the five of

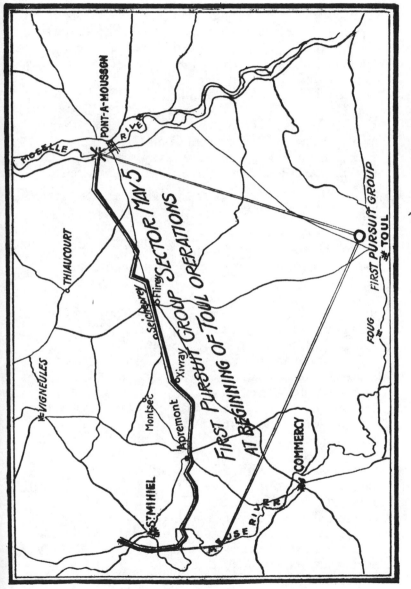

94 SQUADRON'S PATROL OF THE FRONT FROM ST. MIHIEL TO PONT-A-MOUSSON, MAY 5 TO JULY 1, 1918.

us had a merry breakfast. We advised Campbell and Winslow to keep a sharp lookout above the aerodrome that morning, for we intended to stir up the Boches and undoubtedly there would be droves of them coming over our field for revenge.

But upon reaching the field after breakfast we found that the atmosphere was bad and the mist so heavy that the ground was completely hidden a short distance away. Captain Peterson sent Chambers and myself up to reconnoiter at 1500 feet. Away we went. After circling the field two or three times, we noticed Captain Peterson take off and climb up to join us. We continued climbing and just about the time we had attained the frigid altitude, 16,000 feet, I noticed the Captain's machine gliding back to the field.

"Ah!" thought I, "motor trouble! And he told me last night to carry on in case he dropped out! It is my show now. Come ahead, Chambers!"

Unsophisticated as I was, I did not know the danger into which I was leading my companion, and as Chambers knew less about the country than I did, he readily followed my lead and away we flew.

We picked up the valley of the Moselle River and proceeded blandly upon our way and would probably have kept on to the Rhine, but for a sudden bark under the tail of Chambers' machine which announced that we were discovered over German guns. I had been shot up by Archy before and now gloried in the utter contempt I felt for him, but this was Reed's first experience with German anti-aircraft artillery and, as he admitted later, he thought it was all over with him. He sheered in so close to me that we nearly collided. Gradually we maneuvered out of the zone of fire and eventually became so disdainful of the shell bursts that we proceeded grandly on our way without paying any attention to them.

I located Pont-à-Mousson and from there set our

course for St. Mihiel. Four times we made the round trip between these two towns amid intermittent Archy fire but without seeing any aeroplanes in the sky. Then I decided we must turn towards home if we were to close our first patrol at the designated time. To my horror I discovered the whole landscape to the south of us was covered with a dense covering of fog. The whole area was covered; and under the blanket, somewhere in France, was the field upon which we were supposed to land. Land we must in a short half hour, for our fuel would be consumed and we would drop that instant. I began to realize then why Captain Peterson had gone back to the field and I felt cold chills run down my spine as I contemplated the various kinds of mishaps that were in store for Reed and me.

There was nothing for it but a dive through the thick fog clouds. I stuck down my nose, entered them and lost Chambers immediately and only hoped that he had not come in directly behind me. I flew by compass, all the while watching the needle drop down the altimeter. Cautiously I flattened out at one thousand feet, for there are high hills in this sector and some tall trees might show up ahead of me at any instant. Again I put down her nose and crept nearer the earth. At last I saw something below me and immediately zoomed up into the mist again. The nervousness of that foggy ride homewards I shall never forget.

By the sheerest good luck I caught a brief glimpse of a Y and a railroad tunnel that somehow seemed familiar to me. I circled back and got another view of it. Imagine my joy when I discovered it was a landmark near Commercy, that I had flown over just once before when coming from Epiez to Toul. I put about and flying only a hundred feet above ground continued straight into Toul, from which location I easily found the flying field and landed quite perfectly.

Captain Peterson came up to me and informed me I was a bloody fool for flying off in a fog, which I knew was a fact and cheerfully admitted. Then I asked about Reed Chambers and felt a return of all my previous fear when I learned they had heard nothing from him.

With a heavy heart I got out of my flying clothes and walked over to Headquarters to make out my report. I was positive the telephone would ring within a few minutes to inform us that Chambers had crashed and killed himself in the fog. I had barely begun my writing when the telephone did ring. I stood quivering in my shoes, while the Operations Officer answered the call. Then he shouted: —

" Quick! Two Boche aeroplanes are reported over Foug. Send in an alerte!"

But at the same instant we heard two of our machines taking off the field. It was Campbell and Winslow, who had been standing by all the morning for a chance nobody had expected them to get. I started to run towards the hangars; but before I reached the field a private rushed to me saying, " A German aeroplane has just fallen in flames on our field!"

It was true. I could see the flames from where I stood. Before I could reach the spot, however, another yell aroused my attention and I turned and saw a second Boche machine fall nose down into a field not five hundred yards away. The first had been destroyed by Alan Winslow who had shot it down in flames within three minutes after leaving the field. The second was forced down by Douglas Campbell, and it crashed in the mist before the pilot could discover his proximity to the ground. These were the first two enemy aeroplanes brought down by any American squadron and both were miraculously crashed on the very doorstep of our aerodrome on the first day we had begun operations!

Neither of the German pilots was seriously injured.

Upon our questioning them as to how they happened to be about in such weather, they informed us that they had been summoned to go up to attack two patrolling machines that were being " Archied " between Pont-à-Mousson and St. Mihiel. They had followed Chambers and me until they lost us in the fog. Then they tried to find their own way home to their aerodrome near Metz. They discovered our field and came down low thinking it might be their own, when Winslow and Campbell flew up and attacked them at about 500 feet above ground.

This was indeed a wonderful opening exhibition for our Squadron and had the stage been set and the scene arranged for it, could not have worked more perfectly. Then it was added to our joy to receive the congratulations and praise of the French inhabitants of Toul, who had endured so many bombing raids from these Boche machines without seeing any allied planes on the defense of their beloved little city. When they learned that two enemy machines had been shot down on the very first day of the arrival of the Americans their delight knew no bounds. They wrung our hands, kissed us, toasted us in their best Mozelle wine and yelled: —" *Vive la France!* " " *Vivent les Americains!* " until they were hoarse. We each took a souvenir from the German machines, which were to be the first of our long series of " *descendus,*" and the remains of the captured prizes we rolled into Toul, where they remained upon exhibition in the city square until the last vestiges of them disappeared. To complete our joy, we learned that Reed Chambers had landed a short distance away from our 'drome; and that night he came in to join us.

For the next few days the Squadron lived upon its reputation and received the congratulations of our superior officers and the Staff with much mock nonchalance. Lieutenants Campbell and Winslow were overwhelmed with telephone calls and cablegrams. From all parts of the United States congratulations came to them and quite a number of messages were sent to the two victors from England and France. It was particularly fortunate for the squadron that such an extraordinary success should have marked the very first day of our operations and still more lucky that the enemy machines had crashed in sight of us all. The episode put great confidence into all of us and we felt we were a match for the whole German air force. The date of this first American victory was April 14th, 1918.

For several days following, bad weather kept us idle on the ground. But on April 18th an *alerte* was sounded informing us that an enemy plane was seen over Pont-à-Mousson. Reed Chambers and I applied for the job of landing this fellow, and after obtaining permission we jumped into our machines, which were warmed up and ready, and off we started. I was determined to bring down the next victim for our squadron and had it all planned out in my mind just how it was to be done.

It was a thick day and the clouds hung about 3000 feet above ground. We plunged boldly into them and flew straight on. Finally we got above the clouds and began circling about in wide sweeps, looking everywhere for the bold German. After thirty minutes or more of desperate searching, I decided to drop back below the clouds and see where we really were. Certainly there were no Boches in this sector after all.

In ten minutes I was below the clouds and skimming along the landscape with an eye out for landmarks. Suddenly I discovered a large city ahead which looked strangely like Nancy, except that it was in exactly the wrong direction. I drew nearer and couldn't believe my eyes when a closer scrutiny proved it was true. I had been trusting to my boasted sense of direction

all during this flight and had not even consulted my
compass. Consequently I had turned completely
around and had led Chambers in exactly the opposite
direction from the spot where the Boche was waiting
for us. We had not been within ten miles of the lines
the whole morning.

In great disgust I led the way homewards. Landing my machine I went over to the office and put in
a very brief report to the effect that there were no
enemy machines to be seen in our patrol. Quite true
as far as I went, but I could not bring myself to state
just why there were no Boches that morning. But I
learned a very valuable lesson that day and have never
had cause to regret the short discomfiture it gave me.

That same day a Hospital Unit moved into Toul and
settled within a mile of our aerodrome. The nurses
were all American girls, and several of us had the
good fortune to meet a party of them as we were taking a walk into Toul. After seeing only the coarsest
and oldest sorts of French peasant women for so many
months, we thought we had never seen anything so
beautiful as these first American girls at Toul. We
gave them a grand greeting, and as a recompense all
of us were invited to come over for a dance at their
mess. In fact, all the boys in our squadrons were
invited to come and we were instructed to give them
the message. Having discovered this goldmine ourselves, however, we all mutually and instantly decided
we should do nothing of the kind. We walked on into
town, each man thinking of the girl he would ask for
a dance and what a scoop we would have on the other
fellows who would stay at home playing cards at
camp!

However, when the time came we couldn't keep it
to ourselves. We took the whole crowd and introduced them to the girls — and were immediately sorry
we had done so. But on the whole the presence of

these girls from back home so near to our field was the second best thing that had happened to us since the war.

General Liggett, commandant of the First Army Corps and Colonel William Mitchell, commanding the Air Service, came over to see our group the next day. I was sent up to do some stunting for their entertainment, and, upon landing to receive their compliments, found that I had broken a part of my motor. This little catastrophe put me out of the trench strafing party which our squadron carried out at four o'clock that afternoon on the enemy's lines just north of Seicheprey. It was a wonderful success and all the boys came home overjoyed with the scurrying troops on the ground that had been thrown into great confusion by the attack of the aeroplanes. This ground strafing is probably the most exciting sport in aviation and one that is attended with comparatively little danger to the pilot. The aeroplanes swoop down so swiftly and are so terrifying in the roar of their engines and the streams of bullets issuing forth from two rapid-fire guns that an ordinary soldier always looks for a hole rather than for any weapon of defense.

The machine passes overhead so quickly that I imagine no gun can begin to be aimed until we are gone. Only when a steady barrage fire is going up and a pilot happens to pass through its very path does he get injured while upon this work. I have frequently dived down upon a highway filled with marching Germans and put them to flight with one swoop. If they ever fired at me I never knew it and never have seen any evidences of a hit through my wings.

All these little details seemed very important to me at the time, for it must be remembered that every pilot in our group was fearfully inexperienced and overawed by the mysteries in store for him in the future. War to us was very much of a plunge into an unknown planet. We knew something of the wiles of the enemy and were familiar enough with the dangers that every pilot was so fond of describing. But there remained always that unknown fear of a new menace. Ever constant was the impression that luck might for an instant desert us and that instant would end the war for us. We often wondered just what new danger would be thwarted by pure luck each time we went out for a patrol into enemy territory.

So it was that each experience that came to me in those first days of war-flying made a great impression on my mind. I grew more confident each day. Many doubts were removed, more disdain for the enemy came to me and a growing certainty gradually possessed me that I had fathomed all the possibilities that could threaten me and my aeroplane when over the lines of the enemy. And I always tried to remember every incident that happened, so that in the future I might take advantage of familiar circumstances.

I was standing by on the aerodrome on April 23d when at about noon we received a warning by telephone that an enemy aeroplane had just been sighted between St. Mihiel and Pont-à-Mousson, flying from West to East. Major Huffer sent me word to get off immediately and find the Boche. No one else was ready, so I set off alone.

I took off the field and pulling up her nose, I lifted my little Nieuport straight upwards as steeply as she would climb as I set a direct course for Pont-à-Mousson. The day had been rainy and cloudy and it had been several days since there had been any activity in the air. In five minutes I picked up the river and the little city of Pont-à-Mousson crowded along its bank. I was some eight thousand feet up.

The French now held Pont-à-Mousson. Enemy artillery had been doing considerable damage to the bridge and buildings, and this now disclosed itself to my eyes.   Many roofs were torn off and the whole town was badly knocked about.   I took my eyes away from the ground and began to search the skies for a moving speck.

A sudden palpitation of my heart indicated that I did see a speck, on the very first glance I shot into Germany. There at about my own altitude was the wasp-like edge of an aeroplane coming directly towards me.   I began to shiver lest he had seen me first while I was joy-riding over Pont-à-Mousson and had thus had time to form a plot of his own before I had formulated any of mine.   Both of us continued dead ahead at each other for twenty seconds or so until we arrived almost within shouting distance, when I discovered to my great relief that he wore the blue center cocard of a Frenchman and his machine was a Spad.   We had fortunately neither of us fired a shot.

Suddenly I saw the French pilot zoom up over me and attempt to get on my tail.   Whether joking or not, I couldn't permit such a maneuver, so I quickly darted under him and got the best position myself. The Nieuport can outmaneuver a Spad and has a little faster climb; so the stranger soon found he had his match.   But to my amazement the fellow kept circling about me continually trying to bring his guns to bear upon me.   I began wondering then whether he was some idiot who did not know an ally when he saw one. or was he a real Boche flying over our lines in a cap- tured French machine?   The former was evidently the correct solution, for as soon as I came by him again I turned flat over in front of him and let him have a long look at my American white center cocards on my wings.   This performance apparently satisfied my persistent friend, for he soon swerved off and went on home, leaving me to proceed on my mission. This little episode taught me another lesson.   Since that day I have never taken any chances with any aeroplane in my vicinity, whether it was friend or foe. Some friends are better shots than are casual enemies.

My real quarry had made his escape during my little tourney with the Frenchman and I found no game in the sky, though I flew a full two hours along the lines. When I returned home, however, I found myself surrounded by the whole force as soon as my Nieuport stopped rolling along the ground. They fairly overwhelmed me with congratulations for bringing down a Boche, who had been seen to fall by one of our artillery batteries. As he fell in the very sector which I was then patrolling, they naturally credited me with the victory. It was a pity to undeceive them, but it had to be done.

The curious climax to this affair was that we never did discover who shot down that Boche machine. He was never claimed by any one else. But for my part I was convinced that I certainly could not have accomplished my first victory without firing a shot or even seeing my enemy.

Thus I had all the fruits of a first victory without having won it. But what was far more important to me, I had learned something more in the art of war-flying. I had undoubtedly saved my life by keeping out of the gun-sight of a friendly machine!

The very next day I learned another lesson.

Again it was about noon and I was on duty, when an alarm came in that a Boche was flying over St. Mihiel. It was a day of low hanging clouds. I was absolutely determined that day to get my Boche despite every obstacle, so I flew straight into the enemy's lines at about 3000 feet altitude. At that low height my machine was a splendid target for Archy, for after the first shot at me they found exactly the level of the clouds, and they could see I was just under them. Consequently I knew I was in for a warm time with the shell-bursts and I did some extraordinary dodging across two or three of their batteries.

I passed just north of St. Mihiel, and within a minute after the Archy began firing at me I sighted an enemy plane just ahead. I was coming in upon him from the rear for I had decided it would be a brilliant idea to cross the lines half-way to Verdun and catch the Boche from a quarter that might be unsuspected. It had worked perfectly, though I couldn't understand why he had been so blind as to let the black bursts of shell-fire around me pass unnoticed. But still he sat there with apparently no intention of trying to get away. I began to get nervous with the idea that this was almost too much of a good thing. Was he really a Boche?

As this was in reality the first German machine I had ever seen in the air and I had judged his status from the shape of his planes and fusilage, I thought perhaps I had better actually take a look at his markings before firing and see that he really had a black cross painted on his machine. So I dropped my finger from the trigger of my gun and dived a little closer.

Yes! he was Boche. But instead of having a black cross he wore a black cocard! It was a black cocard with white center. This must be something new, as no such markings had ever been reported at our headquarters. However he was no friend of mine and I would now proceed to down him. Why did he linger so complacently about my guns?

Suddenly I remembered the often repeated instructions of Major Lufbery about attacking enemy observation machines. "Always remember it may be a trap!" I hurriedly looked over my shoulder,— and just in time! There, coming out of a cloud over my head, was a beautiful black Albatros fighting machine that had been hiding about, waiting for me to walk into his trap. I gave one pull to my joystick and

zoomed straight upwards on my tail without giving
a second thought to my easy victim below me.

To my delight I found that I could not only out-
climb my adversary but I could outmaneuver him while
doing so. I got above him after a few seconds and
was again pressing my triggers to fire my first shots
in the great war when again it occurrred to me that I had
better look again and see that nobody else was sitting
farther upstairs watching this little party with a view
of joining in while my attention was diverted. I
shot a sudden glance over my shoulder.

Instantly I forgot all about bringing down Boche
aeroplanes and felt overwhelmed with one immense desire to get home as quickly as possible. Two aeroplanes from Germany were coming head-on at me not
500 yards away. How many more there were behind
them I didn't wait to determine. I was convinced that
my inexperience and stupidity had led me into a stu-
pendous plot against my person and I was in for a race
for my life.

On that homeward trip I experienced a great variety of feelings. I had been led to believe that German planes were not very good and that we could
fly away from them whenever we wanted to. As I
looked back over my shoulder and ascertained that
they were gaining upon me in spite of every maneuver
that I tried, I felt a queer sort of admiration for their
misjudged flying ability, mingled with an unspeakable
contempt for the judgment of my instructors who
had claimed to know all about German aeroplanes.
I climbed, dived, tailspun, circled and stalled. They
beat me at every maneuver and continued to overhaul
me. Just when I had begun to despair of ever seeing
my learned instructors again I ran into a cloud.
Dimly I realized I was in a position of advantage for
the moment, so I improved it to the utmost. Half-
way in I reversed directions and began climbing

heavenward. After thirty minutes industriously occupied in throwing my pursuers off my trail, I ventured out of concealment and gratefully made my way home. There on the field two of my dear old comrades were waiting for me to come in. What anxiety they would have suffered if they had known what I had just been through!

"Hello, Rick! Why the devil didn't you wait for us?" Doug Campbell inquired, as I began to climb out of my machine. "We chased you all over France trying to catch up with you!"

"Where did you go, Eddie, after we lost you in those clouds?" demanded Charley Chapman, looking at me interestedly as he leaned against my suspended leg. "We've been home almost half an hour!" Here, it seemed were the two pilots — American instead of Boche — who had been chasing me.

I thought very intently for a quarter of a second. Then I pushed Chapman away and descended from my machine.

"I thought I remembered seeing a Boche back in Germany and went back to make sure," I replied easily. "But I guess I was mistaken."

CHAPTER IV

DOWNING MY FIRST HUN

IT will be noticed that my preparation for combat fighting in the air was a gradual one. As I look back upon it now, it seems that I had the rare good fortune to experience almost every variety of danger that can beset the war pilot before I ever fired a shot at an enemy from an aeroplane.

This good fortune is rare, it appears to me. Many a better man than myself has leaped into his stride and begun accumulating victories from his very first flight over the lines.   It was a brilliant start for him and his successes brought him instant renown.   But he had been living on the cream at the start and was unused to the skim-milk of aviation.   One day the cream gave out and the first dose of skim-milk terminated his career.

So despite the weeks and weeks of disappointment that attended my early fighting career, I appreciated even then the enormous benefit that I would reap later from these experiences.   I can now most solemnly affirm that had I won my first victory during my first trips over the lines I believe I would never have survived a dozen combats.   Every disappointment that came to me brought with it an enduring lesson that repaid me eventually tenfold.   If any one of my antagonists had been through the same school of disappointments that had so annoyed me it is probable that he, instead of me, would now be telling his friends back home about his series of victories over the enemy.

April in France is much like April anywhere else. Rains and cloudy weather appear suddenly out of a clear sky and flying becomes out of the question or very precarious at best.   On the 29th of April, 1918, we rose at six o'clock and stuck our heads out of doors as usual for a hasty survey of a dismal sky.   For the past three or four days it had rained steadily.   No patrols had gone out from our aerodrome.   If they had gone they would not have found any enemy aircraft about, for none had been sighted from the lines along our sector.

About noon the sun suddenly broke through and our hopes began to rise.   I was slated for a patrol that afternoon and from three o'clock on I waited about the hangars watching the steadily clearing sky.   Captain Hall and I were to stand on alert until six o'clock that night at the aerodrome.   Precisely at five o'clock Captain Hall received a telephone call from the French headquarters at Beaumont stating that an enemy two-seater machine had just crossed our lines and was flying south over their heads.

Captain Hall and I had been walking about the field with our flying clothes on and our machines were standing side by side with their noses pointing into the wind. Within the minute we had jumped into our seats and our mechanics were twirling the propellers. Just then the telephone sergeant came running out to us and told Captain Hall to hold his flight until the Major was ready. He was to accompany us and would be on the field in two minutes.

While the sergeant was delivering the message I was scanning the northern heavens and there I suddenly picked up a tiny speck against the clouds above the Forêt de la Reine, which I was convinced must be the enemy plane we were after. The Major was not yet in sight. Our motors were smoothly turning over and everything was ready.

Pointing out the distant speck to Jimmy Hall, I begged him to give the word to go before we lost sight of our easy victim. If we waited for the Major we might be too late.

To my great joy Captain Hall acquiesced and immediately ordered the boys to pull away the blocks from our wheels. His motor roared as he opened up his throttle and in a twinkling both our machines were running rapidly over the surface of the field. Almost side by side we arose and climbing swiftly, soared away in a straight line after our distant Boche.

In five minutes we were above our observation balloon line which stretches along some two miles or so behind the front. I was on Jimmy's right wing and off to my right in the direction of Pont-à-Mousson I could still distinguish our unsuspecting quarry. Try as I might I could not induce the Captain to turn in that direction, though I dipped my wings, darted away from him and tried in every way to attract his attention to the target which was so conspicuous to me. He stupidly continued on straight north.

I determined to sever relations with him and take on the Boche alone, since he evidently was generous enough to give me a clear field. Accordingly I swerved swiftly away from Captain Hall and within five minutes overhauled the enemy and adroitly maneuvered myself into an ideal position just under his sheltering tail. It was a large three-seater machine and a brace of guns poked their noses out to the rear over my head. With fingers closing on my triggers I prepared for a dash upwards and quickly pulled back my stick. Up I zoomed until my sights began to travel along the length of the fusilage overhead. Suddenly they rested on a curiously familiar looking device. It was the French circular cocard painted brightly under each wing! Up to this time I had not even thought of looking for its nationality, so certain had I been that this must be the Boche machine that had been sighted by the French headquarters.

Completely disgusted with myself, I viraged abruptly away from my latest blunder, finding some little satisfaction in witnessing the startled surprise of the three Frenchmen aboard the craft, who had not become aware of my proximity until they saw me flash past them. At any rate I had stalked them successfully and might have easily downed them if they had been Boches. But as it was, it would be a trifle difficult to face Jimmy Hall again and explain to him why I had left him alone to get myself five miles away under the tail of a perfectly harmless ally three-seater. I looked about to discover Jimmy's whereabouts.

There he was cavorting about amidst a thick barrage of black shell-bursts across the German lines. He was half-way to St. Mihiel and a mile or two inside Hun territory. Evidently he was waiting for me to discover my mistake and then overtake him, for he was having a delightful time with the Archy gunners, doing loops, barrels, side-slips and spins immediately over their heads to show them his contempt for them, while he waited for his comrade. Finally he came out of the Archy area with a long graceful dive and swinging up alongside my machine he wiggled his wings as though he were laughing at me and then suddenly he set a course back towards Pont-à-Mousson.

Whether or not he knew all along that a German craft was in that region I could not tell. But when he began to change his direction and curve up into the sun I followed close behind him knowing that there was a good reason for this maneuver. I looked earnestly about me in every direction.

Yes! There was a scout coming towards us from north of Pont-à-Mousson. It was at about our altitude. I knew it was a Hun the moment I saw it, for it had the familiar lines of their new Pfalz. Moreover, my confidence in James Norman Hall was such that I knew he couldn't make a mistake. And he was still climbing into the sun, carefully keeping his position between its glare and the oncoming fighting plane. I clung as closely to Hall as I could. The Hun was steadily approaching us, unconscious of his danger, for we were full in the sun.

With the first downward dive of Jimmy's machine I was by his side. We had at least a thousand feet advantage over the enemy and we were two to one numerically. He might outdive our machines, for the Pfalz is a famous diver, while our faster climbing Nieuports had a droll little habit of shedding their fabric when plunged too furiously through the air. The Boche hadn't a chance to outfly us. His only salvation would be in a dive towards his own lines.

These thoughts passed through my mind in a flash

and I instantly determined upon my tactics. While
Hall went in for his attack I would keep my altitude
and get a position the other side of the Pfalz, to cut
off his retreat.

No sooner had I altered my line of flight than the
German pilot saw me leave the sun's rays. Hall was
already half-way to him when he stuck up his nose and
began furiously climbing to the upper ceiling. I let
him pass me and found myself on the other side just
as Hall began firing. I doubt if the Boche had seen
Hall's Nieuport at all.

Surprised by discovering this new antagonist, Hall,
ahead of him, the Pfalz immediately abandoned all
idea of a battle and banking around to the right started
for home, just as I had expected him to do. In a trice
I was on his tail. Down, down we sped with throttles
both full open. Hall was coming on somewhere in
my rear. The Boche had no heart for evolutions or
maneuvers. He was running like a scared rabbit,
as I had run from Campbell. I was gaining upon him
every instant and had my sights trained dead upon his
seat before I fired my first shot.

At 150 yards I pressed my triggers. The tracer
bullets cut a streak of living fire into the rear of the
Pfalz tail. Raising the nose of my aeroplane slightly
the fiery streak lifted itself like the stream of water
pouring from a garden hose. Gradually it settled into
the pilot's seat. The swerving of the Pfalz course
indicated that its rudder no longer was held by a directing hand. At 2000 feet above the enemy's lines
I pulled up my headlong dive and watched the enemy
machine continuing on its course. Curving slightly
to the left the Pfalz circled a little to the south and
the next minute crashed onto the ground just at the
edge of the woods a mile inside their own lines. I
had brought down my first enemy aeroplane and had
not been subjected to a single shot!

Hall was immediately beside me.   He was evidently as pleased as I was over our success, for he danced his machine about in incredible maneuvers.   And then I realized that old friend Archy was back on the job. We were not two miles away from the German anti-aircraft batteries and they put a furious bombardment of shrapnel all about us.   I was quite ready to call it a day and go home, but Captain Hall deliberately returned to the barrage and entered it with me at his heels.   Machine-guns and rifle fire from the trenches greeted us and I do not mind admitting that I got out quickly the way I came in without any unnecessary delay, but Hall continued to do stunts over their heads for ten minutes, surpassing all the acrobatics that the enraged Boches had ever seen even over their own peaceful aerodromes.

Jimmy exhausted his spirits at about the time the Huns had exhausted all their available ammunition and we started blithely for home.   Swooping down to our field side by side, we made a quick landing and taxied our victorious machines up to the hangars. Then jumping out we ran to each other, extending glad hands for our first exchange of congratulations.   And then we noticed that the squadron pilots and mechanics were streaming across the aerodrome towards us from all directions.   They had heard the news while we were still dodging shrapnel and were hastening out to welcome our return.   The French had telephoned in a confirmation of my first victory, before I had had time to reach home.   Not a single bullet hole had punctured any part of my machine.

There is a peculiar gratification in receiving congratulations from one's squadron for a victory in the air.   It is worth more to a pilot than the applause of the whole outside world.   It means that one has won the confidence of men who share the misgivings, the aspirations, the trials and the dangers of aeroplane fighting. And with each victory comes a renewal and re-cementing of ties that bind together these brothers-in-arms. No closer fraternity exists in the world than that of the air-fighters in this great war. And I have yet to find one single individual who has attained conspicuous success in bringing down enemy aeroplanes who can be said to be spoiled either by his successes or by the generous congratulations of his comrades. If he were capable of being spoiled he would not have had the character to have won continuous victories, for the smallest amount of vanity is fatal in aeroplane fighting. Self-distrust rather is the quality to which many a pilot owes his protracted existence.

It was with a very humble gratitude then that I received the warm congratulations of Lufbery, whom I had always revered for his seventeen victories — of Doug Campbell and Alan Winslow who had brought down the first machines that were credited to the American Squadrons, and of many others of 94 Squadron who had seen far more service in the battle areas than had I. I was glad to be at last included in the proud roll of victors of this squadron. These pals of mine were to see old 94 lead all American Squadrons in the number of successes over the Huns.

The following day I was notified that General Gerard, the Commanding Officer of the Sixth French Army, had offered to decorate Captain Hall and myself in the name of the French Government for our victory of the day before. We were then operating in conjunction with this branch of the French Army. The Croix de Guerre with palm was to be accorded each of us, provided such an order met the approval of our own government. But at that time officers in the American Army could not accept decorations from a foreign Government, so the ceremony of presenta-

tion was denied us. Both Captain Hall and myself
had been included, as such was the French rule where
two pilots participated in a victory.

The truth was that in the tense excitement of this
first victory, I was quite blind to the fact that I was
shooting deadly bullets at another aviator; and if I
had been by myself, there is no doubt in my own mind
but that I should have made a blunder again in some
particular which would have reversed the situation.
Captain Hall's presence, if not his actual bullets, had
won the victory and had given me that wonderful
feeling of self-confidence which made it possible for
me subsequently to return to battle without him and
handle similar situations successfully.

CHAPTER V

JIMMY MEISSNER STRIPS HIS WINGS

FROM the entries in my diary of this April period
one would get rather an unfavorable opinion of
that quarter of France in which our Squadron was
located. "Rain and Mud!" "Dud Weather!"
"No flying to-day!" are a few of the samples.
None of the pilots or enlisted men of our American flying squadrons will be easily enraptured in the
days to come with descriptions of the romance of
this part of La Belle France. The villages are dismal
and dirty. Every householder rejoices in the size and
stench of his manure heap, which always decorates
the entire area in front of his house. Sidewalks there
are none. The streets slop with mud of the clinging
variety, and even in the larger cities themselves the
American finds but little to interest him. An overwhelming love for his own country is the most enduring souvenir the American soldier in France gained

from his visits to these towns of the Vosges and the Meuse.

To add to our irritation, we felt that every day we lost by bad weather was injuring American aviation in the eyes of our Allies. The British and the French had had three years and more of air fighting and the veterans of these squadrons looked upon the American pilots with something of amusement and something of polite contempt. They had believed in the story of our twenty thousand aeroplanes which had been promised by April. Here was April at hand and we were flying ill-equipped machines that we fortunately had been able to wangle out of the French and English. Our pilots were not trained under the veteran leadership that England could provide and our methods were crude and new. Our spirit and determination were perhaps never doubted by our Allies, but we all of us felt that we must show these more experienced squadrons that we could equal them in any department of aviation, even with our inferior machines, if we only might have the opportunity for flying. And still the rain continued!

The day after my first enemy machine was brought down we were unable on account of the fog to carry out our air patrols. That afternoon a group of American newspaper men came out to the aerodrome to talk to me about my sensations in shooting down another man's machine. They took photographs of me and jotted down notes and finally requested me to make a short flight over the field and perform a few stunts. The weather was not too rough for such an exhibition, so I gladly complied and for half an hour I rolled and looped and dived about the clouds a thousand feet or so above the aerodrome. But the visibility was so bad that I could not see the ground a mile away from the field.

On May first Major Lufbery and I made a little attempt to get a Hun, but it ended in a somewhat ludicrous fiasco. Luf was attached to 94 at that time, not as a commanding officer, but as a pilot for instruction. He was America's Ace of Aces and our most distinguished pilot. His long and successful experience in air-fighting was naturally of the greatest benefit to all of us younger pilots and every one of us considered it an honor to be sent out on an expedition with him.

We were sitting about the hangars talking and smoking about five o'clock that afternoon, when the telephone rang and Major Lufbery was informed that a German aeroplane had been sighted over Montsec, just above St. Mihiel. Lufbery hung up the phone; grinned his confident smile and began pulling on his flying suit. I suspected something was up and walking quickly over to where Lufbery was dressing I asked him if I might go with him.

"Where do you want to go?" asked Lufbery.

"Wherever you go!" I replied.

My answer evidently pleased the Major, for he grunted his customary chuckle and said, "Come ahead."

I was delighted at the opportunity of accompanying Lufbery anywhere, and was inside my flying clothes as soon as he was. As we walked out to our Nieuports, he told me we might get a Boche. All I had to do was to follow him and keep my eyes open.

We flew over Montsec for half an hour without getting a sign of a Hun. Thick as the day was, we would have been able to see the French anti-aircraft shells bursting if any enemy aeroplanes had been in that sector. So after cruising about once more over the German lines, Lufbery started for home in the direction of Pont-à-Mousson. We passed directly over the town at an altitude of 6000 feet.

Suddenly Lufbery started diving directly down. I

immediately nosed over and followed in hot pursuit,
thinking he had spotted an enemy below and was about
to open an attack.   But a minute later I saw that the
Major was very evidently in trouble.   His propeller
had stopped turning and he was anxiously looking
about and circling away for a favorable landing place.

Following him at a little distance behind I saw him
settle down into a very respectable field just south of
Pont-à-Mousson.   His machine dropped gently down
to the mud, rolled along a few feet, then to my astonishment it stuck its nose into the mud, stood with tail
pointing heavenward, hesitated there for a second or
two and, as I passed about a hundred feet overhead,
his Nieuport turned gently upside down and lay there
on its back.   I dare say Lufbery was swearing softly
to himself as he saw me glide past.

Circling back I was highly amused to see the Major
crawling out on his hands and knees through the mud.
He waved a dripping hand to me to indicate he was
all right.   I put on speed and hurried on home to send
him help.   His machine had somersaulted less than
three miles from the enemy's lines.

Major Huffer himself took down from my description the exact location of the "panne," and jumping
into a motor car he ran up to the spot I had indicated.
There he found Lufbery, none the worse for his forced
landing, excepting a slight scratch alongside his nose.
One of his cylinders had blown out and he had found
himself at just a sufficient height to glide down and
land at a spot safely behind the observation of the
enemy.

It was on the very next day that Lieutenant Jimmy
Meissner of Brooklyn had another very trying experience with the Nieuport machine.   About noon he and
Lieutenant Davis were sent out to protect a French
observation machine which had been ordered to take
photographs of the enemy's positions back of Pont-à-

Mousson.   The photographing machine went down to
seven or eight thousand feet and was proceeding calmly
on its work, leaving the matter of its defense to the
two American pilots sitting upstairs some four or
five thousand feet overhead.

Suddenly Jimmy Meissner discovered two Albatros
fighting machines almost upon him, coming from out
of the sun.   They were already on the attack and were
firing as they dived swiftly upon the two Nieuports.

Jimmy made a quick maneuver and zoomed up above
the nearest Albatros.   Instantly he utilized his advantage, now that he had the upper floor, and in a trice
he headed downwards upon the tail of the enemy, firing long bursts from his machine-gun as he plunged
after the fleeing Hun.   But the Albatros pilot was an
old hand at this game, and before Meissner could overtake him he had thrown his machine into a tailspin
which not only presented a target difficult to hit, but
almost persuaded Jimmy that the machine was falling
out of control.

Jimmy had heard many stories of this sort of " playing possum " however.   He determined to keep after
the spinning Albatros and see the end of the combat.
Accordingly he opened his throttle and dived headlong
down.   One thousand, two thousand — three thousand
feet he plunged, regardless of everything but the occasional target that whirled periodically before his
sights.   At last he got in a burst that produced immediate results.   The Albatros sent out a quick puff
of smoke that was immediately followed by a mass of
flames.   One of Meissner's tracer bullets had set fire
to the fuel tank of the enemy's machine.   The plucky
victor pulled up his Nieuport and took a self-satisfied
look about him.

There scarcely a thousand feet below him were the
enemy's lines.   From various directions machine guns
and short Archies were directing their fire upon him.

He grinned at them contemptuously and looked away for the expected view of Lieutenant Davis' Nieuport and the other Albatros. Neither was to be seen. Perhaps they were on his other wing. One glance around to the left and Jimmy's heart was in his throat.

He saw that the entire length of his left upper wing was stripped of fabric! And as he turned a horrified gaze to the other wing, he saw that its fabric too was even at that moment beginning to tear away from its leading edge and was flapping in the wind! So furious had been his downward plunge that the force of the wind's pressure had torn away the fragile covering on both his upper wings. Without this supporting surface his aeroplane would drop like a stone. Although it couldn't make much difference whether it dropped into German lines or within his own so far as his life was concerned, Meissner admitted later he always wanted a military funeral; so he eased off his speed and tenderly turned about his wobbling machine and headed back towards France.

Giving the slightest possible engine power and nursing his crippled little 'bus with great delicacy, Meissner succeeded in gaining No Man's Land, then passed over the American trenches. He did not dare to alter either his direction or speed. Less than half a mile further his machine glided into the earth and crashed beyond repair. Meissner crawled forth from the wreckage and felt himself all over carefully, to try to make himself understand that he was in reality in the land of the living — and free.

Such was the climax of James A. Meissner's first victory, and the Squadron's fourth. Meissner lived to repeat his success many times and to add much luster to the reputation of his squadron. But a narrower escape from death has rarely favored any pilot at the front.

Again did the news of the squadron's victory pre-

cede the arrival of the victor. When Meissner arrived
at the aerodrome by automobile an hour or two later,
the American photographers and newspaper men had
already arrived and he was begged to stand for his
photograph. Like an embarrassed schoolboy Jimmy
pushed them away, exclaiming,

" Nobody saw the machine fall in flames but myself.
It may not be confirmed."

Great was his surprise when he learned that a French
observation post had witnessed the whole combat and
had already telephoned us, not only the result of the
fight, but the position where Meissner had been forced
to land. We all took a hand then and forced the embarrassed pilot to stand and face the camera. It was
a custom with which most of 94's pilots had to become
acquainted within the next six months.

But our happiness and satisfaction were short-lived.
Later in the afternoon Captain Peterson returned from
his patrol over enemy's lines and brought back with
him but two of the three companions who had gone
out with him. We all walked out to get the news.
Peterson had shot down another enemy aeroplane in
flames, totaling five for the squadron with this double
in one day. But during his combat, in which five
Pfalz monoplanes had been attacked by our four pilots,
Captain Peterson saw one of his Nieuports pass
swiftly by him, ablaze from stem to stern. He collected his patrol quickly about him and rapidly scanned
their markings. Charley Chapman's was missing!
All were present but Chapman's well known machine.

Then Peterson remembered seeing Chapman leave
the fight to attack a two-seater German machine below
him. Other pilots later filled in the details that were
lacking. Chapman had no sooner dived to the attack
than one of the hostile fighting machines was upon his
trail. Chapman turned to meet his pursuer and in
doing so he brought himself full into the range of

fire of the two-seater.   Set on fire by the first burst,
the mounting flames soon were quickly swept over the
whole structure of Chapman's machine by the rush of
the wind.

It was our first loss in combat and sadly did we feel
that loss.   Charley Chapman was one of the best
loved of our little band and the sudden pang came to
each one of us that we would never see his jolly good-
natured smile again.   The horror of his fate was not
lost upon us, one may be sure.   No form of death is
so dreaded by the pilot as falling to the earth in flames.
Later on our most noted member leaped overboard to
his death to avoid the slower torture of being burnt
alive.

One of the queerest boys who had been wished into
our squadron by an allwise Air Staff was one we will
call "T. S."   He was the source of constant amusement to the rest of us — amusement sometimes tinc-
tured by a spasmodic desire to turn him over to the
enemy where he might amuse the prison camps with
his drolleries.   We will call him T. S. because that is
not his name.   T. S. came to us early in the training
season and was immediately marked as a pilot afraid
of his medicine.   He was frankly a coward and he
didn't care to conceal the fact.   His very frankness
on this subject was very amusing to the rest of us,
who were every bit as much afraid of bullets and war
as he was but who had a certain shame about admitting
the fact.   But T. S. could see no use in playing the
hypocrite about so deadly a business as getting shot
down from on high.   Naturally it required some little
attention to keep T. S. up to the scratch when it came
to patrol work over the lines.   The boy was a fair
pilot and was a strapping big fellow who always was
in the best of health and spirits.   But he did object to
guns and ammunition.

The first occasion of his fluking a military job was

one day when he was left on the alert at the aerodrome. All the patrols were out and he had the secondary responsibility of responding to a hurry call. The telephone sergeant came running out to the hangar and confronted our shameless reserve:

"Who is on duty here this afternoon, sir?" inquired the man.

"I believe I am," returned Lieutenant T. S., languidly eyeing the inquisitive sergeant. "Anything I can do for you?"

"Two enemy aeroplanes have been alerted over our lines, sir, in the vicinity of St. Mihiel. They are two-seater machines sent over by the Germans to observe our positions." The sergeant saluted and made room for the rush of events that usually followed the receipt of such intelligence.

But T. S. never moved an eyelash. He looked the sergeant up and down, finally speaking deliberately and with finality.

"Well," he said, "let them observe! If you think I am going over there to get shot down myself, you are mistaken!"

When questioned later by the Commanding Officer, the lieutenant unblushingly repeated his statement.

"I am simply scared to death at the thought of getting into all those Archies and things over the lines," he admitted, "and I'm not going to do it if I can get out of it. There are plenty of fellows here who do not mind them and they are the ones you ought to send."

The Officer stared at T. S. in amazement, unable to criticize the faultless logic of this frank soldier. After thinking it over, it was decided to send T. S. out in patrols with veteran leaders until he had somewhat accustomed himself to the terrors of Archy. By this means a valuable pilot might be saved for the government.

Accordingly one afternoon Lieutenant T. S. was ordered to accompany Captain Hall and myself, in response to an alert that had just come in. Two enemy observation planes had been reported crossing our lines north of Nancy at an altitude of only eight thousand feet. Captain Hall directed T. S. to stick in formation close behind his left wing, while I was to occupy the same position on his right. The Captain was the flight leader and we were to obey his signals and directions.

We got away from the field without delay and streaked it across the sky in a perfect V formation. Straight towards the lines we flew, climbing as we advanced. As we neared the lines, we searched the neighboring skies but could discover no aeroplanes in sight, enemy or otherwise. So over the lines we went. We had reached a spot almost two miles behind the front, when all of a sudden a dozen magnificent Archies burst simultaneously under, above and all around us. The Germans had planned the whole show, to catch us in just this kind of trap. They had counted upon our coming over at the same altitude at which the two decoy planes had traveled and had prepared their anti-aircraft guns and time fuses thoroughly to drench this certain spot with flying shrapnel.

Fortunately no direct hits were made. But I noticed one shell explode under the tail of T. S.'s machine, lifting his 'bus suddenly and violently into the air, where it hung suspended for a moment with the tail pointing heavenward. The next moment he had recovered control of his Nieuport and making a short half turn, he headed for home and opened up his throttle to its full. Straight for Nancy he flew, looking neither to the right nor the left. Captain Hall and I followed after him, the Captain making desperate efforts to overtake him, all the while dipping his wings and trying to summon the frightened airman back to

the formation. But it was no use. In two minutes
T. S. was out of sight, with an unusually vigorous
engine turning up at least 1700 revolutions of his propeller per minute. We abandoned our pursuit and
continued on our patrol.

An hour later we landed at our aerodrome and inquired for T. S. Nothing had been seen or heard of
him. Somewhat alarmed at this strange climax to
the afternoon's performance, we telephoned all over
the country for news of him, but only to learn that he
had not landed at any of our aerodromes near the
front. Dinner passed and still no news of T. S. We
decided he had become confused in his location and had
landed by mistake in an aerodrome of the Germans.
The lines from Nancy to Switzerland ran in such an
irregular fashion that such a mistake would be quite
possible.

Not until late the following afternoon was our
anxiety relieved. Then came a telephone call from
Lieutenant T. S. himself. He had landed quite safely
at a French aerodrome just south of Nancy and but a
dozen miles from our own field. He informed us that
he would fly back to us at the earliest possible moment.
Pressed as to why he had kept us in such long suspense about him, he replied with great indignation that
he considered he was doing pretty well to have sufficiently recovered from shell-shock within twenty-four
hours to get to the telephone!

The very rarity of such an example in American
aviation makes this story worth the telling. Heroic
conduct in war has become so usual and ordinary a
thing that such a career as that of T. S. seems incredible and even amusing. The very contrast indicates
how thoroughly American boys have smothered their
natural desire for " living through the war " and have
hurled themselves with supreme self-sacrifice into the
thick of dangers over the battle lines.

CHAPTER VI

JIMMY HALL'S LAST FIGHT

ON Monday, May 6th, 1918, the monotony of another "dud" day was happily broken by the arrival at our aerodrome of our old comrades of the 95th Squadron, who had been with us at Epiez. They had just completed their gunnery training at Cazeau and were now ready for the great war. From that day to the end of the conflict Squadrons 94 and 95 continued to occupy the same aerodrome. No other two American squadrons in France ever equaled their victories and number of hours flying over the lines.

Squadron 95 contained much the same quality of material as was found in my own squadron. John Mitchell of Boston, now the Captain of the Squadron, was an old boy from Fay School, St. Mark's and Harvard.

Quentin Roosevelt was one of the newly assigned pilots in 95. Both the enlisted men and his fellow pilots found that Quent relied upon his own attainments rather than upon the reputation of his celebrated father; and it is safe to say that Quent Roosevelt was easily the most popular man in his Squadron. To indicate Quentin's love for square dealing and fairness, I may divulge a little secret that were Quentin still living might not be told.

His commanding officer, moved perhaps by the fact that Quentin was the son of Theodore Roosevelt, made him a Flight Commander before he had ever made a flight over the lines. Quentin appreciated the fact that his inexperienced leadership might jeopardize the lives of the men following him. He accordingly declined the honor. But his superiors directed him to obey orders and to take the office that had been assigned to him. A trio of pilots, all of whom had had more experience in war flying than had Quentin so far received, were placed under his command.   And an order was posted directing Lieutenant Roosevelt's Flight to go on its first patrol the following morning.

Quentin called his pilots to one side.

" Look here, you fellows, which one of you has had the most flying over the lines?   You, Curtis? "

Curtis shook his head and replied:

" Buckley, or Buford,— both of them have seen more of this game than I have."

Quentin looked them all over and made up his mind before he spoke.

" Well, any one of you knows more about it than I do!   To-morrow morning you, Buckley, are to be Flight Commander in my place.   As soon as we leave the ground, you take the lead.   I will drop into your place.   We will try out each man in turn.   They may be able to make me Flight Commander in name, but the best pilot in my group is going to lead it in fact."

Until the day he died a gallant soldier's death, Quentin Roosevelt continued to fly under the leadership of one of his pilots.   He himself had never led a flight.

Sumner Sewell, of Harvard, Bill Taylor, later killed in combat, old Heinie Heindricks, later shot down with ten wounds and made a prisoner in Germany, and a dozen other choice spirits combined to make of Squadron 95 an aggregation second to none other in the world — excepting that of my own, the 94th.

About eight o'clock in the morning of May 7th, 1918, the French alerted us by telephone.   Four enemy aeroplanes were flying over Pont-à-Mousson and were headed for the south.   The First Flight — my own — was on duty at the time — very luckily for us, as Jimmy Hall, Eddie Green and I thought.   We jumped for our machines and anxiously watched the mechanics swinging the propellers.

"Switch off!" yelled the mechanic.

"Coupez!" I replied as I cut the switch with one finger while wriggling the rest of them into my fur gloves. Three or four downward strokes of the stick and the mechanic paused a second to look over the fusilage into my face.

"Contact?" he yelled determinedly.

"Contact it is!" I called back, snapping on the switch. The well groomed motor caught with a roar at the first heave and at almost the same time I saw that Hall and Green were in equal readiness for the business of the day. A moment later and the three machines lifted their spinning wheels from the ground and heading straight towards the little city of Pont-à-Mousson on the Moselle, we began climbing as we flew.

When I looked down and found the roofs of Pont-à-Mousson below me, my altimeter indicated an elevation of 12,000 feet. Nothing appeared to be in sight inside the German lines, so I turned my scrutiny to the west towards St. Mihiel. The winding river there traced an indistinct line around the hills about St. Mihiel, and finally disappeared near distant Verdun. I drew my focus a little closer and instantly detected a moving shadow some two or three miles inside our lines in the vicinity of Beaumont, about half-way to St. Mihiel. It was a Boche — this I saw at the second glance. Looked like a two-seater and was very evidently regulating the Huns' artillery fire against some American position back of Beaumont. I dipped my wings to signal the news of my discovery to my companions and as I did so I saw Jimmy Hall's Nieuport play the same maneuver. The three of us began our direct pique together.

As we neared the vicinity of our unsuspicious prey I noticed a German Archy shell break, not near me but in close proximity to their own machine. The Hun shells emit a black smoke upon bursting, which distinguishes them from the Allies' shells, which show a white smoke. Instantly the two-seater Albatros turned and dived for Germany.

A moment later three more German shells burst ahead of the retreating two-seater. And these three bursts were at about our present altitude. It seemed to be a previously arranged method of conversation which the gunners below were carrying on with the aeroplane high above them. They were telling the Albatros that our three fast fighting machines were approaching from the east, and they indicated by the smoke-bursts the precise altitude at which we were flying.

Many times since have I noticed this marvelous signaling arrangement between the anti-aircraft gunners and the German aeroplanes. Upon one occasion I saw shell-bursts informing the Boche pilots of my presence above a cloud when I was hiding and planning a surprise party for the oncoming Huns. This admirable liaison between German artillery and their aviators might be imitated with great advantage by our own army. For not only does the threatened machine get this valuable warning, but aeroplane reinforcements far distant can see these smoke-bursts and fly to the rescue with full information as to the number, altitude and perhaps the type of hostile machines ahead of them. Almost invariably an overpowering enemy formation appeared shortly after these signals were sent up.

Still another signal was adopted by the Hun batteries to indicate the formation of our machines to their pilots. Through their powerful telescopes they ascertained the relative position of each machine in our formation. If one of our machines climbed high above the rest of the formation in order to perch well upstairs and guard against a surprise from the ceiling, this maneuver was communicated to the Boche pilots by

sending up one shell which burst well above the others.
Immediately the Boche pilots were on their guard
against an antagonist who was hiding in the glare of
the sun and could not be seen by them.   The single
high burst notified them that he was there.

As Captain Hall, Lieutenant Green and myself drew
nearer to the slower two-seater machine, another
smoke-burst signal came from the batteries below.   I
turned my head and looked about me to see if enemy
machines were coming in answer to these signals.
Back towards Pont-à-Mousson I thought I saw something in the sky.   Keeping my gaze fixed in that direction, my suspicions were soon verified.   Four Pfalz
scouts were in hot pursuit after us and were diagon-
alling our course so as to cut off our retreat.

Sheering in ahead of Captain Hall, I wigwagged
my wings and headed away to the right.   This is the
signal given to the leader of a flight, to draw his attention to a danger that he has overlooked.   The next
moment Captain Hall had again taken the lead and all
three of our machines had turned and were headed
eastward.   The oncoming enemy formation was flying much below us, which gave us a decided advantage.
We could dive down to the attack when we chose and
could keep out of their reach so long as we kept above
them.   Our machines were at that time some three or
four miles inside the German lines.

For some unexplained reason Captain Hall began
turning more and more into Germany.   I wondered
what could be the trouble.   Either he saw something in
that direction, or else he still was ignorant of the near
presence of the four Pfalz machines.   I debated the
matter for an instant, then darted in ahead of Jimmy
and gave him another signal   Fully convinced now that
he must see the Boche formation which was hardly
more than a mile from us, I came out of my virage
and headed down for the attack.   With a man like

Captain Hall behind me, I did not fear for the outcome. His machine followed close behind mine.

From our superior height we soon accumulated a speed which brought us into a very favorable position. I selected the rear Pfalz scout and got my sights dead upon him and prepared to shoot. My aim never wavered as the distance between us narrowed. At 200 yards I pressed my trigger and watched my tracer bullets speeding ahead into the Pfalz's wings. My gun continued to fire steadily until I had approached to within 50 yards of the Pfalz. Then the enemy machine turned over and fell into a vrille. I did not dare to follow him farther. I zoomed up until I stood fairly upright on my tail, in which position I looked swiftly around me.

My first thought was that during the intentness of my pursuit against my victim one of his companions might be getting a similar position over my tail. To my great relief no enemy was behind me. But off to the right, not a hundred yards away, I saw a Nieuport diving steeply down, and on his tail was a diving Pfalz pouring streams of living fire into the fusilage and cockpit of the American machine. Even as I watched this frightful death chase, the tables were suddenly turned. Hall or Green, whichever it was, seeming to tire of the monotony, zoomed quickly upwards and looped his machine completely over, coming out of the loop just as the Pfalz went under him. In a twinkling the situation was reversed and the Nieuport was pouring bullets at the rate of 650 per minute into the Boche machine, ahead.

The Boche fell and I piqued down and flew alongside the victorious Jimmy Hall. My surprise can be imagined when I discovered not Hall, but Green looking across at me from his seat! And no other machine was in the sky. What could have happened to Jimmy Hall?

We flew homewards together, Green and I, encountering a furious storm of Archy as we crossed the trenches. Arrived at the landing ground, I immediately ran over to Green to inquire for news of Jimmy. My heart was heavy as lead within me, for I was certain as to what the answer would be.

"Went down in a tail spin with his upper wing gone!" Green informed me without my speaking. "I saw him dive onto a Boche just as I began my attack. The next I saw of him, he was going in a vrille and the Boche was still firing at him as he was falling. He must have struck just back of those woods behind Montsec."

I cannot describe the joy that came to the squadron about a month later when we received a letter from Jimmy Hall himself. He wrote from a hospital in Germany, where he was laid up with a broken ankle. He had not been shot down in the combat, as we had supposed, but had dived too swiftly for the weak wing structure of a Nieuport. His upper wing had collapsed in full flight; and not until he had almost reached the ground had he been able to straighten out his aeroplane. In the crash he had escaped with merely a cracked ankle. In another fortnight he hoped he would be as good as ever.

On November 19th, 1918, when the day came for the French army to march in and occupy the fortress and city of Metz, several of the officers from our squadron flew over from our aerodrome at Rembercourt to witness the ceremony. We appeared to be the first Americans that the Metz populace had seen. One of the first citizens that spoke to us while we were overlooking the triumphal procession through the Plaza, asked us if we knew an American aviator named Captain Hall. We immediately gathered around him and drew him one side.

"Well," he said, half in French and half in German, " your Captain Hall was confined in the hospital here for many weeks and then was in a prison. Only yesterday the Germans evacuated Metz and all their prisoners were et at liberty. Captain Hall left here yesterday in the direction of Nancy. He walked away quite nicely with the aid of a cane, and perhaps he will be able to get a ride part of the way."

Upon our return to the aerodrome from Metz next day, we learned that Jimmy Hall had indeed come through the lines. He had gone to Paris for a rest. A number of his old friends immediately got into their machines and flew to Paris, where they greeted their long lost comrade with appropriate ceremonies at the justly celebrated Inn of Monsieur de Crillon — that American aviator's rendezvous and oasis in Paris.

And from Jimmy Hall himself we learned the true facts of his accident that day over Montsec. He had overtaxed his Nieuport by too fast a dive. A wing gave way and threatened to drop him into the woods below. But by nursing his machine along with engine half on he was succeeding, just as Jimmy Meissner had done the day before, in making appreciable headway towards home, when he felt a violent blow on his engine. His motor stopped dead. Again he dropped utterly out of control and eventually crashed in an open field, suffering a badly broken ankle.

One of the pilots with whom we had just been fighting landed near by and came over and made him prisoner. A brief inspection of his motor showed that the violent blow he had felt in mid-air was the result of a direct hit by a dud shell! By some miracle it had failed to explode!

The Pfalz pilot took Captain Hall to his own Squadron quarters where he dined that night with the German aviators. They admitted to him that they had lost two machines in the fight with our formation that day.

Two machines! Green shot one down, but who got the other? I had seen my man fall in a vrille, but having no time to follow him down, I had concluded that he was shamming and was in reality quite unhurt. I had not even thought that I had won a victory in that combat. Imagine my surprise when Captain Hall later described how he himself had seen my antagonist burst into flames and crash, burnt to a crisp! And the surviving pilots of his Squadron admitted to Captain Hall that they had lost two machines in that day's fight! Thus do victories sometimes come to the air-fighter without his realizing it. This enemy machine was never claimed and never credited to me.

Captain Hall's disappearance that day was known to the whole civilized world within twenty-four hours. Widely known to the public as a most gifted author, he was beloved by all American aviators in France as their most daring air-fighter. Every pilot who had had the privilege of his acquaintance burned with a desire to avenge him.

Within fifteen minutes after I had landed from Hall's last patrol I encountered old Luf walking towards the aerodrome with a set look of determination on his usually merry features that denoted no mercy to the enemies he had in mind. He was, I knew, one of Jimmy's very intimate friends. For many months they had flown together in the famous old Lafayette Escadrille.

His mechanics, seeing his approach, anticipated his wishes and began pushing out his plane and collecting his flying equipment for him. Without uttering a word Lufbery pulled on his flying suit, climbed into his machine and set out towards Germany.

He flew for an hour and a half without encountering an enemy plane. Then with but half an hour's petrol remaining he flew deeper into Germany to attack single-handed three fighting machines which he detected north of St. Mihiel. One of these he shot down and the others took to their heels. The following day his gallant victory was confirmed by an advanced Post which had witnessed the combat.

Pathetic and depressing as was the disappearance of James Norman Hall to all of us, I am convinced that the memory of him actually did much to account for the coming extraordinary successes of his squadron. Every pilot in his organization that day swore to revenge the greatest individual loss that the American Air Service had yet suffered.

CHAPTER VII

NEW RESPONSIBILITIES

IT was on May 8th, 1918, the day following the melancholy disappearance of Captain Jimmy Hall, that I was notified that I was to take his place and henceforth was to command Number 1 Flight in our squadron. While very much gratified by this promotion I could not help realizing that before the day was over some other man in my Flight might be taking over the command in my place just as I was taking it from Captain Hall.

Many small ideas that might enable me to prolong my life in aviation had made indelible impressions upon my mind during the past weeks. Several of them had come to my attention through the ludicrous blunders I had been making. The more foolish I had felt over each mistake, the deeper became the lesson to me. I resolved as soon as I became Flight Commander, that I should begin by schooling the pilots under my care in some of the life-saving tricks that I had learned. The dangerous frailty of the Nieuport's wings was one item to bear in mind.

Another of these little precautions that might spell the difference between life and death was the habit I forced upon myself always to make one or two complete circles of the aeroplane before landing at the end of a patrol. The necessity for such a trifling precaution is reasonable. Diving swiftly and suddenly from 15,000 feet altitude where the air is thin and very cold, to the ground level where the change in the pressure upon the temples is often severe, may very easily make the airman dizzy. He may misjudge his distance above the earth and crash violently when trying only to skim the ground. A circuit or two just above the surface of the landing field will give him time to adjust his vision and accustom himself to the change in the air pressure. It takes but a minute and may save a life. Incidentally one can look about and see that no other planes are preparing to land in the same spot at the same time.

Two days after assuming my new command I was returning with my Flight late in the afternoon from a patrol. As we circled about our field I noticed a plane flattening out for a landing below me. I watched him for a moment and saw that he was coming in perfectly. The next instant I noticed another plane coming in to land from exactly the opposite direction. The wheels of both machines touched earth at the opposite ends of the field at approximately the same moment. I was powerless to do more than watch the climax of this stupid proceeding, though I believe I did try to shout to each of them to look out for the other fellow. Of course I could not make myself heard by anybody, but I couldn't help shouting, for I knew instinctively that they were in for a jolly good crash.

The two machines sped gracefully towards each other head on, very much like a staged railroad collision at a county fair. Exactly in the middle of the field they met, the two wings embraced each other in an "aleman left" figure of the lancers and around and around they went, spinning like a top. In the midst of the revolving dance the synchronizing mechanism on Captain Marr's machine-gun became involved and flaming tracer bullets and incendiary bullets shot out of the merry-go-round at the rate of 650 shots per minute. From my box seat above it looked very much like a Fourth of July celebration, with a gigantic pin wheel shooting out living sparks in every direction.

Fortunately not a soul was hurt during the entire celebration, as seems to be the usual lucky outcome of mimic war maneuvers. Both pilots crawled out of the wreckage, shook hands and walked over to the hangars to tell the men in shelter that the show was over. Then we made our landing.

Next day Reed Chambers accompanied me on a patrol across the German lines and we made another rather interesting discovery. Four splendid Albatros machines were approaching us from over Thiaucourt, which was about four miles inside the enemy's territory. They were in good formation and were at about our altitude. I wigwagged over to Reed and he wigwagged back to me. We both understood each other. We were two against the enemy four, but the two on our side had full confidence in each other and both were fairly well bucked up over the recent successes of our Squadron. Perhaps the opposing four might be lacking in this mutual confidence. At any rate, it was worth the chance of trying a bluff to see if we could not get them separated.

It is half the game to know thoroughly one's partner and his capabilities in air-fighting, as it is in any other accomplishment. Reed Chambers was a dare-devil to all appearances, and was always an eager flyer, but I had noticed that he combined a rare caution with his recklessness, making him an excellent and reliable comrade in a fight. Subsequently Reed accumulated seven official victories to his credit and at the end of the war he stood next to me in the number of hours' flying over enemy's lines.

Turning simultaneously towards the Albatros group, we put on our motors and headed directly into them. We didn't swerve an inch from our parallel course as we shot straight at the center of the approaching quartet. Whether they thought we were two furious expert fighters from the United States or two crazy amateurs who might ram them in mid-air I do not know, but before we had arrived within fair shooting range the leader banked over, turned tail and, the rest of the formation sheepishly following him, they all four dived steeply down into Germany, leaving us a vacant sky over Thiaucourt. We had bluffed out a superior formation through sheer impudence.

May 12th was "dud" as far as aviation was concerned, but it was brightened with one of the pleasantest incidents that marked my stay in France. Colonel Mitchell telephoned over to the aerodrome to invite several of us to make a call with him at Château Sirur, a magnificent estate of an old French family, situated some fifty miles south of our aerodrome. Major Huffer, with several other officers from our squadron, left the mess with me immediately after lunch and we reached the Château within a few minutes of the arrival of Colonel Mitchell and Major Hall. The Countess gave us a most cordial greeting, then took us over a part of the estate, which consisted of a park some ten miles square. The grounds were heavily wooded and beautifully kept. Through the woodland curved a winding stream which was spanned at intervals with quaint and ancient stone bridges. Fish ponds and shooting preserves provided the Château with wild game the year around. Several wild boars crossed our road a few paces in front of us during our walk. Shooting wild boar, we were told, was one of the favorite pastimes of the occupants of the Château.

The Château itself contained many palatial rooms. A dimly lighted little chapel occupied one corner of the Château and this part of the building, we learned, dated back to the days of the Romans.

During tea the Countess very graciously invited us to make this magnificent old castle our home if at any time American aviators became worn out with work at the front. I must confess to the good Countess some day that a scandalous number of our over-tired aviators and perhaps still greater a number of not-at-all tired American aviators did subsequently avail themselves of her very generous invitation.

After cordial good-bys to our hospitable hostess we motored back to Chaumont where we dined with Colonel Mitchell; and then with another long drive we finally reached home tired but happy at 3.30 in the morning. There staring me in the face was an order directing me to lead my patrol over the lines in the morning at five o'clock, sharp! An hour and a half sleep for an utterly worn out aviator!

Heaven must have heard my prayers for rain that night, for the next morning when I woke up at eleven o'clock and rushed to the window I found the rain falling in sheets. The orderly had omitted to call me at the appointed hour, because he saw that the weather was too thick for flying.

Decorations for valor and heroism were coming to several of the boys in our squadron on May 15th; and we all woke up that morning to find a beautiful day dawning. While we all of us assumed a truly American disdain for performances of this kind, we nevertheless clearly indicated by our nervousness the pride which we really felt in receiving this award.

General Gerard, Commander of the 6th French

Army, was to arrive at our field shortly after lunch.
All the forenoon I tried to avoid my gallant messmates,
who were continually seeking me out to advise me to
shave again and to use plenty of powder on the cheeks
where the General would kiss me.   Both Lieutenant
Jimmy Meissner and I were quite new to this decoration business and we were nicely stuffed by all the
other fellows who claimed to know all about it.   Major David Peterson was also receiving the Croix de
Guerre, but he had been through many ceremonies
of this kind and was little worried by the prospect.
Captain James Norman Hall, whom we considered
killed in combat, and Lieutenant Charles Chapman,
who had been shot down a fortnight before, were both
summoned to appear for their well earned distinctions,
but neither, alas, could answer to his name.

Shortly after one o'clock three companies of a crack
Poilu regiment marched onto our field behind a gor-
geous French military band of music.   Then came several more companies of infantry from the famous
American 26th Division, the New England boys.
They had a good snappy American band at their head.
Both French and American soldiers drew up their ranks
in the form of a hollow square in the center of our
aerodrome.

In the meantime we had run out all the Nieuports
from the hangars and they stood cheek by jowl across
the field, shining brightly with their red, white and blue
markings in the sunlight.   All the mechanics and enlisted men formed ranks behind the aeroplanes and
stood awaiting the beginning of the ceremony.

Jimmy Meissner and I stood shaking in our well
polished boots, while our cheery comrades came by for
a last word of comforting advice.   Then, with Major
Peterson beside us, we waited for the fatal word of
advance into the awful presence.   Suddenly, midst a
blare of both bands, the General's party appeared from

behind one of the hangars where they had been in hiding all this time. I tried one minute to think of how proud my old mother would be of me and the next would attempt to stretch my face up to such a height that no ordinary general would ever be able to reach it with his lips. This was the last piece of excellent advice that a delegation of my oldest friends had crossed the aerodrome to give me.

Suddenly a faraway band began playing something that sounded somewhat familiar. It turned out to be the National Anthem, " Oh! Say! Can you See . . .? " Everybody jerked to attention and stood at the Salute until it ended. Then from far away in front of me Colonel Mitchell, the Head of our Air Service, began a brief speech congratulating us upon the honors which the French Army was conferring upon us. And then General Gerard, a kindly looking man with a business-like military efficiency in his features and movements, approached our little line of three. He was carrying in his hands the Croix de Guerre and a printed list of citations from the French Army. Pausing immediately in front of us, he began reading them aloud in French.

The Croix de Guerre is a beautiful medal in bronze, artistically designed and executed. It hangs suspended from a ribbon of striped red and green upon which are fastened the palms or stars for each particular citation given by the army or division. If any individual soldier is mentioned for an act of heroism in especial terms by an army order he is presented with an additional palm for each of such citations. Some of the French airmen have received so many citations that the medal itself would hang down below the waist if the ribbon were properly lenthened to accommodate every palm awarded. I have seen René Fonck, the French Ace of Aces, who has been cited 29 times for his victories, wearing his Croix de Guerre in two sections so as to accommodate all the palms that must be worn upon ceremonial occasions. If the citations come from a division instead of an army the decoration to be worn above the Croix de Guerre is a star instead of a palm. Colonel William Thaw wears two stars and three palms among his many other decorations.

With a quick fastening of the much prized honor upon the breast of our tunics and a hearty handclasp of congratulations General Gerard left us, with a very dignified salute which we all returned simultaneously. The discriminating Commander had not made an attempt to kiss us at all!

Within five minutes the field was cleared and we were running up our motors for a pre-arranged exhibition in stunt-flying, formation flying, farce combats and acrobatics. We flung our lithe little Nieuports about the warm sky in every variety of contortion for half an hour, at the end of which we landed and again received a hand-shake and a smile of thanks from this most courteous of French officials. The troops disappeared behind the dying strains of the " Sambre et Meuse " march, the mud-splashed automobiles bore away the last of our distinguished visitors, the mechanics reappeared in their grease-covered overalls and began trundling in the machines.

Suddenly Jimmy Meissner stood by my side, grinning his most winsome grin. " Rick," said he, " I feel that ' Hate-the-Hun ' feeling creeping over me. What do you say to going up and getting a Boche? "

" Right! " I called back over my shoulder. " Come along. We'll take a real ride."

As luck would have it, we had hardly left the ground when we saw a Hun two-seater, probably a Rumpler machine, very high above us. The Rumpler has the highest ceiling of any of the German two-seaters and frequently they sail along above us at an elevation quite impossible for the Nieuport to reach. It is maddening to attain one's maximum height and see the enemy still sailing imperturbably along, taking his photographs and scorning even to fire an occasional burst at one. We climbed at our fastest to overtake this fellow before he could reach his safety spot. Evidently he got " wind up," for after a few minutes climbing he sheered off towards Germany and disappeared from our view. We completed our patrol of the lines without finding another enemy in the sky and returned to our field, where we landed with the mutual vow that on the morrow we would begin seriously our palm collecting shows until we might dangle our new Croix de Guerre well down below our knees.

Jimmy looked contemplatively down at my long legs.

" Have a heart, Rick! " he said softly, " think of the cost of the red tape! "

CHAPTER VIII

A VICTORY AND A NARROW ESCAPE

REED CHAMBERS and I often used to discuss new tricks and wiles by which we might hope to circumvent the crafty Hun. Take it all in all, this whole game of war aviation is so new that any day some newcomer may happen upon a clever trick that none of us has before thought of. I suppose the Huns are sitting up nights the same as we are, trying to devise some startling innovation in the still crude science of air-fighting. At any rate Reed and I sat up late very often and rose very early the next morning to carry into execution some little plan which had enraptured us the night before.

On the morning of May 17th, 1918, my orderly

routed me out at four o'clock sharp, in accordance with orders I had the night before waked him up to give him. I sent him in to Reed's room to call him.

Over our coffee fifteen minutes later Reed and I hurriedly discussed our clever little scheme for the morning run. We intended to get away from the ground before daylight, climb clear up out of sight and out of hearing long before the Huns were out of bed. By hanging around their front yard we might pick up a stray machine venturing alone across our lines for photographs. It was a wonderful plan. We wondered why nobody had ever thought of it before.

Up over Toul and Commercy and Nancy we circled as we climbed, climbed, climbed. At nearly 18,000 feet we found we had enough climbing. It seemed about 18,000 degrees below zero at this great height. Still I hugged myself with much satisfaction over the thought that we surely had the upper hand of any two-seater that might come over; and as the visibility was good we had a tremendous range of view.

We waited and we waited. Up and down along the prearranged sector, where we expected any reasonable enemy might want to come to get photographs on such a fine morning as this, up and down, back and forth we went. At last I began to get rather fed up with the sport. Our plan had worked perfectly and without a single flaw. Yet the stupid Boches were trying to gum up the whole show by staying home this morning. I finally grew indignant at the thought of our early rising hour, our fortunate weather conditions, our high ceiling cleverly obtained without the knowledge of Archy — all these efforts and accomplishments honestly achieved, only to be nullified by the refusal of the fish to bite.

Major Lufbery used to remind us that it was impossible to get Boches by sitting at home in the billets with one's feet before the fire. I considered this sage advice as I turned back on my beat for the twentieth time and estimated I still had an hour's petrol left in my tank. I was nearly perishing with the cold and with hunger. Bitterly I contrasted the cozy mess fire in the breakfast room with the frigid heights at which I had spent the last hour. And there were just as many Boches to be shot at there as here. I felt I had been badly treated.

Where was Chambers anyway? During my preoccupation I had forgotten to keep an eye upon him. I examined every portion of the sky, but he was not in sight. Nothing was in sight. No other fool in the world was abroad at such an unearthly hour. But still, I had to admit to myself, Luf was right! It was just like going fishing. If there were no fish in the stream that certainly would be hard luck, but still one couldn't expect to catch any with his feet before his fire. I smiled to myself as I thought of the Alabama colored gentleman who spent the afternoon fishing in his water trough. A censorious white man walked by and watched him jerk his line out of the water half a dozen times. Finally the white man yelled,

" You black rascal! Don't you know there are no fish in that mud-hole? "

" Yes, boss! But it's close and handy! " replied the black.

The old story gave me an idea. Perhaps I was selecting a poor fishing place whose only merit was that it was close and handy. I pulled up my machine and started off for Metz. I knew the fishing must be good there. It was 25 miles back of the lines and claimed, besides the famous fortress, one of the best of the German aerodromes.

I was now at 20,000 feet above earth and as I turned east I saw the first ray of the sun that shone over France that day. The sun lay a huge red ball behind the distant mountains of the Rhine. I headed in that

direction in order to cross the enemy's lines east of
Pont-à-Mousson, where I knew lay concealed several
sharp-eyed German batteries. At the extremely high
altitude at which I crossed the lines that early morning the sound of my motor must have been heard by
the gunners below, but I am sure none of them could
have seen me, even with the most powerful telescopes.
At any rate not a shell was fired at me during my entire journey to Metz.

The celebrated fortifications soon lay spread below
my wings. Metz herself lies deep down within a valley — the lovely valley of the Moselle River. Practically sheer bluffs one thousand feet high rise on either
bank of the river, and a sudden turn of the stream a
mile below the city's walls provides almost an entire
circumference of fortifications about the sheltered little city below.

Beautiful as Metz appeared to me, I for once re-
gretted that I was not mounted on a bombing machine
from which I might drop a few souvenirs of my visit
into the crowded camps below. Doubtless Metz contained hundreds of thousands of troops and many officers of high rank, as this secure little city was the
gateway between Germany and her front line on the
Meuse. My machine-gun could inflict no damage from
such a height. Regretfully I made a last farewell
circuit over the Queen City of Lorraine and started
homewards over the Frascati aerodrome, whose hangars topped the hills, and peeped down into the valley
of the Moselle. No aeroplanes from there had yet
thought fit to leave the ground.

But one more chance remained to me to get a Boche
this morning. I knew of an aerodrome just this side
of Thiaucourt, where some activity might be expected.

My time was nearly gone, for my fuel must be rather
far down. The thought of encountering engine
trouble this twenty miles behind the lines made me

accelerate my pace a bit. Germany would be a sad place for an enemy named Rickenbacker to land in for duration of the war.   I stuck my nose down a bit more as I thought of this and further increased my speed.   Ah! here comes the vicinity of Thiaucourt. Cutting down my motor, I glided on almost noiselessly and reached the town at about 18,000 feet altitude.

Two or three complete circles were made over Thiaucourt with silent engine.   My eyes were all the while set upon the enemy aerodrome which I knew occupied the smooth field just outside the little city. Some activity was apparent there and even as I sailed above them I noticed three graceful Albatros machines leave the ground one after the other.   It was evident from their straight-away course that they were going over the lines, accumulating their elevation as they flew southward.   I made myself as inconspicuous as possible until the last of the three had his back well towards me.   Then I returned to my course and gradually narrowed the distance between us.

By the time we reached Montsec, that celebrated mountain north of St. Mihiel, I estimated some 3,000 feet separated me from my unsuspicious quarry.   I was so eager to let them get over our lines before attacking that I quite forgot I was now a conspicuous figure to the German Archies.   Two quick bursts just ahead of me informed me of my error.   Without waiting to see whether or not I was hit, I put on the sauce and dived down headlong at the rearmost of the three Huns.

Again I saw the warning signal sent up ahead of the three Albatros pilots.   A single black burst from the battery below caused the German airmen to turn about and look behind them.   They had not expected any attack from this quarter.

When the leader made the first swerve aside I was less than 200 yards from the rear Albatros.   I was descending at a furious pace, regardless of everything but my target ahead. Fully 200 miles an hour my Nieuport was flying. Without checking her speed, I kept her nose pointing at the tail of the rear Albatros, which was now darting steeply downwards to escape me. As the distance closed to 50 yards I saw my flaming bullets piercing the back of the pilot's seat. I had been firing for perhaps ten seconds from first to last. The scared Boche had made the mistake of trying to outdive me instead of out-maneuvering me. He paid for his blunder with his life.

These thoughts flashed through my mind in the fraction of a moment. All the while during which my fingers pressed the trigger I was conscious of the extreme danger of my position. Either or both of the other enemy machines were undoubtedly now on my tail, exactly as I had been on their unfortunate companion. And being alone I must rely solely upon my own maneuvers to escape them.

I believe I should have followed my first target all the way to the ground regardless of the consequences, so desperately had I determined to get him. So I perhaps prolonged my terrific speed a trifle too long. As the enemy aeroplane fell off and began to flutter I pulled my stick back close into my seat and began a sharp climb. The notorious weakness of the Nieuport quickly announced itself. A ripping crash that sounded like the crack of doom to my ears told me that the sudden strain had collapsed my right wing. The entire spread of canvas over the top wing was torn off by the wind and disappeared behind me. Deprived of any supporting surface on this side, the Nieuport turned over on her right side. The tail was forced up despite all my efforts with joystick and rudder. Slowly at first, then faster and faster the tail began revolving around and around. Swifter and swifter became our downward speed. I was caught in a vrille, or tail-spin, and with a machine as crippled as mine there seemed not the possibility of a chance to come out of it.

I wondered vaguely whether the two Albatros machines would continue to fire at me all the way down. Twice I watched them dive straight at me always firing more bullets into my helpless little craft, notwithstanding the apparent certainty of her doom. I felt no anger towards them. I felt somewhat critical towards their bad judgment in thus wasting ammunition. No, that was not exactly it either. My senses were getting confused. What I felt critical about was their stupidity in believing I was playing 'possum. They were fools not to know when an aeroplane was actually falling to a crash. The whole spread of my fabric was gone. No pilot ever could fly without fabric on his machine.

Where would I strike, I wondered. There were the woods of Montsec below me. Heavens! how much nearer the ground was getting! I wondered if the whole framework of the machine would disintegrate and fling me out to the mercy of the four winds. If I struck in tree tops it was barely possible that I might escape with a score of broken bones. Both Jimmy Meissner and Jimmy Hall had escaped death when betrayed through this same fault of the Nieuport. Never would I fly one again if I once got out of this fix alive! But no use worrying about that now. Either I should not be alive or else I should be a mangled prisoner in Germany. Which would my mother rather have, I wondered?

This sudden spasm of longing to see my mother again roused my fighting spirit. With that thought of her and the idea of her opening a cablegram from the front telling her I was dead, with that picture before my mind a whole series of pictures of childhood scenes were vividly recalled to me. I have never before realized that one actually does see all the events of one's life pass before one's eyes at the certain approach of death. Doubtless they are but a few recollections in reality, but one's natural terror at the imminence of death multiplies them into many.

I began to wonder why the speed of my vrille did not increase. With every swing around the circle I felt a regular jar as the shock of the air cushion came against the left wing after passing through the right. I felt a growing irritation at these monotonous bumps. But although I had been experimenting constantly with rudder, joystick and even with the weight of my body I found I was totally unable to modify in the slightest the stubborn spiral gait of the aeroplane. Fully ten thousand feet I had fallen in this manner since my wing had collapsed. I looked overboard. It was scarcely 3,000 feet more — and then the crash! I could see men standing on the road in front of a line of trucks. All were gazing whitefaced at me. They were already exulting over the souvenirs they would get from my machine — from my body itself.

With a vicious disregard for consequences, I pulled open the throttle. The sudden extra speed from the newly started engine was too much for the perpendicular tail and before I had realized it the tail was quite horizontal. Like a flash I seized the joystick and reversed my rudder. The pull of the propeller kept her straight. If only I could keep her so for five minutes I might make the lines. They seemed to beckon to me only two miles or so ahead. I looked above and below.

No aeroplanes in the sky. My late enemies evidently were sure I was done for. Below me I saw the landscape slipping swiftly behind me. I was making headway much faster than I was falling. Sudden elation began to sweep over me. I boldly tried lifting her head. No use! She would fly straight but that was all. Ah! here comes friend Archy!

It is curious that one gets so accustomed to Archy that its terrors actually disappear. So grateful was I to the crippled little 'bus for not letting me down that I continued to talk to her and promise her a good rub down when we reached the stable. I hardly realized that Archy was trying to be nasty.

Over the lines I slid, a good thousand feet up. Once freed from the danger of landing in Germany, I tried several small tricks and succeeded in persuading the damaged craft to one more effort. I saw the roofs of my hangar before me. With the motor still running wide open I grazed the tops of the old 94 hangar and pancaked flatly upon my field.

The French pilots from an adjoining hangar came running out to see what novice was trying to make a landing with his motor on. Later they told me I resembled a bird alighting with a broken wing.

I had passed through rather a nervous experience, as I look back upon it now. Yet I do not recall that I felt anything unusual had happened, as I slid over the edge of my cockpit and inquired for Reed Chambers. This is one of the curious results of flying in wartime: A species of fatalism soon possesses a pilot to such an extent that he learns to take everything as a matter of course. Rarely does a pilot betray much excitement over the day's work, no matter how extraordinary it is.

So I inquired for Reed Chambers with some anger as I got out of my machine. I felt that he had deserted me. I remember that was the principal feeling that attended me across the aerodrome.

Reed hadn't been heard from. But a few minutes later he blew in, full of some cock-and-bull story about my running away from him in violation of our agreement. He had been back in Germany also, and in coming out he had met the two Albatros machines who were then returning home to their aerodrome, possibly to get a motorcar and hurry down to view my remains. Reed had not seen my combat nor did he notice me flying my crippled bird homewards. But his report of seeing only two Albatros confirmed my expectations that the third had actually gone down to a final crash.

Early next day the French notified us that they had indeed seen the Albatros machine crash and had noticed my crippled Nieuport staggering homewards from the fight, surrounded with Archy. They thus confirmed my victory without any request on my part. And the extraordinary part of the whole affair was that the dead German pilot — my latest victim — had so fallen upon his controls that the machine flew towards France and landed with his dead body a few hundred yards inside the French line

CHAPTER IX

DOWN IN FLAMES

THE 94th Squadron had been at the front about one month when there arrived Lieut. Kurtz, one of my companions of the training school days. On completion of his course at the flying school Kurtz had been selected to make a special study of aerial gunnery, in order to become an instructor to the thousands of young men who were now being drafted into Uncle Sam's aerial fleet. For this purpose he had been sent to England, and on returning to France from that country Kurtz had received orders to report to the 94th Squadron at the front in order to secure actual war experience and to make trips over the enemy's lines.

After the newcomer had asked thousands of questions and received answers to them to the best of our ability, he suggested that he should proceed to the more advanced stage of an actual combat with the enemy. As I was second in command of the Squadron, being Flight Commander of the 1st Flight at that time, it was my duty to arrange for him to accompany a patrol into enemy territory. No matter how much natural ability a man may possess, or how carefully he has been trained, his first experiences over the enemy lines, his first contact with enemy machines are rather trying to him. A moment's forgetfulness, a trifling foolhardiness, a slight miscalculation, and even a man who has been carefully and expensively trained and who possesses all the characteristics of a successful pilot, may fall before the skill of a more experienced enemy flyer.

For this reason I always made it a practice to accompany new pilots on their first trip over the enemy's lines, and by my advice and by actual protection when aloft, assist them over that delicate period between the theory of the school and the hard practice of battle.

We were still flying the well-known Baby Nieuport single-seater " chasse " or fighting machine, equipped with a Gnome Monosoupape motor. It was then the best machine of its kind in service, although it had some faults undeniably. Having just arrived from the rear, Kurtz was not acquainted with the peculiarities of this machine. I therefore arranged for him to make a few short flights from our field and to practice frequent landings, so that if he ever should have sudden motor trouble he would be able to come down on any ground he found available. After a few days of this practice, he expressed himself as being capable of handling the machine under all circumstances and ready for that greatest adventure of the young pilot: that first trip over enemy's lines.

We agreed that Lieut. Kurtz should accompany Lieut. Chambers and myself on what is familiarly known as a voluntary patrol. Chambers and I were in the habit of undertaking these extra patrols when the regular day's work was over, provided we were still, to use an aviator's slang expression, "Mad at the Boche." It was a beautiful summer morning, bright, clear and still — just such a morning as the Hun observation pilots would select to come over our lines and take photographs.

Our plan of action was carefully explained to our new comrade. We were to fly in V formation; I was to lead, Chambers on my left, and Kurtz 100 meters behind and above us. He was not to engage in a combat, should we meet with any Boche airmen, unless the advantage was with us. I have always made it a point to avoid a fight unless I can maneuver to get the best advantage. He was at all times to maintain his position behind and above us, playing the rôle of a spectator. He was instructed to try out his machine-gun occasionally with a few short bursts if he had his plane pointing towards Germany. Finally, if we became scattered and he was unable to find us, he was to remember that the sun rose in the east, and, keeping it on his left was to fly south until he felt certain that he was over French territory before making a landing.

It was decided that we should start after breakfast, promptly at 8 o'clock, meet over the field at 1500 feet, get our full altitude between Nancy and Toul, and cross over the lines at 15,000 feet. Before starting I noticed that Lieut. Kurtz appeared rather nervous, but this was not a matter for surprise under the circumstances. Little did I understand the reason for this nervousness then, or suspect in what a tragic manner it would later be revealed to me.

Lieut. Kurtz's machine was climbing badly, so we got up to an altitude of 14,500 feet rather slowly; at that height I decided to pass from the comparative safety of our own side of the line to the hazard and adventure of the German positions. Mr. Hun was abroad, for I caught sight of the shimmer of what I believed to be a photo plane six miles inside our lines and very high up — probably 19,000 feet. As this enemy was certainly beyond our reach, I decided to keep the nose of my machine headed towards Germany and to continue to gain altitude as steadily as possible, at the same time keeping an eye on this nearby enemy, for there was just a chance that we might be able to reach his altitude and head him off before his work was done.

Suddenly, little fleecy white puffs appeared in the clear atmosphere ahead and above us. This anti-aircraft activity of ours meant that more Huns were abroad in our vicinity. A few minutes more and we had spotted them; three powerful single-seaters of the Albatros type, 1500 feet above us, and about half a mile ahead. As a signal to the others I wig-wagged my wings, which is the aviator's way of saying " Look out, and keep your eye on the leader." I had time to look back and see that Lieut. Kurtz was well in the rear, and a little higher than the enemy then appeared to be. There was then no reason to fear for him. It was not necessary to give any thought to an experienced fighter like Lieut. Chambers. I had been out enough with Reed to know that he was the equal to any two Huns. Doubtless Reed had seen the Boches before I had, for he was keeping close by me, probably wondering what my plan was going to be.

Keeping a close watch on our opponents, I rapidly analyzed the situation. The enemy had the advantage in height; they were three, probably all experienced men, while we were two fighters and one novice, who was catching sight of a German plane for the first time in his life. But the enemy pilots were inside our lines. Down below, several hundreds of men in the trenches were watching what to them was to be an equal fight — three Americans against three Germans. With their field glasses the French officers had picked out the black German crosses, and noted the red, blue and white rings of the U. S. machines. Doubtless at that very moment they were discussing the outcome of the impending fight. They had the right to expect a fight, since we were 3 to 3. So a fight it should be.

In the minds of the Germans there appeared to be no element of doubt or hesitation. Having the advantage of height, they suddenly, all three, swooped down on us; first one, then the second and third dived down and sprayed us with bullets from their machine-guns. I had time to notice that Lieut. Chambers banked up on a wing tip and dived down; I did a half vrille, and in less time than it takes to tell, we were both out of range. The Germans in their diving attack had not only failed to get any of us, but had also lost their advantage of height. The tables were turned, or at any rate the conditions were equal, and retreat was evidently the uppermost thought in the minds of the Huns.

We gave chase and in a few minutes I had succeeded in separating one of the planes from the formation. It was then either his life or mine! Perhaps I should get in the fatal shot; or maybe luck would be on his side; in either case, I was determined that it should be a fight to the death. Occupied as I was with my own enemy, I yet had time to notice that Lieut. Kurtz was doing well. He and Lieut. Chambers were in full cry after the two remaining Albatros planes; the whole show was proceeding in the direction of St. Mihiel.

Mine was a running fight until we arrived over Thiaucourt, the little city about six miles inside the German lines. Here my enemy decided that conditions were in his favor, for he swung around and headed straight for me. But I was satisfied to accept the challenge, for I was 100 yards behind and about 200 yards above my opponent, and this gave me a not to be despised advantage. Nearer and nearer he came, heading towards me in a climbing virage, and working both his machine-guns furiously. It is a sensation which almost defies description: there we were, only a few yards apart, sparring around one another like two prize-fighters in a celestial ring. His incendiary explosive bullets were cracking all around me, and any one of them, if it touched a vital spot, was capable of putting an end to the fight. But my feelings were not personal; indeed, in those few critical moments which constitute the turning point of a fight the aviator usually has all thoughts of self driven away. With a quick half-turn of a vrille I secured a position on the tail of my enemy. I was then in such a position that he was unable to turn his gun on me. It was my chance, a chance which probably would be lost in the next fraction of a second. But I had no intention of losing it. With a pull on both triggers, a hail of bullets swept towards the German plane.

Down he swooped. Apparently he was out of control. Would he crash, or would he be able after that giddy dive to pull out and make a safe landing? That I could not tell, for while the spinning nose-dive of an enemy always looks like certain destruction, it is often, in the hands of an artful pilot the only highway to safety. Had I been over our own lines, I might have followed him down, and made certain of his crash. If I saw that he had regained control I could then immediately renew the fight at a lower altitude.

But I was well inside enemy territory and only 10,000 feet above ground. It was quite possible that while I had been occupied in this fight other enemy planes had gathered overhead and were preparing to wreak vengeance. Personal safety and the elementary rules of aerial fighting require the pilot in such circumstances to "regain altitude, or get back to the lines as soon as possible."

Thus I had to leave the issue of my fight in doubt. I had a faint hope that some other observer might be able to confirm the enemy's crash, and so allow me to place one more Hun to my credit. A few minutes later and I realized that my recent instinctive fears were only too true. High above, but fortunately a considerable distance away from me, approached two German planes, which I rapidly concluded were the two machines which had succeeded in escaping from Kurtz and Chambers and were now determined to punish me when they discovered me so remotely isolated from my formation.

My only hope of safety lay in speed. Often and often on the race track, with wide open throttle, every nerve taut, every pent-up ounce of energy concentrated in my arms, have I wished that I could infuse just a little more power into my engine, could give just a little more speed to my car, in order to draw away from the man whose car was creeping up to and overhauling mine inch by inch.

But this case was even more crucial. Speed now meant safety, speed here meant life. My motor was flung wide open, the nose of my machine was turned down, and I raced as I had never raced before, for the prize was life itself. But do what I could, it was impossible to shake off one of my opponents. Now I was directly over the lines; a few minutes more and I should be in our own territory and in a position either to land or get away from my persistent rival. However, the advantage the other fellow had in height was too much for me, and I realized that it was best for me to turn round and fight. In a flash I had kicked my tail around and was heading towards my opponent. He swooped down, reserving his fire, while I kept my fingers on the triggers of my guns. I had him in range, but I hesitated; the thought had flashed through my brain that perhaps in three seconds more I should be able to shoot with more deadly effect.

Now I had my sights on him; now was the time to release both guns. At that very moment his machine banked up on one wing tip, and there under the lower wing I saw the concentric red, blue and white wings of the United States Air Service. The supposed Hun was friend Chambers, who was returning from chasing the enemy, and the second plane was that of Lieut. Kurtz back from his first aerial scrap. God only knows why I held my fire for that brief fraction of a second. In talking it over later, Chambers said, "When I saw Rick swing round in that wild fashion I realized that he was still 'mad at the Boche,' and thought the time had come to let him see my colors."

It is not often that a man rises to the degree of joy I felt as we headed for home, the fight over, and all three safe. I had every reason to believe my German was down, possibly Chambers had got another, and Kurtz for his first time over had deported himself wonderfully.

I searched around for the pilot Kurtz, whom I regarded as being in my care, but to my surprise was unable to find him. I cruised around for a few minutes, searching in every direction, but not one plane could I see in the sky. I argued to myself that he must have gone home, and in consequence I turned my machine towards our aerodrome, hoping to pick him up at any moment. Just as I got sight of our landing ground my anxiety was relieved, for there, ahead of and below us was Lieut. Kurtz making rings above our field, exactly as I had advised him to do.

Lieut. Kurtz was evidently on his last turn over an adjoining field prior to landing when to my unspeakable horror I saw his Nieuport drop into a vrille and crash straight to earth, after which bursts of angry flame shot up all around him. What could possibly have happened?

If help could be got to him without a moment's delay he might be pulled out of that wreckage before the flames consumed him. But I could not get to him, for the place where his machine had crashed was among barbed wire entanglements and trench works so thick that a safe landing was impossible. Below was a road, only 50 yards from the burning machine, and on the road was a French " camion." I speeded down, shut off my motor, and by signs and voice urged the driver to go to the rescue. The man stood still and watched. I realized later that he understood it was a hopeless task, for all the ammunition in the wrecked plane was exploding, and for any man to approach meant almost certain death.

Unable to land close by, I sped on to our own field, jumped out of my plane almost before it had stopped rolling; vaulted into the saddle of a motorcycle and raced towards the scene of the disaster with a vague wild hope that I might yet be able to do some good. Could I live for a million years I should not forget that awful sight of the charred remains of the man who had been my companion in the schools, and who only one brief hour before had set out with me full of life and hope.

A few hours later the mystery of that crash was revealed. As has already been mentioned, I had noticed before starting that Lieut. Kurtz appeared nervous, but had not given the matter any great consideration. The explanation was given by a brother officer who had come with Lieut Kurtz to the squadron. Before starting on his last flight, Lieut. Kurtz had confided to him that he was subject to fainting spells when exposed to high altitudes, and the only thing he was afraid of was that he might be seized with such a fit while in the air.   Alas, his fear had been only too well founded.   But what a pity it was he had not confided this fear to me, his Flight Commander!

The next morning a simple funeral procession wound its way down the leafy lanes, the while shells passed overhead with an incongruous whine.   Awaiting me at the camp on my return from this sad ceremony was an official notice from the French commander.   It stated, briefly, that an infantry officer, on outpost duty in No Man's Land, had observed that the German I had fought with had crashed to the ground a total wreck.   I had got my Boche; but I had lost a friend, and he had perished in the manner most dreaded of all aviators, for he had gone down in flames.

CHAPTER X

LUFBERY IS KILLED

LIEUTENANT WALTER SMYTH, of New York, came to me on the morning of May 10th, 1918, and said:

"Rick, where do you find all these Boches of yours over the lines?"

I asked him what he meant by "all."

"Why," he said, "I've been over the lines two or three times and I haven't had a single look at an enemy machine.   I would like to go across with some one like you who always gets into some fun.   Will you take me with you on a voluntary patrol?"

This was the spirit I liked to see in a pilot and I immediately told Smyth I would take him over at nine o'clock this very morning if he could get ready.   My regular patrol was not on until late in the afternoon, so I had all the morning to myself.   Smyth was delighted with the invitation and immediately made himself ready.

We left the field together and sped quickly towards St. Mihiel. Our altimeters indicated 17,000 feet as we finished our first patrol and found ourselves over the city of Pont-à-Mousson. No enemy machines had been encountered.

Considering it · uite probable that a Rumpler might be coming out for photographs on such a nice morning as this, I determined to cut a slice off the German territory on our next patrol and run directly from Pont-à-Mousson to Verdun. Accordingly I set off with Smyth close by my right wing. A slight northerly course brought us directly over Mars-la-Tour, where I knew was located a fighting squadron of Germans. We should satisfy Smyth's curiosity even if we had to descend onto the Hun aerodrome.

As we crossed the little town of Mars-la-Tour I detected a German two-seater making off towards Verdun almost directly ahead of us. It was an Albatros and was several thousand feet below us, and about two miles ahead. We were in excellent position, for not only was our presence entirely unsuspected so far in his rear, but once discovered we had the sun at our backs and had the advantage in height and in numbers. I felt certain of the outcome of the fight and was warmly congratulating Smyth upon his good judgment in picking me as his leader in to-day's expedition as I dipped him a signal and began setting our course into the sun. By the time we reached Conflans I was just above the enemy's tail and in an excellent position. As yet we had remained unperceived.

I stuck down my Nieuport and began my dive. My tracer bullets sped by the startled observer and gave him the first intimation he had of my proximity. The German pilot must have seen them flash past too.

For the next thing I knew was that in some way or other I had passed the Albatros and was still wildly firing into vacancy, while the two-seater enemy machine by one masterful maneuver had given me the go-by and was now on top of me. Clearly he was an old hand at this game and it behooved me to be careful.

I zoomed up again and got the upper berth. But this time I found it extremely difficult to get into a position for shooting. The pilot kicked around his tail so adroitly that every time I prepared to dive upon him I found the observer coolly sighting a brace of machine-guns full into my face. Moreover, I found that at this high altitude the Albatros could maneuver as well or just a little better than could my lighter Nieuport. Once I tried to make a sharp bank to the right. I had quite forgotten the rarity of the air and, instead of a virage, I found I had thrown my machine into a vrille. Two complete revolutions were made before I could get myself straightened out. Then looking about me for my enemy I found the Albatros nearly a mile away from me making a fast spurt for home. Smyth was composedly sailing along above me, appearing to be quite enchanted with the entertainment.

I had encountered an expert pair of airfighters on the Albatros and I looked after their departing shadow with some admiration salving my disappointment. Then much of my self-satisfied abandon evaporated instantly when I began to realize that Smyth and I were over twenty-five miles inside Germany. I decided to retreat while retreating was good, fully satisfied that I had given Smyth his money's worth in the shape of a " first show."

As we passed over St. Mihiel on our way home I perceived white Archies bursting, back in the direction of Verdun. Closer scrutiny disclosed the same Albatros two-seater quietly riding the air-bumps and making steadfastly for our side of the lines. The pilots thought they had me bluffed and were going on with their work in full view of Smyth and myself.

I wiggled a signal to Smyth and started again in pursuit of the foxy Albatros. But immediately the enemy made an about face and reentering the barrage of Archy set out at a stiff gait for Mars-la-Tour and home. I swerved a bit to the right to cut him off and glanced about me as I did so to ascertain the exact position of Smyth. He was nowhere in sight!

Below me was Etain. I was at least ten miles back of the lines. When had Smyth left me, and in what direction had he gone? Feeling more than a little uncomfortable in my thoughts at having neglected to look out for him in the last few minutes I made a half-bank and set my course straight for home. As I learned, late that afternoon, Smyth had landed inside our lines with motor troubles and was unable to reach our aerodrome until near nightfall.

As I neared our aerodrome, I saw a large crowd gathered together on the center of the field. It was just ten-fifty in the morning when I landed beside them and hastened up to learn what calamity had overtaken my poor friend Smyth. If through my carelessness Smyth had become engaged in an unequal combat and had been wounded or had crashed upon landing, I could not escape the responsibility for his loss. I hurried over to the hangars, filled with apprehension.

The exclamations I heard only bewildered me the more. Major Lufbery's name was on everybody's lips. I asked if any one had seen Lieutenant Smyth come in. The boys only looked at me vacantly and made no reply. Finally I demanded the reason for this extraordinary gathering on the field. The answer left me dumb with dismay and horror.

Our beloved Luf was no more! Major Raoul Lufbery, the American Ace of Aces, the most revered

American aviator in France had just been shot down in flames not six miles away from our field!

This sad story is so well known to the whole world that I would not repeat here the details of Lufbery's last fight were it not for the fact that numerous false stories of his heroic death were spread broadcast throughout America immediately after the news of his loss had been cabled home. Several of these garbled accounts later came to my attention.

As our Commanding Officer, Major Huffer, tells the story, it was about ten o'clock when the anti-aircraft guns on top of Mt. Mihiel began belching great white puffs of smoke overhead at a very high altitude. An alerte came to us immediately that a German photographing machine was coming our way and was at that moment almost directly over our field.

Lieutenant Gude was the only pilot on the field ready for flight. He was sent up alone to attack the intruder, an incident which brought vastly regrettable results. It was Gude's first actual combat. His encounter with the enemy was plainly seen by all the spectators who gathered about our hangars.

Just as Gude left the ground the French Archy ceased firing. Evidently they had scored a hit, for the German observing machine at that moment began a long vrille, spinning faster and faster as it drew nearer to the ground. Just as the onlookers were convinced that the enemy machine was falling for its last crash the Albatros recovered its poise, straightened out at less than 200 feet above earth and turned back towards the German lines. Almost immediately Lieutenant Gude flew in to the attack.

Gude began firing at an impossible range and continued firing until his ammunition was exhausted, without inflicting any appreciable injury upon the two-seater Albatros. As he came flying home the Archy batteries in the neighborhood again took up the battle and poured up a violent barrage, which surrounded and encompassed this lone enemy on every side. But all to no purpose. The Albatros continued steadily on its retreat, climbing slightly and setting a course in the direction of Nancy.

In the meantime, Major Lufbery, who had been watching the whole show from his barracks, jumped on a motorcycle that was standing in the road and rushed to the hangars. His own plane was out of commission. Another Nieuport was standing on the field, apparently ready for use. It belonged to Lieutenant Davis. The mechanics admitted everything was ready and without another word Lufbery jumped into the machine and immediately took off.

With all his long string of victories, Lufbery had never brought down an enemy aeroplane within the allied lines. All seventeen of his early successes with the Escadrille Lafayette and his last success — when he had gone out to avenge Jimmy Hall — all had been won across the German lines. He had never seen the wreckage of a single one of his victories. Undoubtedly he seized this opportunity of engaging in a combat almost within sight of our field with impetuous abandon. Knowing nothing of the condition of his guns nor the small peculiarities of his present mount, Lufbery flew in to the attack.

With far greater speed than his heavier antagonist, Major Lufbery climbed in pursuit. In approximately five minutes after leaving the ground he had reached 2,000 feet and had arrived within range of the Albatros six miles away. The first attack was witnessed by all our watchers.

Luf fired several short-bursts as he dived in to the attack. Then he swerved away and appeared to busy himself with his gun, which evidently had jammed. Another circle over their heads and he had cleared the jam. Again he rushed the enemy from their rear, when suddenly old Luf's machine was seen to burst into roaring flames. He passed the Albatros and proceeded for three or four seconds on a straight course. Then to the horrified watchers below there appeared the figure of their gallant hero emerging in a headlong leap from the midst of the fiery furnace! Lufbery had preferred to leap to certain death rather than endure the slow torture of burning to a crisp. His body fell in the garden of a peasant woman's house in a little town just north of Nancy. A small stream ran by at about a hundred yards distant and it was thought later that poor Lufbery seeing this small chance for life had jumped with the intention of striking this water. He had leaped from a height of 200 feet and his machine was carrying him at a speed of 120 miles per hour! A hopeless but a heroic attempt to preserve his priceless life for his needy country!

While I was listening to the details of this shocking story the telephone rang. We were informed by a French officer of the exact spot upon which our late hero had fallen. Jumping into a motor we sped across the intervening miles at a prodigious rate and arrived at the scene of the tragedy less than 30 minutes after Luf had fallen. But already loving hands had removed his body. The townsfolk had carried all that remained of poor Raoul Lufbery to their little Town Hall and there we found him, his charred figure entirely covered with flowers from the near-by gardens.

I remember a conversation we had had with Major Lufbery on the subject of catching afire in the air a few days previous to this melancholy accident. I had asked Luf what he would do in a case of this kind — jump or stay with the machine? All of us had a vast respect for Major Lufbery's experience and we all leaned forward to hear his response to this question.

"I should always stay with the machine," Luf responded. "If you jump you certainly haven't got a chance. On the other hand there is always a good chance of side-slipping your aeroplane down in such a way that you fan the flames away from yourself and the wings. Perhaps you can even put the fire out before you reach the ground. It has been done. Me for staying with the old 'bus, every time!"

What an irony now to recall old Luf's instructions! His machine had received a flaming bullet in the fuel tank. The same bullet evidently cut away the thumb of his right hand as it clasped the joystick. The next instant the little craft was but one mass of flame, from which there was no means of escape.

Leaving instructions to send the body to the American Hospital near our aerodrome, we returned to our field. There we learned one or two climaxes to Lufbery's combat and death.

Captain DeRode, the Commanding Officer of a French escadrille near by, met us and stated that one of his pilots, in fact his leading Ace, had witnessed the death of Lufbery and had immediately taken up the pursuit of the Albatros to revenge him. At the first attack he too was shot through the heart and fell immediately. His machine had crashed but a mile or two from the spot where Luf had fallen. But the German machine was finally shot down by another French machine, and it fell a mile inside our lines, where both pilot and observer were captured.

Upon inquiring for Doug Campbell, we then learned he too had gone up to seek revenge for Major Lufbery's death. An hour later he returned and reported that the Albatros had secured too great a start for him, but that he had encountered a two-seater Rumpler, over Beaumont and after a brisk combat he had killed the rear gunner and wounded the pilot. The machine fell within our lines, both wings having been torn off in its rapid descent without control.

Stoically receiving our congratulations, Douglas assured us that this Rumpler was but one of many that the Huns would give us in the attempt to pay for the loss of Raoul Lufbery.   And well has Douglas Campbell kept his promise!

His brother came to lunch with us that day.   Doug had expected him.   His brother was an officer in a corps of engineers which was stationed but a short distance away, at Gondrecourt, and Douglas had invited him over to mess with us on this particular day.

As soon as he arrived, Lieutenant Campbell informed Douglas that it was very gallant of him to go up and shoot down an enemy aeroplane before his very eyes on this day of his luncheon party.   He said he would like to drive over and see what the wreck of the German aeroplane looked like after falling 16,000 feet. So immediately after lunch Major Huffer took the two Campbells and myself in his car and we crawled up to the front and parked the car in some woods as near to Beaumont as we could get.   Our own big guns were well behind us, sending their long whining shells over our heads about ten every second.

We walked forward half a mile with due caution, and finally came to the spot where Douglas Campbell's victims lay.   Two or three French poilus had been placed on guard over the wreckage by the French Colonel in charge of this sector.   The wings lay several hundred feet away from the fusilage.

We collected some souvenirs of Doug's victory and made our way homeward.   It was rare enough that an aviator ever set eyes upon any part of the machine he had shot down.   Usually the enemy machine fell far within the German lines, for the German policy was to fight only above their own territory.   If we were ever fortunate enough to catch a Boche inside our lines and down him there the last scrap of his machine was carried away by the men in the trenches or by the lorry drivers, who happened to be in the vicinity, long be-

fore the victorious pilot appeared upon the scene. As
we reached home with our enemy souvenirs we were
again faced with the sorrowful realization that old Luf
would never more sit in the group around our cheerful
mess table.

It was on the following day, May, 20th, that the
last remains of our beloved hero was to be laid away
in our little "Airman's Cemetery." Already the little
plot bore this name, and quite half a dozen of our
fellows lay side by side in this foreign clay, so far
distant from the land and dear ones they loved. They
were now to be joined by one whom all France and
America considered preeminent in aviation.

General Gerard, Commander of the Sixth Army,
arrived with his entire staff at one o'clock. General
Liggett, commanding the 26th Division, came with
Colonel William Mitchell, commanding the Air Forces
of America. All bore with them quantities of beautiful flowers. Hundreds of officers from all branches
of the service came to pay their last act of respect to
the memory of America's most famous aviator.

I watched the great assemblage gather. Their
flowers covered the casque of the dead airman and
formed a huge pyramid beside it. At one-thirty I
hurried back to the aerodrome. I had one last flight
to make in conjunction with my comrade of so many
patrols.

The pilots of Flight No. 1 were strapped in seats
and awaiting me. Our mechanics silently handed us
our baskets of flowers. Leaving the field in flight
formation we circled over the hospital plot until five
minutes to two. The last of the procession had
passed up the short stretch of road and the aviators'
last resting place was filled with Lufbery's friends.

I flew my formation twice across the mass of uncovered heads below, then glided with closed engine
down to fifty feet above the open grave. As his body

was being slowly lowered I dropped my flowers, every pilot behind me following in my wake one by one. Returning then to our vacant aerodrome we sorrowfully faced the realization that America's greatest aviator and Ace of Aces had been laid away for his last rest.

CHAPTER XI

SQUADRON FESTIVITIES

THE monotony of dud days on the aerodrome exacts a cost from aviators which can not be computed nor definitely ascertained, but seasoned squadron commanders have learned that their pilots live longer and fight better if they are helped through these dull periods with occasional amusements. Especially is this true where leaves of absence are infrequent. The British, who are past masters in this art of caring for their men, not only established a regular schedule of holidays for their pilots, but even while they lived on aerodromes all pilots were required to take part in a certain amount of athletic sports, games and friendly visits back and forth between squadrons. Movie shows, whist tournaments, long walks and other methods of inducing the pilots to take their minds off their work served to produce a morale and esprit in the British aviators that has not its equal in the world.

With the American forces several influences prevented this happy solution to a trying problem. We were new to the game and had not yet learned to study the psychology of the flyer; we had too few aviators at the front to permit them regular and frequent leaves of absence; we had pressing work before us that could not be disturbed for experimentation. Those high in authority considered it more necessary to ship infantry to France than to increase the number of pilots in aviation; consequently the few that were first sent to the front served steadily through to the end, almost without a day's leave being granted for rest and recuperation of spirits.

It is said that the work of the war-pilot exacts more strain from the individual than is the case with his brothers-at-arms in any other arm of warfare. Perhaps he does live under a more constant strain. I cannot judge of the truth of this, for I am not familiar enough with all the details of the other man's work. But the fact that the aviator knows he is constantly under the possibility of sudden death every time he sets foot in his machine, whether it be death from bullets and shells or from the possible collapse of his machine in mid-air — this constant nerving of mind and body against the daily perils which surround him undoubtedly counts heavily against his strength after many weeks of daily service. The wise commanding officer therefore provides as much amusement and recreation for his pilots as the circumstances of war permit.

On May 25th, our squadron adjutant, Lieutenant Smith, had the good fortune to meet in Menil-la-Tours the two Herring sisters from the old U. S. A., who were at the front giving entertainments for our soldiers in France under the auspices of the Red Cross organization. Lieutenant Smith immediately called upon the two young ladies and secured a promise from them to come out to Toul and give us a performance at our aerodrome. They very kindly agreed to come the very next afternoon.

Upon receipt of the news we began our preparations at the field. One of the largest French hangars, which was then in use by a photographing squadron, was emptied of its machines and equipment and was cleaned up for the occasion. Everybody enthusiastically turned in to help and after a few hours' work we had the theater ready. A stage was set up at one end and electric lights were arranged with artistic theatrical effect. A captured German piano was brought over from one of the messes and the dirt floor was swept and polished.

The Misses Herring arrived at four o'clock and found officers and men all impatiently awaiting them. Even the Frenchmen who still occupied part of our aerodrome were on hand, anxious to see and hear this "All-American" show.

It was a wonderful entertainment for all of us and I am sure the Misses Herring have never received more enthusiastic and sincere applause from any audience. After the "show" was over we invited the girls over to our squadron mess and at the end of a very merry meal we all went out to put them in their car and see them safely started on their way.

Just as the car was starting, I put my head inside the curtains and inquired of them their next destination. They told me they were going to Langes, a town not many miles distant from Toul, and very cordially invited me to come over and see them and have dinner with them some evening during the following week. I naturally accepted with every indication of pleasure and proceeded to make definite arrangements with them as to just what afternoon I should arrange for a flight and come down a panne in neighborhood of Langes, when I heard a chuckle behind me. I withdrew my head from the curtains and found myself face to face with the C. O. Major Huffer eyed me for a moment with the ghost of a smile on his face, as much as to say: "I overheard everything, my boy, and I don't think you *will* 'panne' near Langes during the next week." C. O.'s can take a lot of joy out of life!

Next day Douglas Campbell, who was running neck and neck with me for the squadron record, won a celebrated victory. He went out on a little private expedition of his own and while in the vicinity of Pont-à-

Mousson he saw a formation of the British Independent Air Force coming home from a bombing raid on Thionville, an important railway town some thirty miles north of Metz. Some of these British bombing squadrons occupied an aerodrome only a few miles south of our own and we frequently met them going or coming across the lines. They flew De Haviland two-seaters with the Liberty motor and each machine carried almost a ton of bombs. About twenty of these bombing squadrons were under command of General Hugh Trenchard, the greatest authority on war aviation in the world, in my opinion, and they were designated as the Independent Air Force because they were not subject to any army orders. Their one function was to drop bombs on German cities.

Lieutenant Campbell noticed one of the British machines had dropped back almost a mile behind the others as they were returning homeward from their expedition. No fighting machines ever accompanied these bombers. They relied solely upon their close flying formation to beat off all attackers. Evidently this straggler had motor trouble for he could not keep his altitude and was slowly dropping farther and farther behind his formation. To make his situation more desperate he was at that moment being attacked simultaneously by three Pfalz fighting planes.

Without hesitation Doug dived down to his rescue.

Keeping the eastern sun at his back, Campbell executed a long but rapid circle which brought him onto the rear of the enemy formation without being seen. He aimed for the nearest Pfalz and neatly shot him down with almost his first burst. Turning savagely upon the other two Pfalz machines, he gave them burst after burst. Both turned tail and began diving for safety.

Chasing the two Huns back for a few miles until he was satisfied they would not check their speed this side their aerodrome, the American turned back and quickly overtook the crippled British De Haviland. Escorting the pilot and observer well back to their destination, Campbell waved them good-by and made for home.

An hour later the Commanding Officer of the English squadron telephoned us, asking for the name of our plucky pilot who had downed one Hun and driven away from their intended victim two others. He stated that the British pilot and the observer had both been wounded by the Pfalz attackers and had it not been for the timely arrival of Lieutenant Campbell both would undoubtedly have been killed.

The next morning Lieutenant Campbell and I started out together on a voluntary patrol to see if we couldn't bag a few Hun machines. It was May 28th. We set out from the aerodrome at about nine o'clock under a beautiful clear sky and drove straight for the lines in the direction of Pont-à-Mousson. We were careful to keep inside our own lines so that the Hun Archy would not betray our presence to the enemy aeroplanes. Four or five patrols were made, back and forth, back and forth, between Pont-à-Mousson and St. Mihiel.

About an hour after we had left home I noticed a formation of machines approaching us from the vicinity of Mars-la-Tour. It was evident that they must be enemy machines since they came from that direction and were attracting no bursts of Archy from the German gunners of that locality. I dropped a signal to Campbell and began a southerly climb for greater altitude.

Reaching 18,000 feet I turned and headed back towards the enemy's lines. Now the members of the advancing formation were quite distinguishable and I made out two Albatros two-seater fighting machines coming towards us at about 16,000 feet and above them four Pfalz single-seater fighting machines were accompanying them as protectors. Undoubtedly the expedition was planned for taking important photographs and a strong defense had come along to enable the Albatros to accomplish their missions despite any attacks from our side.

We had about 2,000 feet altitude over them, but we needed all the advantage we could possibly get against such odds. So I withdrew, still into the sun, and waited until the whole formation had crossed the lines and were well on our side before turning for the attack.

As soon as we began our dive we were observed. The two Albatros immediately turned tail and started for the lines. The four fighting planes drew closer their formation and also turned back, keeping themselves between us and the machines they were protecting. Although the long range was hopeless Campbell and I both fired occasional bursts as we continued after them, always preserving our advantage in altitude and never permitting them a shot at us. In this fashion we all crossed the lines again and soon were above the city of Thiaucourt, Campbell and I still holding the upper floor.

Apparently the Huns began to tire of this humiliating game, for at this juncture we suddenly noticed a breaking up of their formation, the two Albatros machines began circling back of Thiaucourt, while the four Pfalz struck off for the east and began climbing towards the Moselle valley. We watched this neat little maneuver for a few moments. Then to test the crafty trap which was so evidently being laid for us we suddenly dived, or made a feint at a dive, upon the two abandoned Albatros machines. Campbell went straight down upon the nearest one while I stayed above him and kept an eye upon the four fighting machines.

Instantly the four fighting planes reversed their direction and came hurrying back for a rescue. Douglas zoomed craftily back to a position just below me and we continued a slow retreat towards our lines. The Pfalz maintained a safe position well in our rear.

Again the tricky Huns undertook a fancy maneuver. We saw one of the Albatros suddenly draw away towards the west, flying directly towards St. Mihiel, while the other ceased its circling and hastened to overtake the four fighting planes ahead of him. They waited until he had overtaken them; then all five turned to the east towards the Moselle leaving the lone Albatros an attractive bait for us some two miles in their rear.

With extreme care we estimated the exact distances that now separated us. Fully aware of the new trap that was laid for us, it was only a question of our ability to get down at the bait and dispose of him and then regain our altitude before the superior enemy formation could descend upon us. Our judgment was as good as theirs. Our position was a little better, for we could estimate better than they the distance from our point in the sky to the slow moving Albatros left as a decoy in the west. Better still, we knew to an inch the capabilities of our Nieuports and perhaps the Huns would underestimate our speed. A fraction of an instant was all the mistake they need make. And they made it!

Like a flash we turned our aeroplanes and side by side dived swiftly down at the lone Albatros with our throttles full open. The Pfalz machines instantly turned to the pursuit. But even as they did so they must have realized the futility of the chase, for not only did we have a mile or more handicap, but we rapidly increased this distance between us. As we neared our target we nursed our machines until our gun sights were directly upon the enemy Albatros.

About one hundred shots each we fired before we eased off our machines and began to climb away to regain our altitude. Looking back we saw we had done a complete job with our Albatros. It swooped one way and then the other and, finally falling into a last vrille, we saw it crash at the edge of the town of Flirey just inside the Ratta Woods.

Long before the final crash of our victim Campbell and I had regained our former altitude. Then came the surprise of the day!

Instead of dashing after us to wreak their well earned revenge, the four Hun fighters returned hastily to their remaining Albatros and surrounding it began carefully conducting it northwards still deeper within their own territory! Many times later did I observe this craven characteristic of the enemy air-fighters. No matter what their superiority in numbers or position, if we succeeded in bringing down one of their number the others almost invariably abandoned the combat and gave us the field. It may be military efficiency but it always appeared to me to be pure yellowness.

Campbell and I were both content to let them go. No sooner had the Pfalz machines pulled away than the Archy batteries below us began target practise. They had had time to calculate our position to a relative nicety in all this time and they got in some really creditable work. I sheered off towards home, but Campbell, who comes from the same breed as Jimmy Hall, made me wait for him while he returned into the barrage and captivated the German gunners below with his American aerial contortions, the barrage of shrapnel in the meantime getting very much like an Iowa hail-storm. After satisfying himself that they understood his contempt for them Doug consented to come along home with me. We crossed the lines without suffering a hit and soon were taxying our victorious little Nieuports across the field to the doors of our hangar.

We had scarcely gotten out of our seats when Douglas received news that completely dissipated the joy of his victory. Lieutenant John Mitchell, a brother of our colonel and dear chum of Douglas Campbell had been killed that morning in landing his machine at Columbey-les-Belles. Campbell and Mitchell were college chums, had entered aviation together and had sailed for France from New York on the same steamer. They were inseparable and all their friends thought of them as two brothers. Poor Doug was inconsolable.

Friendships in flying squadrons are curious affairs. Where it is one's daily business to go out looking for trouble it is plainly imperative that one keep oneself always fit and clear-minded. It would never do so to occupy one's mind with emotions of love or friendship that one's fighting perceptions are dulled. The enemy's mind can be counted upon to be burdened with no such heavy weight. It is a matter of life or death to every airfighter — this quick-thinking, unburdened mind.

Hence I had steeled my heart against that intimate kind of friendship with my comrades that prostrates one upon the death of a friend. When Jim Miller went down I learned that necessary stoicism. Later Jimmy Hall went, and Lufbery. Many others were to follow and well I knew it. Close as our friendships were, living and working side by side with common purposes and mutual interdependence, all the pilots of 94, I believe, eventually came to look with a callous indifference upon the sudden death of their dearest chum. This necessity is to my mind one of the greatest horrors of the war.

Lieutenant Smyth used to talk to me about his old mother in New York. She was a widow and he an

only son. She was in ill health and he was haunted
with the belief that a visit from him would do much
to bring her back to good health and spirits. I liked
Smyth immensely from the first, possibly at first because he had so flattered me with his request to go
with me on voluntary patrols, but subsequently I found
that he had the ability and character of a wonderful
pilot and he was a reliable companion in a fight. Various men in my squadron appealed to me in various
ways, but Smyth got so close to me by some attractive quality in his nature, that I sometimes
dreamed of him at night, picturing him battling against
desperate odds in the air or being shot down in flames.

Smyth had an unfailing fund of good nature and
humor. One morning shortly after my last exploit
with Douglas Campbell, Lieutenant Smyth again came
to me and asked me to take him on a second expedition.
We agreed to go on the following morning at four
o'clock.

I might say for the benefit of those who have never
been out of bed at four o'clock that it is always raw
and chilly at that hour in the morning. And when
one climbs up 20,000 feet in the air and cruises about
for an hour or so with nothing more than a cup of
coffee under one's belt it requires some little enthusiasm in one's nature to derive unmixed pleasure out
of it.

On this morning in question Smyth and I got up
to 22,000 feet over Pont-à-Mousson and Flirey. The
temperature at this altitude was probably close to fifty
degrees below zero. We expected to find some early
bird of the Germans coming over the lines to take their
customary photographs, and it was necessary for us to
have the topmost ceiling to escape his attention.

After an hour of fruitless searching, I led off again
to the west, this time a little deeper within the German
lines. To my surprise I noticed Smyth suddenly turn

towards home and soon disappear from my sight. Supposing he had been let down by a faulty motor, I continued my patrol for another hour, saw one enemy plane which also saw me and escaped me without a combat, until finally despairing of finding any game before my fuel was completely exhausted I returned to the field after almost two and one-half hours in the air.

Lieutenant Smyth came up to my machine as I shut off the motor.

"Hello! Esquimo!" he greeted me with some savageness. "Why didn't you stay up all day?"

I asked him why he had come down. He looked at me a moment and then began to laugh.

"Rick!" he said, "I am frozen so stiff yet that if I laugh out loud I will break in two. I don't know just how high up we were but I'll swear that I saw the sun rising for to-morrow morning!"

The Nieuport is a cold berth in high altitudes and one must dress for the part. When I learned that Smyth had worn only his ordinary clothing I could easily fancy that to-day's sun might look to him like the one due a week hence.

CHAPTER XII

JIMMY MEISSNER AGAIN

SUCH was the liaison between the allied forces on our sector of the front in the Spring of 1918 that we were frequently called upon to act in concert with the infantry or the air forces of the French and British. Thus on Decoration Day, when all the thoughts from our aerodrome were directed towards the significance of the celebration that our people back home were planning for this occasion, a call came from the British

Independent Air Force Headquarters that an important expedition was being carried out that morning at
eight o'clock against the German railroad station at
Conflans, and it would be appreciated if we Americans
could furnish them some protection on their homeward
journey.

Accordingly Lieutenant Meissner was given charge
of a formation of six Nieuports from 94 Squadron
and Lieutenant John Mitchell led a similar formation
of six machines from the 95th, all of which left our
aerodrome on this mission.   They were to rendezvous
over Thiaucourt, which was about half-way to Conflans
from the front.   This Lieutenant John Mitchell of 95
Squadron must not be confused with the other John
Mitchell, our colonel's brother, killed, as already stated,
at Columbey-les-Belles.

Thinking the chances good for a little private scrap
of my own, I got my machine ready and left the aerodrome at seven-thirty.   The two large flights were just
fading away in the distance as I left the ground.

By the time I reached Flirey I had attained an
altitude of 15,000 feet and was in a splendid position to
witness the whole show.   There were the English
squadrons returning from this expedition against the
supply depots of Conflans.   They had evidently
dropped all their bombs and had quite as evidently
aroused a hornets' nest in so doing.   A large formation of enemy planes were following them hot-foot
and our fighting machines were climbing up to intercept them.   Ahead of the British aeroplanes a furious storm of shrapnel indicated that Archy was not
caught napping.   The German shells burst below and
ahead of the bombing squadron but ceased as soon as
the pursuing Hun machines approached that area.
Those German batteries were putting up a beautiful
performance but they were lacking in just one essential.
They couldn't hit the target.

My own formations were at that moment passing over Thiaucourt and were dashing forward with all speed to the rescue of the approaching Englishmen. It looked like a regular dog-fight that was preparing before my very eyes. The Americans should reach the Englishmen at about the same time that the Huns overtook them from their rear.

Suddenly I noticed something going wrong with the American formation below me. Evidently another enemy flight had come up from the west and had started a free-for-all fight to prevent the Nieuports from giving aid to the bombers. As I watched this encounter I noticed one of our Nieuports, probably three thousand feet below me and a little to the west, first flutter and then begin to fall out of control. Ever since the beginning of the stage setting I had been edging my way towards the center of the field where the opposing forces must meet. Now they were fairly under me.

The stricken Nieuport had no sooner begun its uncontrollable spin than I noted two Albatros fighting machines set themselves on his tail. Instantly I descended pell-mell onto one of them, firing at long range and continuing my fire until to my great relief I saw my target falling steeply to earth, quite beyond control. The other Albatros veered off and hastened away.

I did not know who was the hapless pilot of the Nieuport and could not tell in what condition he was. I started swiftly down beside him to ascertain whether he was beyond further help or whether his whole performance was simply a ruse to get away from an overwhelming force. Before I had reached him I saw the Nieuport come gracefully out of the spin and with one long bank begin again its upward climb. It was only a ruse! The boy was coming back to the fight!

Climbing above him, I again turned my attention to the thickest of the fray.   The attacking Fokkers had been met by the remaining strength of the Americans by now and the English bombers were nearing the allied lines.   A number of individual combats were waging in various parts of the heavens.   I ran about from one to the other with a savage sort of elation urging me on.   It is a glorious feeling to down an enemy in combat and the sweetness of such a victory is more than doubled if it includes saving a comrade from a fall.   Who this comrade was I did not know, but I saw that he was following me along as we searched the sky from place to place for a favorable opening.   Finally it came!

About five kilometers away in the direction of Pont-à-Mousson I saw a running fight which had passed quite through the rest of the combatants.   I had been flying in almost the opposite direction and had not noticed their passing us.   My recent protégé had left me and was already streaking it in their direction. I pulled over and started in pursuit, straining my eyes to distinguish what machines were involved in this new mêlée, to what sides they belonged and how our fellows were faring.   A glance at the lines told me that the British squadron was well away and unpursued.

The little Nieuport ahead of me continued straight on and while I was still half a mile away I saw him dart in to the attack.   There were four or five Nieuports against the same number of Albatros machines and the whole show was drifting east toward the Moselle River.   I slightly increased my altitude and prepared to select the most favorable door for my entrance.   But whilst I was in the very act of entering it a sudden change in the situation attracted my attention.   The same little Nieuport that had been in trouble so recently over Thiaucourt and which had again gone in red-headed against these Albatros was diving down on the tail of one enemy while a second Albatros perceiving his advantage had gotten into a similar position on *his* tail. Even while I was starting down to make the fourth in this headlong procession I saw the leading Albatros suddenly zoom sharply up and loop over onto his back. The Nieuport went under him at headlong pace.

Both Albatros were now on the Nieuport's tail and I was firing intermittently at each of them, hoping to divert their attention for the fraction of a second necessary to relieve the pilot on the Nieuport. With a careful aim I settled a long burst of bullets into the Albatros ahead of me. I saw at once that he was finished. The machine continued straight ahead until it crashed full into the forest that lines the east bank of the Moselle.

In the midst of this diving battle the pilot in the Nieuport had tried the same maneuver that the enemy Albatros had so recently achieved. Pulling back his joystick with great suddenness, the Nieuport rose and let the two machines, one a pursuer, the other my victim, and now pilotless, pass beneath him. But at the same instant came the sound of that sinister crackling that indicated to me that the strain had again been too much for the strength of the Nieuport's wings. The whole surface of the canvas on the right wing was torn off with the first wrench! It was the same familiar old accident that had so nearly claimed Jimmy Meissner a fortnight previously — that had indeed landed Jimmy Hall a prisoner in German lines and that had so terrified me a few days before. And here we were again at least four miles north of No Man's Land! Would he disintegrate here or would he be able to make some sort of landing in the forest-covered mountains below? It was a pitiable choice.

Fortunately we were left alone with our problem —

the pilot of the other Nieuport and myself.   The two
Albatros had evidently decided to call it a day and go
in. They may never have known the catastrophe
which overtook their coveted victim.   The other enemy
machines had carried on their attacks or retreats well
beyond the Moselle.   I took a rapid survey of the
heavens before turning my helpless attention to the
ugly situation in which my protégé now found himself.
Truly, if he gets out of this alive, I thought to myself,
he will certainly survive the war!

"The boy who can pilot a machine without any
fabric on it, as that chap is doing, is certainly something
of an artist," I again said to myself as I put on the
sauce and hastened to overtake my wobbly companion,
who was staggering towards our lines much like a
drunken man.   But at any rate he *was* getting there.
I came up to within twenty feet of him and looked
curiously into the pilot's seat.

There was Jimmy Meissner again, turning a cheery
grin towards me and taking his ease while he waved a
hand to me!   Jimmy Meissner indeed!   No wonder he
could fly a machine without canvas.   With the practise he was getting he would soon be flying without
wings.   This was the second time he had gone through
with practically this same experience, and I had saved
him from attack on both occasions.

I stayed close beside Jimmy all the way in.   When
he finally settled down on our field for his final little
crash he came wobbling over to me from the wreck as
blithe and merry as ever.

"Thanks, old boy, for shooting down those Boches
on my tail," said Jimmy, trying to be serious.   "I'm
beginning to like coming home without any wings on
my machine."

Just here Doug Campbell came out of the hangar
and ran up to my machine.

"Rick!" said Douglas, "who was the poor fellow

who ripped the canvas off his wings and fell just beyond Pont-à-Mousson? I saw the thing go down."

"Doug!" I returned seriously, "you simply can't kill some people!"

"But I've put in a report that he crashed!" retorted Doug. "Taylor and I were in on that show that you just left. We beat you home. We both saw the wing come off that Nieuport when he came out of the dive. Who was he?"

I pointed sadly at Jimmy without speaking. Then I pointed to the remains of his machine in the center of the field.

"Jimmy Meissner!" I said, climbing down from my machine, "I got two Huns through you to-day and I thank you for them, but you must really stop this sort of thing. It's getting on my nerves."

"Was that really you, Jimmy?" queried Campbell, coming up and hugging the unabashed Meissner. "And this is the second time you've gotten away with it!"

"You will never be shot down in air fighting, my son," contributed Thorn Taylor, who was also regarding our lucky pilot with unbelieving eyes. "Wait till Flatbush hears about this new stunt of yours!"

Jimmy Meissner comes from that part of Brooklyn known as Flatbush.

While we were thus congratulating Jimmy upon his second miraculous escape on a collapsed machine John Mitchell of 95 Squadron settled upon the field beside us. And he had another interesting story of the day's adventure.

He had noticed an enemy two-seater and two protecting fighting planes of the enemy accompanying it just east of the British bombers who were returning. His entire formation dived down to the attack and a brisk little battle took place at only 3,000 feet above

ground. One after another Mitchell's formation of
six machines piqued down at the two-seater and let go
a burst. At the last swoop the enemy plane burst into
flames and crashed.

Then they took up the pursuit of the two defending
planes and Mitchell chased one of them as far north
as Vigneulles, which is half-way to Metz from the front
line trenches. At this point the fleeing Hun evidently
decided that he was no match for the American who
dared to follow him so deep within his own territory,
for he dived suddenly to earth and attempted to land
in a large open field just outside the town. Mitchell
followed him all the way down, firing continuously as
he attempted to land. The Boche pilot made a miscalculation of his distance, being probably scared out
of his wits, ran full into a fence and turned a double
somersault before ending in a total smash.

Just how the pilot came out of this misadventure
Mitchell had no way of ascertaining, but as long as
the wreckage remained in his sight no person attempted
to emerge therefrom.

It was a glorious day for 94 and 95 Squadrons.
We had brought down in combat four aeroplanes of
the enemy without the loss of a single one of our own.
We lost one machine through accident in this fight,
but there were so many amusing incidents connected
with this accident that none of us took it seriously.
It happened in this way:

The comedian and life of 95 Squadron was Lieutenant Casgrain, of Detroit, Michigan. Lieutenant
Mitchell took him along on this expedition, although
it was his first trip over the lines. Casgrain kept in
the formation and took a gallant part in the attack on
the two-seater machine which ended in its destruction
in air.

But in recovering from the downward dive Casgrain made the same mistake which so many of us had made in pulling up the Nieuport too quickly. He lost his canvas, just as Meissner had done.

Being unaware that proper manipulation would permit him to fly home in that condition Casgrain put his nose down immediately and began a long glide to earth. Evidently he thought he was much nearer home than he was. For as we were told later by an artillery observer who had seen him land, Casgrain floated blandly half-way across No Man's Land, which is about a mile wide at this point, selected a smooth piece of ground and landed with the ease of an eagle.

He stepped out of his machine with a nonchalant manner, map in hand, and set about quietly perusing it as much as to say, "Well, here I am! Now just where am I?"

At this moment several rifle balls dug up the dirt at his heels. He dropped his map and made a jump for some nearby trees. After a short consideration of his position he was seen to leave the trees and advance straight towards the German trenches, his hands held up in the air!

Poor old Casgrain evidently thought he was well behind the German lines, after his first rude awakening. As a matter of fact he might just as well have walked in the other direction and passed through into our own lines if he had only known that he was in No Man's Land.

The officers' mess at 95 Squadron do not tire of repeating this story to the present day. A few days after the cessation of hostilities they learned from released prisoners with great satisfaction that their star comedian had been well cared for in German prisons, where he had been the wit of the camp. A fortnight after his capture he was caught hoarding his food in order to have a supply on hand when an opportunity

came for an escape. For this offense Casgrain was
sent north to a distant camp in Prussia just before the
armistice was signed.

The American gunners who witnessed Casgrain's
landing in No Man's Land brought their 75's to bear
upon his aeroplane as soon as they discovered he had
abandoned it. It lay somewhat nearer the German
trenches than our own. All the rest of the day they
hammered away at it without scoring a single hit.
Presumably the novices in this battery were experimenting at range finding, for they shot away much
ammunition without damaging the machine. This
particular battery evidently had not had much practise
before they left the United States.

That night the humorous Boches in the trenches
went out and secured the little machine. The next
morning the American gunners saw the top plane
of the Nieuport standing upright in the German front
line trench. The bulls-eye cocard, which was brightly
painted with red and blue circles around the big white
center, stood directly facing them as much as to say:
"Now! Here is the target! Take another try
at it!"

From the frequency of these accidents to our Nieuports it may be wondered why we continued to use
them. The answer is simple — we had no others we
could use! The American Air Forces were in dire
need of machines of all kinds. We were thankful to
get any kind that would fly.

The French had already discarded the Nieuport for
the steadier, stronger Spad, and thus our Government
was able to buy from the French a certain number of
these out-of-date Nieuport machines for American pilots — or go without. Consequently, our American
pilots in France were compelled to venture out in Nieuports against far more experienced pilots in more

modern machines. None of us in France could understand what prevented our great country from furnishing machines equal to the best in the world.

Many a gallant life was lost to American aviation during those early months of 1918, the responsibility for which must lie heavily upon some guilty conscience.

CHAPTER XIII

AMERICA'S FIRST ACE

AT the close of the war 94 Squadron not only held first place among all American squadrons in length of service at the front, but we held the record in number of enemy planes brought down and the record number of aces for any one squadron as well. I believe no single squadron in the world has won similarly so many victories as the American 94 Hat-in-the-Ring Squadron had credited to it during the first six months of its existence. Our victories which were confirmed, totalled 69, ending with the last aerial victory of the war — that of Major Kirby, who shot down his first and last enemy machine just northeast of Verdun at about noon on Sunday, November 10th, 1918.

Many of the pilots who had gone out on their first patrols with me counted themselves later among the American Aces. While many Americans had secured five or more victories in the air before the pilots of 94 began their full strides, these early Aces, such as Lufbery, Baylies and Putnam of French escadrilles, and Warman, Libby and Magoun, who were enrolled with the British, all were trained under foreign methods and flew foreign machines. The first official American Ace is therefore claimed by our squadron. This simon-pure American air-fighter who entered the war with the Americans, received his training with

Americans and did all his fighting with the Americans was Lieutenant Douglas Campbell, of St. José, California.

Douglas Campbell was 22 years of age when he made his first trip over the lines. His father was the head of the Lick Observatory on Mount Hamilton, California. Douglas had received an unusually good schooling before he entered the war, being an old boy of Hotchkiss, and later graduating at Harvard with the class of 1917. The outbreak of the war caught him traveling in Austria with his family. They avoided the active theater of war by going through Russia and getting thence from Denmark to England.

After finishing his college course Doug began preparing for aviation by entering the ground school work at Cornell University. He was among the first cadets to be sent to France, arriving in Paris in August, 1917. He had not as yet received any training in flying but was thoroughly familiar with wireless operation, aerial navigation and aeroplane motors.

Made adjutant under Captain Miller, who was then in command of the American Flying School at Issoudun, Lieutenant Campbell had great difficulty in extricating himself from this indoors work, where every day's stay made him more and more valuable to his superiors. He determined to learn to fly, with the expectation that, once possessed of his wings, he might find his transfer to an active service at the front more quickly obtainable.

There were no beginners' training machines at Issoudun. Only the 23 Model Nieuports were there. Pilots were supposed to receive initial training on the slower Curtiss machines, or the Caudrons, before attempting to fly the fast Nieuports. But Campbell feared he would never get necessary permission to take this preliminary training, so he determined to get through without the beginner's course.

Little by little he edged his way into the advanced training school. He finally considered himself well enough schooled in the principles of flying to make his first essay on a solo flight. He went up all right, flew away all right, landed all right. In other words Lieutenant Campbell learned to fly alone on a fast scout machine—a feat I do not remember any other American pilot having duplicated.

Douglas Campbell was always a silent and self-possessed fellow. He was popular among his fellows from his first appearance in 94 Squadron. Quiet and thoughtful in manner and gentle in speech when on the ground, Lieutenant Campbell in the air was quite a different character. He went after an enemy pilot like a tornado, often exposing himself to deadly openings. His very impetuosity usually saved him from danger unless his opponent was an old hand at the game and knew how to measure up the proper amount of defensive and offensive tactics in the same maneuver.

On May 31st, the day after our big celebration just recorded, Lieutenant Campbell went out on a voluntary patrol alone—i. e., Doug went out looking for trouble. He made quite a long flight inside the German lines at a great altitude, but discovering too many enemy aeroplanes aloft he decided to return back to the lines. When still three or four miles behind the German front, he discerned a German Rumpler machine evidently taking photographs of our advanced positions just south of Flirey. Flirey lies just inside our lines about half-way between Pont-à-Mousson and St. Mihiel.

The Rumpler aeroplane was the machine used by the enemy for observation and photographing. It was a two-seater and both the pilot and the observer who sat behind, had machine-guns so mounted that they covered both the front and the rear. The pilot's gun was fixed, that is, it lay flat on top of the engine hood and could not be raised or lowered. The pilot must raise or lower the nose of the aeroplane itself to bring his sights upon a target. The bullets shoot straight through the revolving propeller and the trigger of the gun is so connected with the propeller shaft by a synchronizing gear that the hammer of the gun falls only when the propeller blade is out of the way of the issuing bullets.

The observer in the rear seat, however, is able to move his twin guns about and point them in any direction. An attack is therefore usually made upon such a machine from a position under its tail. If an attack comes from below the fusilage the observer cannot shoot without cutting holes through his own tail. The forward pilot cannot use his guns at all. The only defense against such an attack is a quick swing to the left or right so that the observer can see the attacking enemy and bring his guns into action. This move the attacking aeroplane must anticipate.

Campbell was coming into the enemy's range from a very favorable direction. He had the sun at his back and moreover, he was coming from Germany into France. His presence in that direction would not be suspected.

Maneuvering until he was sure of his position Lieutenant Campbell first tried a diving attack, from above and behind the Rumpler. He had an excellent chance of killing the observer with the first burst long before the latter could swing his guns around and aim them. But no such easy victory awaited him.

As he began his dive he began firing. Six or seven shots issued from the Nieuport's single gun, and then it jammed. The observer turned around and saw the diving Nieuport almost upon him. He quickly seized his own gun mount and got to work. Campbell was compelled to fly a wide circle away out of range while he worked the breechblock of the Vickers and freed the jam. Now it must be a contest between a one-man scout and a two-man fighting 'bus. The best pilotage and the coolest nerve must win.

As Doug returned to the attack he discovered at once that he had a veteran pilot against him. The Rumpler crew showed no sign of panic or fear. The Heinies did not even propose to retreat!

Campbell approached somewhat warily and began a study of the enemy's tactics. The Nieuport could turn and twist with much greater agility than the heavier machine. It had greater speed and a faster dive. Underneath the Rumpler was a safe position from which the American could keep out of view and occasionally point up his nose and let go a burst of bullets through the enemy's floor. Campbell darted in, braving a few hurried shots, and secured his position. But he didn't keep it long!

With a skill that won from Campbell still greater respect for his pilotage, the German pilot suddenly banked over, giving his observer an excellent shot at the Nieuport below. It was no place to linger in and Douglas quickly vacated. He dived again and came away at a safe distance. Again he turned the proposition over in his mind. These fellows were evidently desirous of a real battle. Well, thought Campbell to himself, let the best man win. Here goes!

Circling the enemy again and again at such speed that no careful aim at him was possible, Campbell smiled grimly to himself as he saw the observer frantically continue his firing. At this rate he must soon exhaust his ammunition and then Campbell's turn would come. Doug continued his maneuvers, at times firing a shot or two to tempt the Boche into still greater activity. Round and round they went, the Hun pilot attempting to kick his tail around to keep pace with the quicker circles of the flitting Nieuport.

The pilot was surely a wonder. The observer, however, was not in the same class as an air-fighter.

For fifteen minutes Campbell continued these maneuvers. So far as he knew not a single bullet had entered his plane. Then suddenly he noticed that the pilot had changed his tactics. Instead of trying to keep the Nieuport within range of the observer, the German pilot was now keeping his tail behind him and sought always to get a shot himself with his forward gun. Campbell flew in closer to the tail to get a look at this situation.

Coming in towards the observer from a diagonal direction Campbell approached to within fifty feet of the enemy and saw a curious sight. The observer was standing proudly upright and his arms were folded! From the edge of his cockpit the empty ammunition belt floated overboard and flapped in the wind. He had indeed exhausted his ammunition and now stood awaiting his doom without a thought of asking for mercy. He wore a haughty expression on his face as he watched the American approach. As Doug said later, he was so impressed with the bravery of the action that he felt he could not continue the combat against an unarmed enemy. The Prussian's expression seemed to say: " Go ahead and shoot me! I know you have won."

Upon second thought Lieutenant Campbell realized this was not a game in which he was engaged. It was war. These men had photographs of our positions within their cameras which might be the death of hundreds of our boys. They had done their best to kill him and he had endured their bullets in order to obtain just this opportunity. And the pilot was still continuing his effort to outwit the American and get him beneath his guns.

With his next maneuver Campbell began firing.

With almost his first burst he saw that he had won. The machine of the enemy suddenly descended very rapidly, the next second it began falling out of control, and a few minutes later Lieutenant Campbell saw its last crash in our lines, a few hundred yards north of the little village of Menil-le-Tours.

Campbell returned to the field and immediately jumped into a car and drove over to the scene of the crash. Here he quickly found the mangled Rumpler and in the midst of the débris were the bodies of the two late occupants with whom he had had such a prolonged duel. Both had been killed by the fall.

The brave observer whose demeanor had so aroused Campbell's admiration was in truth a Prussian lieutenant. The pilot held the same rank. Both were subsequently given a military funeral and their personal effects were sent back to Germany in their names.

Lieutenant Campbell detached from the conquered Rumpler the black crosses which decorated its wings and brought them home with him as first evidence of his well won victory. As the machine crashed within our lines it required but a few more hours in which to have Lieutenant Campbell's victory officially confirmed. It was his fifth! He had been the first American pilot to win five official confirmations. Douglas Campbell that night received the heartiest congratulations from all the boys in the squadron as the first American Ace. The news was telegraphed to the whole world and for a month the congratulations of the world came pouring in upon him. Almost self-taught and equipped with not the safest machine at the front, Douglas Campbell had within six weeks of his first flight over the lines fought five successful duels with the boasted air-fighters of the Germans.

During the early hours of the same day on which Campbell was bringing this distinguished honor to the

94th Squadron an episode occurred which illustrates the great aid that aeroplanes give to the land forces in warfare. Sadly enough this illustration is negative rather than affirmative, for it shows the misfortune that resulted from the failure of our troops always to use our aeroplanes before a contemplated advance.

Northwest of Seicheprey a small offensive movement had been planned by the American infantry. By some means or other the enemy had received advanced information of this attack and had prepared a trap for them.

According to the pre-arrangements our artillery began the show with a terrific bombardment of shells along the German trenches. Something like 20,000 shells were poured into a small area of ground inside of one hour. Then the doughboys got the word and went over the top.

They raced along across No Man's Land, dropped into the first line trenches of the Germans, crawled out of them and went on to the second. All the way on to the third line trenches of the Germans they continued their victorious course. When they arrived there they counted up their prisoners and found the whole bag consisted of but one sick Heinie, whom the Germans had been unable to remove!

While they were scratching their heads over this extraordinary puzzle German gas shells began to drop among them. The enemy had calculated to an inch the exact positions they had just evacuated and they quickly filled the trench lines with deadly fumes. Over 300 of our boys were gassed more or less seriously before they had time to meet the devilish menace. Then they realized they had wasted their ammunition upon vacant trenches and had blindly walked into a carefully prepared trap!

One single preliminary aeroplane flight over this area before beginning the offensive would have disclosed to our troops the whole situation. In fact I believe this function of " seeing for the army " is the most important one that belongs to the aviation arm in warfare. Bombing, patrolling and bringing down enemy aeroplanes are but trivial compared to the vast importance of knowing the exact positions of the enemy's forces and " looking before you leap."

On the morning of June first I had an interesting little fracas with an enemy two-seater Rumpler some distance within the German lines. But this pair of Boche airmen was evidently not related to the team that Doug met on the day before. They dived for the ground and continued their course homeward regardless of my earnest invitations to come back and fight it out. Much disappointed with a fruitless day's work I went home and arranged to take a little joyride by automobile over to Nancy, the principal city in this part of France.

Nancy is a city of thirty thousand or thereabouts and is called by Frenchmen " the Little Paris of the East." After four years of war its shops are now almost empty and its glory considerably dimmed; but a visit and walk about the city's streets did all of us good after so many weeks standing on the alert.

We heard rumors there that the American aeroplane squadrons were to be moved soon to another sector of the front to meet a " big push " on Paris that was anticipated. Rumors were rife in Nancy on every topic, however, so we were not fully convinced by them. Nancy is darkened by night, as is every city or village so near the front where bombing raiders may be expected. Nothing daunted by this possibility of a raid however, we investigated the chances for a good meal as dinner time approached. Imagine our gratification when we stepped into a restaurant on Stanislas Plaza and found a list of good old American dishes on the menu!

Upon inquiry we found that the place was called "Walter's" and was quite the most pretentious café in Nancy. I called for the proprietor and learned that his name was Walter. He had formerly been the Chef at the Knickerbocker in New York. Visiting his old home in France Walter had been caught by the war, joined the infantry and after a few months at the front was wounded and retired from service.

Being a native and a lover of France, he decided to stay and see the war out. Accordingly he selected "little Paris in the East" and opened up a first-class restaurant which has now become the favorite rendezvous for the many American officers who find their headquarters in this vicinity.

CHAPTER XIV

RUMPLER NUMBER 16

LIEUTENANT SMYTH went out with me again on June 4th, 1918. He had now become a valuable companion and I placed the utmost dependence upon his reliability and good judgment. We crossed the lines near Pont-à-Mousson to take a look into the enemy territory and see if any inquisitive aeroplane might be coming over for photographs.

Within a dozen minutes after passing the trenches I picked up the distant silhouette of two enemy machines approaching us from the direction of Metz. I saw at first glance that these fellows had more than a thousand feet advantage of us in the matter of altitude. Without waiting to discover whether or not they had any friends behind them, I turned sharply about and began climbing for a greater height. We could neither attack the enemy nor defend ourselves advantageously so far below them.

While flying south and climbing steeply I noticed ahead of us, in the direction of our own aerodrome, an enormous number of white shell-bursts dotting the heavens at about our altitude. These were American anti-aircraft shells and they told me clearly that an enemy aeroplane was operating over Toul; likewise they indicated that no American planes were in the sky there, else our gunners would be more cautious in firing.

Up to this time I had downed five German aeroplanes, every one of them behind their own lines. Confirmation for my last victory, won on May 30th had not yet come in, so officially I was not yet an ace. That was of little consequence but the matter of dropping a Boche plane within our own territory where I might land beside him and have the satisfaction of seeing what sort of prize I had bagged — this was a pleasure that I rather ardently desired. Consequently I forgot all about the late object of our attack, who presumably was still coasting along five or six miles behind us. I wigwagged my wings to attract Smyth's attention, pointed the nose of my Nieuport towards the city of Toul and forged with all possible speed ahead in that direction. Smyth understood and followed close behind me.

As we drew nearer we easily distinguished the outline of a two-seater Hun photographing machine tranquilly pursuing its way amidst the angry bursts of shrapnel. I wouldn't have taken a million dollars for my opportunity at that moment. The enemy was in our very front lawn and would drop within a few kilometres of my own hangar. He hadn't even noticed my approach but was lazily circling about, no doubt photographing everything of interest in the vicinity with calm indifference to the frantic efforts of our Archy batteries.

It was a Rumpler, just as I had thought. I had

him in a tight position. He couldn't see me as I was exactly in the middle of the sun. I had just the right amount of elevation for a leisurely direct attack. Smyth stayed above me as I pushed down my joystick and began my slide.

Painted in big black letters on the side of his fusilage was the number " 16." The outlines of the " 16" was beautifully shaded from black into orange color. Just ahead of the " 16" were the ornate insignia, also in orange which represented a rising sun. I pictured the spot on the wall over my sleeping cot where those insignia would hang this evening after dinner as I directed the sights of my machine-gun past the rising sun, past the observer's seat, raised them a trifle and finally settled them dead into the pilot's seat only a hundred yards ahead of me. Absolutely certain of my aim I pressed the trigger.

Words cannot describe my chagrin and rage as I realized that my gun had jammed after the first two or three shots. I dashed on by my easy target at the rate of two hundred miles per hour, cursing madly at my gun, my ammunition and at the armorer at the aerodrome who had been careless in selecting and fitting my cartridges. The two or three bullets that I had fired merely served to give the alarm to the Huns in the machine. They would turn at once for home while I withdrew to repair my miserable firearms.

It was too true. Already they were headed for Germany and were moving away at top speed. I directed my swifter climbing machine upon a parallel course that would soon distance them as well as regain me my former superior height; and as we flew along I disengaged the faulty cartridge from the chamber of the Vickers and fired a few rounds to see that the mechanism was in good firing order. All again arranged to my satisfaction, I looked below to see how far my craft had carried me.

I had crossed over the lines! There lay Thiaucourt below me, not more than a mile away. The enemy machine had been steadily diving for home all this time and I had a very few seconds left me for an attack of any kind. All hopes of getting a victory inside of my own lines had now disappeared. I should be lucky if I got confirmation for a victory at all, since we were now so far inside Germany and so near to the ground. I dived on to the attack.

Most of one's troubles in this world come from something wrong inside one's self. If I hadn't been so stupidly optimistic at the outset of this engagement I should have been more cautious and my first disappointment would not have made me forget to keep an eye out for other enemy machines. Even Smyth I had forgotten, in my rage at losing the best chance for a brilliant shot that had ever come my way. I had been flying for five minutes with almost no thoughts except angry disappointment. Now I had a rude awakening.

Even as I began my last dive upon the Rumpler I heard, saw and felt living streaks of fire pass my head. They crackled and sparkled around me like a dozen pop corn roasters, except, that they had a far more consistent and regular rhythm. I saw a number of these tracer bullets go streaming past my face before I realized what a blessed idiot I had been. Almost scared out of my wits with the dreadful situation in which I now found myself I did not even stop to look around and count the number of enemy machines on my tail. I imagined there were at least a thousand from the streaks of fire which their tracer bullets and incendiary ammunition cut through my wings. I kicked my rudder with my right foot and shoved my joystick to the right with a single spasmodic jerk. My machine fell over onto its wings and slid sideways for a few hundred feet and then, seeing a clear country between me and dear old France, I pulled her back into line and fed in the gas.   The suddenness of my maneuver must have caught the Heinies quite by surprise, for as I straightened out I looked behind me and saw the two fighting single-seaters which had been on my tail still on their downward dive.   I had gotten away so quickly they did not even yet know I had gone.

Number 16 and the orange-colored Rising Sun that I fancied would be decorating the walls over my sleeping cot were still leering at me from the fat sides of the Rumpler as it descended leisurely to the ground.

As I took my melancholy yet grateful way homeward I reviewed and checked up the events of the morning.   I resolved then and there never again to permit premature elation or circumstances of any kind, good or bad, to rile my temper and affect me as they had this morning.   Fate had been extraordinarily good to me and I had escaped miraculously with only a few bullet holes through my wings, but I could never expect to be so fortunate again.

It was with a chastened spirit that I confronted our armorer a few minutes later and told him about my jam.   Instead of bringing a severe punishment to the careless mechanics who had tested my gun and ammunition I mildly suggested that they make a more stringent examination of my cartridges hereafter.

At this time I was second in command of Squadron 94 and, as one of the privileges of the office, I could go off on voluntary patrols at any time I desired so long as such proceedings did not interfere with my required duties.   I naturally preferred going by myself, for I felt no responsibility for other pilots under such circumstances and I had a much better chance of stealing up close to enemy aeroplanes without discovery.   In formation flying the whole flight is limited to the speed and altitude of its weakest member.   Formation flying is very valuable to an inexperienced pilot;

but after one has learned to take care of oneself one prefers to go out with a roving commission.

The morning following my disappointing encounter with No. 16 of the Rising Sun Squadron, I went over to my hangar at an early hour to see that all was right with my machine. Inside the shed I found the mechanics busy with my Nieuport. The gun had been dismounted and was still in the repair shop. Some defect had been discovered in the mechanism, they told me, and it had been necessary to take it to the gun repair shops for examination. My machine was out of commission for that day.

Looking over the available machines I found that Lieutenant Smyth's Nieuport was in good condition, although the guns were not correctly aligned, according to Smyth's judgment. He readily consented to my using it for a little patrol, though this necessitated his remaining behind. I knew nothing of the capabilities of his machine, yet I was pleased to try the efficacy of his twin gun mounting. My own Nieuport carried but one gun.

Flying high over Nancy and Toul and Commercy I tried first to learn the topmost ceiling of Smyth's machine. The highest altitude, it should be explained, to which any machine can climb, is controlled by the steadily increasing rarity of the atmosphere. The higher one rises, the greater speed is required, to enable the thinner air to sustain the weight of the aeroplane. Consequently, the limit of altitude for any given machine depends upon two factors: its horsepower and its weight. In order to climb an extra thousand feet, you must appreciably increase the horsepower or diminish the weight. To resume: I reached 20,000 feet and found that Smyth's machine would go no higher. I fired a few bursts from each gun and found that they operated smoothly. Everything appearing to be all right, I headed for Germany and began to scour the hostile skies.   For a time nothing appeared.   Then, again coming from the direction of Metz, I observed a photographing two-seater, accompanied by two scouts acting as protectors.

Acting upon the same tactics that had appealed to me yesterday I turned back into the sun and awaited their passing over our lines.   To my delight I saw the two fighting machines escort the Rumpler fairly across our lines and then themselves turn back into Germany. They had not seen me and evidently considered their protection no longer necessary.   I hugged the sun closely and let the Rumpler sail by below me.   Imagine my extravagant joy when I again made out the painted Rising Sun in orange colors along the side of the Rumpler's fusilage, and the big black numerals " 16 " following it!   My escaped prize of yesterday was again within my clutches.   It would never escape again.

The barren walls of my sleeping quarters again rose before my eyes.   Manfully I choked down all unwonted feelings of optimism as I thought of yesterday's mishaps, but still I felt every confidence in the outcome of to-day's encounter.   This was too good to be true.

Compelling myself to patience I followed my enemy along as he made his way still further to the south. He had some special mission to perform, of this I was sure.   I wanted to know just what this mission was.   At the same time the farther back he ventured the better would be my chances for dropping him within our territory.   He was now almost over Commercy.   My sole fear was that some careless move of mine would disclose me to the attention of the observer.

As he left Commercy behind him and approached I made up my mind to delay no longer.   I suddenly left my position in the sun and darted out to the rear to intercept his retreat. It was to be a straightforward battle in the open. Let the best man win!

Again my luck was with me, for I reached a point directly behind him and had turned towards him for my first shots before they were aware of my presence. I had decided upon my tactics. Diving upon him from a diagonal direction my first bursts would doubtless cause him to put his machine into a vrille. I would anticipate this and zoom up over him and catch him dead under my next diving attack. As I neared the Rumpler's tail from three-quarters direction I saw the observer suddenly straighten himself up and look around at me. He had been down in the bottom of his office, probably taking photographs of the scenery below. The pilot had seen my machine in his mirror and had just given the warning to the rear gunner. As he faced me I began firing.

Two unexpected things happened immediately.

Instead of falling into a vrille, as any intelligent German would certainly have done, this pilot zoomed sharply up and let me go under him. In fact I had about the thousandth part of a second in which to decide to go under rather than ram the monster. Thus my clever plans were all upset by the refusal of my antagonist to do the maneuver that I had assigned to him. Our positions were reversed. Instead of my being on top and firing at him, he was on top and by some extraordinary miracle he was firing at me.

I circled away and looked back to unravel this mystery. I quickly solved it. From out of the belly of the Rumpler a wicked looking machine-gun was pumping tracer bullets at me as fast as any gun ever fired! It was a new and hitherto unheard-of method of defense — this shooting through the floor. No wonder he had climbed instead of trying to escape.

To add to my discomfiture I jammed both my guns on my next attack. There appeared to be no justice in the world! I circled away out of range and moodily cleared the jam in one of my guns. The other absolutely refused to operate further. In the meantime I had not failed to keep an occasional eye upon the movements of my adversary and another swift glance at intervals to see that no other enemy machines were coming to interrupt the little duel that was to ensue. I sobered up completely and considered the exact chances of getting in one swift death-blow with my more adroit Nieuport before the more heavily armed Rumpler could bring its armament to bear upon me. The enemy machine was flying homewards now, straight in the direction of St. Mihiel.

Coming at him again from below, I got in two or three good bursts that should have made an impression upon him — but didn't. The lower berth I found altogether too hot a position to hold, owing to the floor guns of the enemy, so I zoomed suddenly up overhead and circled back to try to catch the observer unprepared to receive me. Several times I tried this dodge but I found one of the most agile acrobats in the Germany army on duty in that back seat. He would be lying face downwards in the tail of his machine one second, firing at me. I would zoom up and come alongside and over him within two seconds, yet I always found him standing on his feet and ready for me. We exchanged bursts after bursts, that observer and I, and soon came to know all about each other's idiosyncrasies. I do not know what he thinks of me, but I am willing to acknowledge him the nimblest airman I ever saw.

We had been at this game for forty minutes and the Rumpler pilot had not fired a shot. I had long ago given up hope of their ever exhausting their ammunition. They must have had a week's supply for the rear guns alone. And now we were well back of the German lines again. I continued to circle in and fire a short burst of half a dozen shots, but found it impossible to break through their defensive tactics long enough to get a steady true aim upon any vital part of their machine.

We were getting lower and lower.   They were preparing to land.   I fired a farewell burst and in the middle of it my gun again jammed.   The pilot waved his hand " good-by-ee " to me, the observer fired a last cheery burst from his tourrelle guns, and the show was over for the day.   My coveted " 16 " would not decorate my bedroom walls this night.

I flew thoughtfully homewards, wondering at the curious coincidence that had brought No. 16 and myself together for two days running, and the strange fate that seemed to protect it.   It was unbelievable that a heavy two-seater could escape a fighting machine with all the circumstances in favor of the latter. It must have been something wrong with me, I concluded.

Just then my motor gave an expiring " chug " and I began to drop.   I leveled out as flat as possible and looked ahead.   I should be able to glide across the trenches from here if Smyth's machine was any good at all.   So fed up with disappointment was I that I did not much care whether I reached the American lines or not.   What could have happened to the fool motor anyway?

I glanced at my wrist-watch and found the answer. I had been so absorbed in my pursuit of No. 16 that I had forgotten all about the passing of time.   It had been two hours and thirty-five minutes since I had left the ground, and the Nieuport was supposed to carry oil for but two and a quarter hours' flight.   The oil completely exhausted, my motor was frozen stiff and a forced landing in some nearby shell hole was an imminent certainty.

The continued favors of Providence in keeping

enemy planes away from me in that homeward glide served to restore my faith in Justice. I crossed the lines and even made the vicinity of Menil-la-Tours before it became necessary to look for a smooth landing ground. There was little choice and what choice there was appeared to be worse than the others. Barb wire stretched across every field in close formation. Selecting the most favorable spaces I settled down, just cleared the top of the wire with my wheels and settled without crashing into a narrow field.

As I climbed out of my machine several doughboys came running up and inquired as to whether I was wounded. A few minutes later Major Miller drove up the road in a touring car, having seen my forced landing from a nearby town. I left a guard in charge of the stranded aeroplane and drove away with the Major to telephone to my aerodrome for the aeroplane ambulance and to report that I had landed without injury. As it proved impossible to " get through " by telephone, the Major very kindly offered to drive me home in his car. In half an hour I was back with my squadron, none the worse for the day's adventures, but, on the other hand, none the better save for a little more of that eternal fund of experience which seemed to be forever waiting for me over the enemy's lines.

But as soon as I stepped out of the car I learned of an occurrence which dispelled all thoughts of my own adventures. Douglas Campbell had just landed and was dangerously wounded!

CHAPTER XV

CAMPBELL'S LAST FIGHT

SHORTLY after I had left the aerodrome that morning for my second rendezvous with my *bête noire*, No. 16, Jimmy Meissner and Doug Campbell had followed me on a little expedition of their own. They had chosen the vicinity to the east of Pont-à-Mousson.

Doug and Jimmy were two of the best pals in the world. Indeed it would be a very difficult matter for anybody to be in Jimmy Meissner's company for more than an hour without becoming his pal. Both these boys had companionable natures. They were constantly in each other's company, Jimmy and Douglas, and very frequently they went off on these special hunting parties together.

On this occasion it appears that after a short tour together back of the lines they became separated. Jimmy went off on a wild goose chase of his own, leaving Lieutenant Campbell reconnoitering back and forth over the same locality to the east of Pont-à-Mousson. Upon one of his patient tacks Campbell discovered a Rumpler coming from Germany and evidently aiming towards the vicinity of Nancy. He hid himself in the sun and awaited its approach.

The actual encounter took place at about the same time I was fighting my No. 16 some twenty miles to the west of them. Douglas began his battle with everything in his favor. He caught the Boches completely by surprise and put enough bullets into the enemy craft to sink an ordinary 'bus. But the Hun wouldn't drop. He simply sailed along and continued to pot Doug's Nieuport every time he swung in for an attack. They had very much the same sort of a running fight as I was having with my antagonist, No. 16.

Finally Meissner saw something going on over the Nancy sky and came speeding back in to take a hand in the combat. Just as Jimmy drew near to the scene of the scrap, he saw that he was diverting some of the pilot's attention to himself. Campbell saw this too and immediately took advantage of the opportunity.

Coming diagonally in towards the observer from behind, Doug suddenly changed his course and swerved around to the front for a shot at the preoccupied pilot. He got in a fairly long burst before he was compelled to turn aside to avoid a collision. Though he had not touched the pilot, he had the good fortune to shower the motor with bullets; and to his great joy he saw that the machine was really out of control. The pilot, unable to maintain headway and maneuver at the same time, had put down his nose and was gliding northwards for his lines.

At this juncture Jimmy took a hand in the scrap, and both the pilot and observer had their hands full to prevent a surprise attack from one of the two circling Nieuports.

But the Americans' time was short. The lines were but half a dozen miles away. With his present height the German pilot could glide his machine well behind his own lines. The *coup-de-grace* must be delivered at once if the Americans were to prevent the morning's photographs from falling into the hands of the enemy.

There was no way of communicating a plan of simultaneous attack between the two Nieuports. But both pilots had the same intention and watched each other jockeying around the Rumpler until a favorable opening presented itself. Suddenly both Meissner and Campbell came in upon the enemy from opposite sides. Campbell got a faster start and braving the fire from the observer, dived below for a hundred feet, only to zoom suddenly upwards and direct another long burst through the floor of the Rumpler. Swerving then off to the right he again came by the side of the observer. The latter unfortunately had changed his position to fire at Meissner after Campbell had darted below him on the other side. As Doug now reappeared from below the Rumpler, he came full into range of the observer's guns.

Doug was just coming out of his zoom and beginning a flat circle to the front when a loud explosion at the small of his back told him that he had been hit. He felt a burning pain run up the length of his spine. He was still some two miles above Mother Earth and his first thought was to retain his senses until he could bring his machine safely to ground. He immediately flew for home, leaving the outcome of the battle to his comrade.

Meissner saw Campbell draw away and immediately jumped to the conclusion that he had been wounded. He had not seen the bullets strike him, however, and there was always the chance that merely an engine failure had compelled Doug to withdraw. No matter what was the cause, Jimmy's duty was to prevent the safe return of the enemy machine to its own lines. He could be of no help to his companion anyway. He continued his harassing of the pilot and so occupied that gentleman with maneuvers that by the time the trenches were reached Jimmy had the satisfaction of seeing that the Rumpler could not possibly get to a safe zone for landing.

Just a hundred yards beyond the German first-line trench the Rumpler crashed. Both the pilot and observer scrambled from their seats and ran for their lives. Our doughboys gave them a shower of bullets which greatly accelerated their speed. The Boche soldiers in their trenches stood up and leveled a machine-gun fire at our men to protect their aviators' foot-race for safety. The next moment the American artillery directed a heavy shell-fire of high explosive against the abandoned Rumpler. These were better marksmen than the last I mentioned. After half a dozen shots nothing but fragments remained.

All this spectacle Jimmy gleefully observed before he turned his machine homewards and hastened to find out what had happened to Douglas Campbell. He reached the aerodrome just about the same time I did. Doug was safely landed and had climbed out of the machine without assistance. Although suffering much pain, he would not leave the field until he had learned just how he had been hit. A short inspection disclosed the whole story.

An explosive bullet fired by the observer had come through the floor of Campbell's machine just at the instant he was making a turn. It had penetrated the bottom of the fusilage, gone through the bottom of his seat and then had struck a wire which had exploded the missile not three inches from Campbell's back.

The fragments had scattered backwards and to the side, riddling the framework and fabric which covered the fusilage behind the seat. Very few of the fragments had gone forward. This miraculous circumstance had undoubtedly saved Doug's life.

Jimmy and I gazed with stupefaction at the smiling and imperturbable Doug. He stood beside us refusing all aid and appeared more deeply interested in the condition of his machine than in his own wounds. In the back of his Teddy-bear suit a long jagged tear showed us where the missile had entered his body. Frightful blood stains covered his back. Yet he was deaf to all our entreaties and refused to let us lead him away.

I asked what had been done about getting an ambulance down and found that Campbell had sent for a motorcycle! I could not help laughing at this childish desire to avoid making a scene, which I very well knew had actuated Doug's request for a motorcycle. I immediately commandeered an automobile, and, putting Douglas carefully in it, several of us accompanied him to the hospital.

With continued fortitude Doug refused an anesthetic while the surgeon was removing the bullet. It was found that the steel nose itself had been deflected by the wire into Doug's back. By some miracle it had not touched his spinal column but had traveled up alongside it for five or six inches and finally buried itself in the muscles under the shoulder! This little memento Doug now preserves as his most cherished souvenir of the great war.

With splendid grit Doug smiled and talked while the doctor proceeded with the operation. He drew all the details of the finish of the Rumpler from Jimmy and learned with great satisfaction that this was his sixth official victory. In reality Douglas Campbell's victories total seven, but for one which was downed to my certain knowledge he never received official confirmation.

Had it not been for this unfortunate accident Lieutenant Douglas Campbell would undoubtedly have one of the highest scores of victories claimed by any air-fighter, for he was just entering upon his full stride. As it was, he never fought again. Upon his return in November from America, where he was sent to recover his strength after leaving the hospital, Doug rejoined his old squadron, only to find that its days of fighting were over.

The subject of my encounter with Rising Sun No. 16 occasioned no end of amusement about the mess and many bets were laid as to the outcome. I dreamed about No. 16 at night and was up bright and early on the lookout for him every morning. I took a few of the bets myself naturally enough. I never in my life wanted anything so much as those orange-colored insignia as decorations for my quarters. I planned to build a house some day suitably designed to set off those works of art to the best advantage.

The fates were surely laughing at me all this time. My further adventures with No. 16 would have appeared comic to me if they had not been so infuriating.

The very next day I went up in my own machine with just the one resolve burning in my brain. I saw nothing else in the sky and searched for nothing else. In fact I had scarcely gained my very topmost altitude and set forth in the direction of what I now knew was the favorite path of this daily visitor before I saw him coming to meet me. It was almost as though we had met by appointment.

As I have said, I reached my very highest altitude before going forth to this tryst. Some Nieuports have a higher ceiling than others. It depends upon the quality and natural fitness of the motor. My 'bus reached 18,000 feet that morning. It had just been fitted with two Vickers guns instead of the one it formerly carried. This additional weight of thirty or forty pounds hampered the climb somewhat and lowered my ceiling by at least 500 feet.

Try as I would I could get her no higher. As we approached each other, No. 16 and I, the Rumpler was at 20,000 feet and was still climbing. My Boche friends knew perfectly well they could climb higher than any Nieuport. It might make their photographs a little indistinct but even those were better than our own taken from 12,000 feet. They came steadily on and I turned as they passed me and continued a parallel course some two thousand feet below them.

The railroad stations at Nancy and Toul were their objectives this morning. Without deigning to pay any attention to me they proceeded over their course and deliberately snapped their pictures. Occasionally the observer amused himself with a little target practise at me. At such times I realized that he had nothing else to do, so concluded obviously that he did not desire photographs of those parts of his voyage.

I too fired vain long bursts upwards. I had no idea of hitting them at that long range. It merely served to keep them informed that I was still in their company. They knew they had me at their mercy as far as giving me a chance at a combat.

So we continued along all over the northeast of France. I suppose most of the films they developed that afternoon showed the wings of my Nieuport below them.

My one chance was to keep below them and follow them until they came down. As there is no record of any German machine not coming down finally I determined to follow the Boches back to Berlin if necessary, in order to get a shot at them when they passed my level. Thus we crossed the lines and proceeded steadily northwards. I could outfly the Rumpler and outdive him, but his superior engine power and greater wing spread gave him a much higher ceiling.

After seeing mile after mile slip away beneath my wings and still no evidence of change of heart in my antagonists I began to speculate upon the quantity of gasoline the Rumpler carried. I knew too well the limits of the Nieuport's fuel supply. And the disadvantage again lay with me. For if we both became exhausted at the same time the Rumpler would be in his own territory while I would be many hostile miles from my own.

With savage realization that I was again defeated I turned around and took my way homewards. I could imagine my two Boche adversaries laughing at me as I gave up the chase. They began to glide downwards as soon as I turned my back. I sheered back at them just to have the satisfaction of showing them

I was still their master. Very obediently they altered their tactics and again climbed for their superior ceiling.

When I reached camp I scoured the hangars for information of the highest climbing machine on the aerodrome. My comrades followed me about, supplying me with much gratuitous information and advice. They advised me to leave off both guns next day which might permit me to reach 20,000 feet. Or if I took no fuel along I might go to 30,000 feet. Uncomplimentary references to the weight of my shoes and the heaviness of my grouch aided me considerably.

The result of my researches indicated that Captain Marr's machine had the best reputation for climbing and I immediately set off to obtain his consent for the loan of his Nieuport on the morrow. He readily consented to let me have it, adding that he knew I could reach 22,000 feet with it if I coaxed it properly. I assured him I would coax it all right and left to make my preparations.

The ideal fighting machine is of course one that will outperform every enemy machine in every variety of movement. And there are several kinds of performances that are almost equally valuable in combat fighting. A swift speed is essential. A rapid climb, the ability to dive directly down without overstraining the structure or ripping off the fabric by too sudden an alteration of direction; a high ceiling, which necessitates high engine power and perfect carburetion; quick maneuverability — all these characteristics if combined would make an ideal fighting machine.

This naturally is just what the fighting nations were striving to obtain. Each machine had a superiority in some one particular but failed in another. The famous German Fokker held the skies in 1916 and 1917 for it combined more of these essential details than did any one fighting craft of the Allies. Then came the Spad which the French designed to out-speed and out-maneuver the Fokker, but still the Fokker had a higher ceiling and a swifter dive.

The British produced the S. E. 5 in 1918 which out-dove and out-maneuvered the Fokker, but could not overtake it on a flat race nor out-climb it. The Sopwith Camel likewise came from England and proved superior to the best German fighting machines except in the matter of diving and high-ceiling. As for the Americans, we had to take what machines the Allied nations could spare us. Naturally they kept the best for themselves; and our squadrons of American pilots did the best they could with the second best.

It was at this time that we heard rumors of a new English fighting machine called the Snipe. Like the Camel, it was a Sopwith production. A new engine that was shrouded in much secrecy and mystery was reputed to have carried this little scout machine to the incredible altitude of 33,000 feet. And the speed with which it made this climb broke all the world's records. Our boys of 94 Squadron were naturally desirous of providing themselves with a quantity of these wonderful machines and then trying a few combats with the Richthofen Circus Fokkers.

For the present, however, we had to take what was given to us. We felt that we were not fulfilling the expectations of the people back home, who had been told that we had 20,000 of the best aeroplanes in the world, and all made in America. The truth is that not one American-made fighting machine came to the front, until the war was ended.

Considerably discouraged over the prospects of securing my bedroom trophies from Rising Sun No. 16 I nevertheless climbed into Captain Marr's machine the next morning at exactly 8.15 and amid the cheers of the boys who gathered to see me off I bade the mechanics to pull away the chocks. I made a direct path

to our rendezvous of yesterday, climbing as I flew
northward and east.

Like every enthusiastic owner, Captain Marr had
given his 'bus all the credit that he consistently could.
I have driven automobiles whose owners got a regular
performance of twenty miles to a gallon of gasoline,
but try as one might it would make but about one-
half that mileage for anybody else.

I put Captain Marr's Nieuport up to a little over
19,000 feet that morning, and there she hung. Every
artifice that ever moved an engine was experimented
in but without increasing her capacities an inch. Just
as I had satisfied myself that I had exhausted her
possibilities, I discovered my old friend, No. 16,
winging his way calmly towards me. He was certainly
prompt and business-like in the way he kept his appointments.

Just as yesterday, the Rumpler was some two thousand feet above my highest possible elevation. With
rare magnanimity my old friends kindly came down
a few hundred feet to keep me company. I joined in
the procession as of yore and the two machines made
another grand tour of the northeasterly cities of France
where we photographed all the railroad lines and
canals, took a turn over several aerodromes, French,
British and American, surveyed the charming landscape in all directions and finally decided to call it a
day and go home. My presence served to prevent our
batteries from firing noisy shells at my friends, and
they must have appreciated this act of courtesy on my
part, for during the whole morning's promenade they
did not fire a single shot at me from the machine-gun
which I could plainly see protruding out of the belly of
the monster overhead.

I accompanied them back to their aerodrome, sedulously maintaining the proper distance between us.
Seeing they wanted to alight and mindful of their most

delightful courtesy to me throughout the day I turned about and made for home.

That night I came down with the fever and was immediately sent to Paris on leave.

CHAPTER XVI

BECOMING AN ACE

PARIS in wartime is well enough known to millions of my fellow countrymen, but the scene that presented itself to my astonished eyes as I alighted at the Gare de l'Est on the morning of June 6th, 1918, merits a description. That date, it will be remembered, marked probably the lowest ebb in the spirits of the Parisian populace.

The Germans were along the Marne and but thirty miles from the capital. Château-Thierry was in their hands. The villagers in that vicinity who had braved four years of adjacent warfare were now swept away from their homes. Thousands of these poor refugees were arriving in Paris on the morning I entered it.

Used as I was to the various horrors of war, there was a terror in the countenances of these homeless people that made a new impression upon me. Old women, young women, all clothed in wretched garments and dishevelled head-gear wandered blindly through the streets adjoining the stations, with swarms of crying children clinging to their skirts. Pathetic as this scene was, it had its comic features in the extraordinary articles that these fleeing peasants had chosen to carry with them.

Umbrellas seemed to be the most precious thing that they had tried to save. A little bundle, probably containing a loaf of bread and a few articles of clothing was carried by each woman. The children were loaded down with such strange treasures as axes, parrot cages, wooden buckets and farm implements. The few old men who accompanied them hobbled along empty-handed, with the utmost patience and abandon. Evidently the whole care of the migration was left to the energetic women of France.

They had all been walking for many miles; this was very evident. Their clothing was dusty, worn and crumpled. Their faces were pinched and wretched and an indescribable look of misery and suffering filled every face. The pathos of this scene will never leave my memory.

And here I desire to express my appreciation of the magnificent work of the American Red Cross and American Y. M. C. A. organizations. In that one case of the Château-Thierry refugees these American societies repaid their American subscribers for the sacrifices they made to support them. Indeed, without the help of this American agency I can easily imagine that the French capital, overwhelmed and crushed under the burden and horror of these calamities would long since have abandoned all hope, and riots and disorders would have prostrated the authorities in control of the nation.

Thousands of refugees swarmed throughout a more or less demoralized Paris. They had no money, no food, no idea of where they wanted to go. The spirit was gone from their bodies. Only the call of hunger served to remind them that they still must live.

Preparations were immediately made to care for this new demand upon the American charitable organizations. It was a very critical period of the war. Every available soldier was at the front and these must have the undivided attention of the supply officers, the commissary department and government authorities. Refugees were of no consequence towards winning the war. They deserved pity but could not be permitted to divert the attention of the defenders of a nation.

How dangerous this subtle menace might have been will never be known, for the American Red Cross threw itself into the situation and cared for this increasing army of unfed in Paris. Had they been neglected a day or two longer such riots might have been started in Paris as would have demoralized the whole system of the French organization.

The secret of their success was undoubtedly due to the elasticity and absence of red tape in their organization. But whatever it may have been, the fact that the American Red Cross did successfully feed and clothe these bedraggled thousands was in itself a marvel and made me appreciate how valuable an asset our Red Cross Society was and is in war time.

At the aerodromes and at other military camps all along the front I had abundant opportunities to appreciate this unofficial, or rather unmilitary, aid that was given to the soldiers by these organizations. At our group aerodrome the Red Cross later established a small club-room for the pilots and officers. Here hot chocolate and toast was served in the afternoon and a cheery fire always was found to tempt us out of the mud and rain for a few minutes of recreation. Card tables and writing tables were there; and a piano and phonograph, together with all the old magazines that were sent over by American readers, whiled away many a " dud " afternoon which must have otherwise been spent in more or less solitary confinement within a dripping billet.

The Y. M. C. A. authorities provided in a similar way for the enlisted men. Candy, tobacco and toilet articles were provided at these places at a lower figure than they would have cost at home. Most of these things were absolutely unattainable at the stores in France.

After a good night's sleep far away from the customary roar of artillery, I woke up to find the sun

shining in my Paris window and a fine day well
progressed. After breakfast I took a stroll along
the Champs Elysées under the Arc de Triomphe
and through the beautiful walks of the Bois de Bou-
logne. It was easy to read upon the faces of the
people one met the deadly fear that gripped them.
Thousands had already fled from Paris. The authorities were even that morning considering again moving
the seat of the government to more distant Bordeaux.
The capture of Paris before the American aid could
arrive was a possibility that worried every Parisian.

I tried to fancy the exulting German officers walking down these same beautiful avenues, driving their
motor cars through these splendid woods and occupying such of these magnificent palaces as happened to
tempt their cupidity. Then I thought of the " Spirit
of the Marne " which had so strengthened the French
people in those cruel days of 1914. Studying the set
faces of these passers-by I could discover that the same
indomitable spirit still held them. Their faces held
something of the same expression that was pictured
on that famous French Liberty Loan poster — a Poilu
standing with fixed bayonet defending his native land.
Underneath the poster was written that immortal
phrase, " Ils ne Passeront Pas ! "

After a few days in Paris I returned to my aerodrome by way of Army headquarters, then situated in
Chaumont just south of Toul. Good news awaited
me at my mess. I learned that General Foulois had
been out to see us, and after hearing the repeated stories of the narrow escapes we had had with the fragile
Nieuports, he had promised to secure Spad aeroplanes
for our whole squadron. They were to be driven with
the 220-horsepower Hispano-Suiza motor and would
serve to equip us second to none of the squadrons in
France.

Furthermore, confirmations had been secured for

my fifth victory and several cablegrams from America were handed me, congratulating me on becoming the second American Ace. The news had reached the States before it had found me in Paris!

We had had another victory too. Jimmy Meissner, Alan Winslow and Thorn Taylor had encountered a Hanover two-seater on June 13th, and after a ten-minute combat had the satisfaction of seeing the enemy go down in flames and crash just north of Thiaucourt. The boys were very much elated over the additional news of our contemplated removal to a busier sector of the front. Hunting had become very poor along our old sector. The enemy machines were infrequently met and almost no fighting machines of the Germans were now opposing us. An occasional observing machine came our way and he usually fled long before we had an opportunity for an attack.

We had been for two months on this sector and had received all the preliminary practise fighting that we desired. All the boys were restless and were anxious to get to the thick of the battle down on the Marne where the " Big Push " was now taking place. Fresh from the rumors of Paris, I naturally inflamed their appetite for the contest by picturing to them the state of affairs as I had seen it in the capital. We all felt that we could intercept the Hun invasion and save Paris, if we but had the chance.

At this period we began to notice that the German air tactics seemed to pin all hopes for success upon formation flying. Larger and still larger numbers of enemy aeroplanes clung together when they ventured into hostile skies. From flights of three to five machines in one formation, their offensive patrols now included whole squadrons of twenty or more machines in one group.

Certain advantages undoubtedly accrue to such formations. Mere numbers serve to scare away the more cautious air-fighters, and even the most daring find themselves confronted with such a bewildering and formidable number of antagonists that to attack one must necessarily include defending oneself against several. The Germans were limited in the territory they covered by thus combining their aeroplane strength, but while directing their attack upon one especial sector, such as the Château-Thierry sector, they could operate very successfully with these large formations, and were able to sweep away all opposition from their paths.

Squadron 94 therefore began sedulously to practise flying in similar large formations. Day after day we called together all our available machines and took the sky together, met at a designated altitude and forming a compact group we circled about, executed the various maneuvers that must attend an offensive or defensive movement, and strove always to keep all our aeroplanes in such a position that no single one could ever be cut out and subjected to an attack by an enemy formation. This was a valuable lesson to all of us, and later on we accumulated quite a respectable number of victories by reason of our familiarity with this method of squadron formation flying. Especially valuable is this formation flying to the inexperienced pilot. One illustration will serve to demonstrate my meaning.

On the evening of June 18th, 1918, a few days after I had returned to the command of my First Flight in Squadron 94, we were notified by the British bombing squadrons that they were undertaking a raid upon the railroad yards of Thionville that evening at seven-thirty o'clock. Thionville, or Diderhofen as it is called by the Germans, lies west of Metz and is the favorite gateway to the front from the German interior in the direction of Coblenz and Cologne. Huge supplies were kept there and several squadrons of enemy machines were always on the alert to repel these bombing raids upon their city.

Calling the boys together, I asked for volunteers to go with me on this protective mission for the British. Six pilots stepped forward and we immediately prepared our plans.

Lieutenant Hamilton Coolidge had just joined our group and had not yet made his first trip over the lines. He asked permission to accompany us, and thinking this would be a good opportunity to keep an eye upon him, I consented to his going. We were to meet the bombing machines over Thionville at seven-thirty sharp, and at an altitude of 16,000 feet. We arranged to get above our field and circle about at 2,000 feet until all were ready, then form our positions and fly over in close formation.

As we were getting off the field I noticed that Squadron 95 was likewise sending up a number of machines. Later I learned that they too had heard of this bombing expedition of the British and were going over to see it safely home. Unfortunately they had picked upon the same altitude and the same place for their rendezvous that I had selected.

In ten minutes more I realized that there would be a hopeless tangle of the two formations if I persisted in collecting my followers at the prearranged rendezvous. All the machines were circling about the same position and collisions would be inevitable if the newer pilots were permitted to maneuver about in all this confusion. I accordingly flew about in a wide circle, signalling to my pilots to draw away and follow me. Time was pressing and we must get to Pont-à-Mousson by seven-thirty, even if we were not in our best formation. Two or three of the pilots understood my signals and followed after me. The others got into the other formation and came with it. Some of the inexperienced pilots, including Ham Coolidge, lost both formations and came on alone.

Arriving over the Moselle River at Pont-à-Mousson exactly on the minute, I saw in the direction of Metz a heavy Archy fire. This meant that allied machines were there and were attracting German fire. I flew in to see what it was all about and found a single Salmson machine, belonging to the American Number 91 Squadron falling in a sharp vrille. At 4,000 feet he picked himself up and regaining control of his machine he leveled off for home. I accompanied him back over the lines and saw him safely off for his aerodrome and then turned my attention again to the British bombing machines. Near St. Mihiel I found part of my formation following Lieutenant Loomis. Ham Coolidge had attached himself to this party.

We cruised about together until dusk began to gather, and still there was no sign of the British machines. Suddenly Loomis left me and started for home with Coolidge in his wake. I decided one or both of them had experienced motor trouble and watched them disappear with no misgivings. It was indeed time we got in as the ground would be considerably darker at this hour than one would expect to find it, with the western sun still shining in one's eyes at 15,000 feet elevation. I dropped down over Pont-à-Mousson and getting fairly into the twilight, turned my machine towards home.

Arriving in the vicinity of my landing field, I was suddenly surprised to see a Nieuport flash past me going in exactly the opposite direction. I didn't know who it could be, but it was now so dark that longer flying would be almost suicidal. Feeling instinctively that it might be one of the new pilots, I banked over and started in pursuit. A mile or so this side of the lines I overtook him.

Swerving in closely ahead of the stranger, I wig-wagged my wings and circled back. To my great relief, I saw that he understood me and was following. We soon made our way back to the Toul aerodrome and landed without accident. Getting out of my machine I went over to ascertain the identity of my companion. It was Hamilton Coolidge.

After a question or two Ham admitted that he had become confused in the darkness, had lost sight of Lieutenant Loomis and for some reason or other became convinced that he was flying in the wrong direction. He had reversed directions and was flying straight into the enemy's lines when I had so fortunately passed near by and had intercepted him.

Formation flying then has its uses in other ways than in combat fighting. We had made a confused mess of our formation on this occasion and but for a miracle it would have ended in the loss of a new pilot who later was to become one of the strongest men in 94 Squadron.

One of the comic little incidents that are always rising unexpectedly out of the terrors of war came from my meeting that day with the Salmson machine from Squadron 91. I was just going to bed that night when they called me to the telephone. A member of 91 Squadron wanted to know who was in the Nieuport machine that had escorted him across the lines that evening from the vicinity of Metz. I told him I thought I was the man he sought.

"Well," he said, "I am Lieutenant Hammond of the 91st, and I want to thank you for your help."

I told him there had been very little to thank me for, since there were no enemy aeroplanes about, but I thanked him for calling me up. Then I asked him what had caused him to fall into a vrille.

"Those blooming Archibalds!" he informed me. "They've got the finest little battery over that vicinity

that I've ever seen. I was coming peacefully home
with all my photographs when hell suddenly busted
loose below me. Their first shell exploded just under
my tail and I went up a hundred feet tail first. Then
I began to fall out of control. Evidently my control
wires had been severed, for I couldn't get her out of
the spin for four or five thousand feet. Just as I
finally straightened out along came another shell and
did the same thing to me all over again.

" I fell again, this time feeling certain that I was a
goner. You came along while I was going down the
second time. I managed to get her straightened out,
as you know, when you and I crossed safely over the
lines without any more hits.

" But say, Rickenbacker," he went on, " do you
know what I'm going to do? I've got a sharpshooter's
badge that I won while I was in the Light Artillery.
I've wrapped it up in a small package and tied a long
streamer on to it. I've written a note and put it in,
telling those Heinies that they are more entitled to that
badge than I am — and here it is. Come along and
go with me to-morrow morning and we'll drop it down
on their battery! "

I laughed and told him I would be ready for him
to-morrow morning over my field at eight o'clock.
We would go over and brave the Archy sharpshooters
once more, just for the satisfaction of carrying out a
foolish joke.

But the next morning I was awakened at three o'clock
by an orderly who told me Major Atkinson wished to
talk to me over the telephone. Even as I stood by the
telephone I could hear a tremendous barrage of artillery fire from the German lines. Something big
was on.

CHAPTER XVII

A PERPLEXING BANK OF FOG

THE heavy firing that was now so apparent to me had awakened Major Atkinson in his bed at headquarters, which was in a building adjoining us. He had immediately called us up to order us to take a patrol over the lines at the first break of day and ascertain what this unusual demonstration could mean. I looked at my watch. It was then just five minutes past three. In another hour it would be light enough to leave the field.

Running over to Lieutenant Meissner's billet, I roused him out and then went on to waken the three or four pilots in his flight. In ten minutes all five of us were in the kitchen stirring up the cooks to faster efforts in the heating of coffee and toast. I had already telephoned the hangars and ordered all our machines out on the field in full readiness.

At a quarter to four we were in our machines and were leaving the field. Two other pilots had joined us. It was just beginning to grow light enough to make out the tails of our machines ahead of us.

I directed Lieutenant Meissner to have three of his pilots fly at an altitude of 5,000 feet, and for him to take the other two pilots in his formation and fly below them at 1,500 feet above ground. I, myself, was to keep as close above the contour of the ground as possible and see what the Germans were doing in their first and second line trenches.

With all details of our mission fully understood, we set off and made directly for the north, where the heaviest shooting seemed to be going on. As we neared the lines I could see the constant flashing of the German guns in the darkness. The greatest activity appeared to be just half-way between Pont-à-Mousson and St. Mihiel. Here in the vicinity of Seicheprey the country lies comparatively flat between the mountains which border the Moselle on the one hand and the Meuse on the other. I knew this locality well and could fly at only a hundred feet from the ground without fear of striking against some mountain side in the darkness.

The Huns were doing most of the firing. This was plainly evident from the continuous flashes. The noise of the exploding shells was deadened by the roaring of my aeroplane motor. As I neared the center of all this excitement I sheered off to the north and flew down low enough over the German trenches to permit the tornado of German shells to pass well over my head. Along this course I followed the entire length of the trenches, back and forth, back and forth, until I was convinced that there were no massed bodies of enemy troops waiting for the barrage to cease before they poured forth over the top.

The more I studied the situation the more puzzled I became. I saw the German shells bursting close behind our lines. From the nature of the bursts I knew they were high-explosive shells. This was the usual preliminary to a sudden rush over the top, yet there were no German troops there waiting for the moment of attack.

The whole vicinity of the German front was covered with a dense fog. The intermittent gun-flashes showed but dimly through this mist. Off to the east and the west, where the Meuse and Moselle rivers might be supposed to emit a fog of this sort, the landscape was clear. It was all very puzzling to me.

On each of my excursions back and forth over the German trenches I piqued down from my low level and fired long bursts into their lines with my two machine-guns. I could see my flaming tracer bullets cutting through the night and burying themselves within the enemy's trenches. It was still too dark to distinguish the ground at any distance from the trenches, but I was positive that if any considerable number of men were there they were well under cover.

At last I ran out of ammunition. I decided to fly home, make a report of what I had seen and replenish with fuel and cartridges.

I telephoned my report to Major Atkinson while the mechanics were looking after my 'bus, and in ten minutes I was back again for the region of Seicheprey. By this time the first streaks of dawn were lighting up the ground. While still a great distance away I again noticed the strange clinging bank of fog which began at the German line and covered a space about three miles east and west and half a mile deep. On the American side of the lines the ground was entirely free from this mist.

As I again approached the German trenches I saw more activity there. I dived upon them, letting go long bursts from my guns. Instantly they disappeared from view. It was a very enjoyable game I had as long as any heads remained in view, but after one or two dashes along this front I could find no more targets. The Huns had retired to their underground dugouts.

Many a German fled in terror before my approach that morning. I found myself chuckling with delight over the consternation I single-handed was spreading throughout that German camp. Coming down immediately over the trenches, I would observe a group of soldiers standing outside a dugout, all leveling their rifles at me. With a sudden swerve I would bring them before my sights, and long before they could all cram themselves within the opening I would have a hundred bullets inside their group and would be beyond their reach. I could imagine the terror and helplessness my single presence inspired among the slow moving troops below.   I was having the time of my life.

One particular battery of 77's lay a mile back of the lines and seemed to be having a particularly jolly party. Their flashes almost doubled the other batteries in rapidity.   I determined to fly over and pay them a visit, since none of the infantrymen seemed to care to stick up their heads in the trenches.   Accordingly I turned a bit to the rear and came in upon the battery from behind and at about one hundred feet above the ground.

As I neared them I saw six or eight three-inch guns standing side by side in a little clearing, the line of gunners all rushing swiftly to and fro, picking up and passing forward the fifteen-pound shells.   The guns were firing at the rate of almost one shot each second. A continuous flash could be seen from this little battery, so rapidly did the gunners work.   In a twinkling after my first shot the whole battery became silent.

Pointing my nose directly at the end of the line, I pressed my triggers and raked the whole line before straightening out my aeroplane.   Then with a quick bank I came about and repeated the performance.   Before I had started back every man had fled for shelter and not a gun was firing.   I circled about again and again, chasing the scattered groups of gunners to their respective dugouts and firing short bursts at their heels as they fled.   It was the most amusing little party I had ever attended.   I couldn't help wondering what kind of reception I would get if a sudden panne dropped me within their clutches.

One more dash at the next battery and my ammunition was again exhausted.   I returned to the aerodrome, where I found that Lieutenant Meissner and his pilots had returned without anything new to report. At seven-thirty we all reassembled for breakfast.

We were still discussing the extraordinary episode

of the morning and had none of us arrived at any reasonable explanation for the enemy artillery activity when a visitor was announced for breakfast. He came in and introduced himself as Frank Taylor, representing the United Press Association. We welcomed him heartily and began plying him with questions as to the latest news.

He told us he was out of touch with events lately himself for he had been up all night with the American Gas Organization, who had just been experimenting with their first gas attack on the German trenches north of Seicheprey! Then we all shouted! The whole circus became as clear as daylight to us.

The attack had not been announced generally and Major Atkinson himself was in ignorance as to its hour for demonstration. The Germans, awakened by the fumes at three o'clock this morning, had very naturally imagined that it would precede a sudden attack by our troops. Consequently they ordered out all their available artillery to shell the advanced positions of the Americans, thinking they would destroy our masses of troops in waiting.

The fact was that none of our troops were there, but were soundly sleeping in their beds until the terrible uproar of the German guns compelled them to stay awake. The whole gas attack was but an experiment by our forces, and so far as I have learned was the first time gas was used in war by our American troops.

This cleared up the whole mystery for the Toul aerodrome and we made a particularly merry breakfast over it. Personally I would have refused a great deal in exchange for the morning's experience, for I had felt the gratification of knowing I was putting to flight some hundreds of the enemy soldiers while enjoying the choicest hour of hunting I had ever experienced.

Mr. Taylor invited me to accompany him to Baccarat, a small metropolis of that region of France, lying between Lunéville and Dijon. As we passed Lunéville and proceeded eastward I again noticed the unusual tranquillity of this sector of the war zone. The British Independent Air Force had its hangars of large Handley-Page Bombing Machines along this road. These huge aeroplanes carried bombs of high explosive weighing 1650 pounds each. Nightly these squadrons flew over to the Rhine cities and laid their eggs in and about these railroad centers and factory localities. To my amazement I discovered that this British aerodrome was but twelve miles behind the lines. The German Rumplers came overhead every morning and photographed the field, but no attempts were made to destroy the Handley-Page machines by either shelling from the lines or by aeroplane raids. The Germans are a funny people!

As Mr. Taylor and I were scudding along over these smooth roads through the forests of the Vosges we noticed a family of wild boars rooting in the edge of a field. We backed up the car and I asked Mr. Taylor to be good enough to wait for me a minute while I went over and picked up one of the little pigs for a mascot for our squadron. He very kindly complied. I did not notice the expression on his face until I returned a few minutes later.

Armed with my walking stick I made a detour, so as to come upon the enemy and surprise them from their rear. My plans were to make a sudden attack and divert one of the youngsters from the formation, then close in upon him and complete the capture. My tactics were unusually successful and I bore down upon my prize and was just stooping over to pick him up when I heard a rush from the rear.

I hesitated for the fraction of a second. Old Mother Boar was about ten yards abaft my stern and was piquing upon me at some sixty miles per hour. Further delay upon my part would have been a mistake.

I performed a renversement, put on the sauce and zoomed for the roadway at sixty-one miles per hour. Amid the enthusiastic cheers of Mr. Taylor, I successfully escaped the charge of the enraged enemy by putting myself through two or three virages en route to the car. The beast rushed by me, snorting fire from both forward guns and covering me with a shower of dirt from her hoofs.

I finally made a leap for the running-board of the car, minus my walking stick and a good deal of breath.

"What's the trouble, Rick?" inquired Taylor, enthusiastically. "Did you come back to tell me something?"

"Yes," I panted. "I looked them over and decided they were too young to be torn from their mother. Let's go on."

"But you forgot your stick," retorted Taylor. "I'll wait for you while you go back and get it."

"Oh, never mind the stick," I answered. "It didn't belong to me anyway."

A few weeks later I had an opportunity to see how the French sportsmen proceed in their wild boar hunts. The Mayor of a little French village invited several of us to come over one Sunday morning and take part in the hunt.

By nine o'clock there were fully a hundred persons gathered together in the little plaza facing the village church. About twenty carried guns; the balance were duly sworn in by the Mayor to act as beaters-up. It was a very impressive ceremony and the whole village stood by to witness the scene.

After walking a mile or two through the woods we were halted. The Mayor addressed us and gave explicit orders for further proceedings.

There was one old boar in these woods, he informed us, who had now three dum-dum bullets inside his anatomy. He was a very tough and very dangerous customer. The Mayor strongly advised us to first pick out a convenient tree and take our positions in its immediate vicinity. If the boar came along we could take a shot at him, or not, just as we individually happened to view the situation. Personally he advised us to climb the tree and let some other fellow do the shooting.

The beaters-up, who were all standing at attention, thereupon saluted and disappeared within the forest. We lighted our pipes and measured the distance to the adjacent overhanging limbs. For an hour nothing happened to relieve the monotony. Some one made the brilliant suggestion that we take our cartridges out of our rifles and make dum-dum bullets out of them. This we all did, thereby regaining something of our former jaunty composure.

At last we heard hoots and yells from the forest. The party of beaters-up were advancing towards us, beating the saplings with their sticks and uttering strange cries. I took a last glance at my tree overhead and then crouched down to have a look between the tree trunks at the approaching enemy. It was a strange sight.

There, not fifty feet in front of me, I saw a motley gathering of animals of all descriptions. Red foxes, black foxes, wildcats, two or three innocent-eyed deer, a number of partridges and grouse and quite a flock of wild boars stood stock-still, gazing back at me. Not fifty feet in their rear came the village boys, hooting and yelling to let us know where not to shoot. They were bringing us our game along ahead of them like a flock of barnyard fowls!

It seemed quite impossible to fire in that direction without inflicting casualties among the beaters-up. I therefore continued staring at the animals, until they tired of posing for me and turned their procession *en masse* towards the south.

One of the Frenchmen shot a fox that Sunday morning and we all returned to the village tavern for a glass of wine, highly delighted with the successful day's sport. The Mayor especially congratulated us upon our fortunate escape from the savage wild boar.

Upon my suggesting to His Honor that his beaters-up had occupied a somewhat dangerous position at the crucial moment for firing, he shook his head sorrowfully and replied:

"Yes, it is too true! They are unfortunately wounded at times." Then clearing up his countenance, with a gleam of pride he added:

"But they are good boys. They have accustomed themselves to the danger and they do not shrink."

And thus is the great national sport of the Vosges carried on. Upon the occasional victory over the toothsome wild boar of the forest a triumphant procession follows behind the champion, who strides gallantly through the village street with his trophy hanging head down over his back. If the village is not too densely populated every inhabitant within it dines upon a delicious meat that night.

CHAPTER XVIII

STRAFING THE DRACHEN

OBSERVATION balloons, or "Drachen" as the Boches call them, constitute a most valuable method of espionage upon the movements of an enemy and at the same time are a most tempting bait to pilots of the opposing fighting squadrons.

They are huge in size, forming an elongated sausage some two hundred feet in length and perhaps fifty feet in diameter. They hang swinging in the sky at a low elevation—some 2,000 feet or under, and are pre-

vented from making any rapid movements of escape
from aeroplane attack by reason of the long cable
which attaches them to their mother-truck on the
highway below.

These trucks which attend the balloons are of the
ordinary size — a three-ton motor truck which steers
and travels quite like any big lorry one meets on the
streets.   On the truck-bed is fastened a winch which
lets out the cable to any desired length.   In case of an
attack by shell-fire the truck simply runs up the road
a short distance without drawing down the balloon.
When it is observed that the enemy gunners have again
calculated its range another move is made, perhaps
back to a point near its former position.

Large as is its bulk and as favorable and steady a
target as it must present to the enemy gunners three
miles away, it is seldom indeed that a hit from bursting shrapnel is recorded.

These balloons are placed along the lines some two
miles back of the front line trenches.   From his ele-
vated perch 2,000 feet above ground, the observer can
study the ground and pick up every detail over a radius
of ten miles on every side.   Clamped over his ears are
telephone receivers.   With his telescope to his eye he
observes and talks to the officers on the truck below
him.   They in turn inform him of any especial object
about which information is desired.   If our battery is
firing upon a certain enemy position, the observer
watches for the dropping of the shells and corrects the
faults in aim.   If a certain roadway is being dug up
by our artillery, the observer notifies the battery when
sufficient damage has been done to render that road
impassable.

Observation balloons are thus a constant menace to
contemplated movements of forces and considered as
a factor of warfare they are of immense importance.
Every fifteen or twenty miles along the front both

sides station their balloons, and when one chances to be shot down by an enemy aeroplane another immediately runs up to take its place.

Shelling by artillery fire being so ineffective it naturally occurs to every aeroplane pilot that such a huge and unwieldy target must be easy to destroy from the air. Their cost is many times greater than the value of an aeroplane. They cannot fight back with any hope of success. All that seems to be required is a sudden dash by a swift fighting aeroplane, a few shots with flaming bullets — and the big gas-bag burst into flames. What could be more simple?

I had been victorious over five or six enemy aeroplanes at this time and had never received a wound in return. This balloon business puzzled me and I was determined to solve the mystery attending their continued service, in the face of so many hostile aeroplanes flying constantly in their vicinity.

Accordingly, I lay awake many nights pondering over the stories I had heard about attacking these Drachen, planning just how I should dive in and let them have a quick burst, sheer off and climb away from their machine-gun fire, hang about for another dive and continue these tactics until a sure hit could be obtained.

I would talk this plan over with several of my pilots and after working out all the details we would try it on. Perhaps we could make 94 Squadron famous for its destruction of enemy balloons. There must be some way to do it, provided I picked out the right men for the job and gave them a thorough training.

After discussing the matter with Major Atkinson, our Commanding Officer, who readily gave me his approval, I sought out Reed Chambers, Jimmy Meissner, Thorn Taylor and Lieutenant Loomis. These four with myself would make an ideal team to investigate this proposition.

First we obtained photographs of five **German balloons** in their lairs, from the French Observation Squadron.   Then we studied the map and ascertained the precise position each occupied: the nature of the land, the relative position of the mountains and rivers, the trees and villages in the vicinity of each, and all the details of their environment.

One by one we visited these balloons, studying from above the nature of the roadway upon which their mother-trucks must operate, the height of the trees above this roadway and where the anti-aircraft defenses had been posted around each Drachen.   These latter were the only perils we had to fear.   We knew the reputation of these defenses, and they were not to be ignored.   Since they alone were responsible for the defense of the balloons, we very well knew that they were unusually numerous and accurate.   They would undoubtedly put up such a thick barrage of bullets around the suspended Drachen that an aeroplane must actually pass through a steady hailstorm of bullets both in coming in and in going out.

Willie Coppens, the Belgian Ace, had made the greatest success of this balloon strafing.   He had shot down over a score of German Drachens and had never received a wound.   I knew he armed his aeroplane with flaming rockets which penetrated the envelope of the gas-bag and burned there until it was ignited. This method had its advantages and its disadvantages. But another trick that was devised by Coppens met with my full approval.

This was to make the attack early in the morning or late in the evening, when visibility was poor and the approach of the buzzing motor could not be definitely located.   Furthermore, he made his attack from a low level, flying so close to the ground that he could not be readily picked up from above.   As he approached the vicinity of his balloon he zoomed quickly up and began his attack. If the balloon was being hauled down he met it half-way. All depended upon the quickness of his attack and the sureness of his aim.

On June 25th, 1918, my alarm-clock buzzed me awake at 2:30 o'clock sharp. As I was the instigator of this little expedition, I leaped out of bed with no reluctant regrets and leaned out of my window to get a glimpse of the sky. It promised to be a fine day!

Rousing out the other four of my party, I telephoned to the hangars and ordered out the machines. The guns had been thoroughly overhauled during the night and straight incendiary bullets had been placed in the magazines. Everything was ready for our first attack and we sat down to a hurried breakfast, full of excitement and fervor.

The whole squadron got up and accompanied us to the hangars. We were soon in our flying suits and strapped in our seats. The motors began humming and then I felt my elation suddenly begin to leak out of me. My motor was stubborn and would not keep up its steady revolutions. Upon investigation, I found one magneto absolutely refused to function, leaving me with but one upon which I could rely! I debated within myself for a few seconds as to whether I should risk dropping into Germany with a dud motor or risk the condolences of the present crowd which had gathered to see us off.

The former won in spite of my best judgment. Rather than endure the sarcasm of the onlookers and the disappointment of my team, I prayed for one more visitation of my Goddess of Luck and gave the signal to start.

At 4:30 o'clock we left the ground and headed straight into Germany. I had decided to fly eight or ten miles behind the lines and then turn and come back at the balloon line from an unexpected quarter, trusting to the systematic discipline of the German army to have its balloons just beginning to ascend as we reached them. Each pilot in my party had his own balloon marked out. Each was to follow the same tactics. We separated as soon as we left the field, each man following the direction of his own course.

Passing high over Nancy I proceeded northward and soon saw the irregular lines of the trenches below me. It was a mild morning and very little activity was discernible on either side. Not a gun was flashing in the twilight which covered the ground and as far as my eye could reach nothing was stirring. It was the precise time of day when weary fighters would prefer to catch their last wink of sleep. I hoped they would be equally deaf to the sounds of my early humming Nieuport.

Cutting off my motor at 15,000 feet over the lines, I prayed once more that when the time came to switch on again my one magneto would prove faithful. It alone stood between me and certain capture. I could not go roaring along over the sleeping heads of the whole German army and expect to preserve my secret. By gliding quietly along with silent engine as I passed deeper and deeper within their territory I could gradually lose my altitude and then turn and gain the balloon line with comparatively little noise.

"Keep your Spunk Up — Magneto, Boy!" I sang to my engine as I began the fateful glide. I had a mental vision of the precise spot behind the enemy balloon where I should turn on my switch and there discover — liberty or death! I would gladly have given my kingdom that moment for just one more little magneto!

At that moment I was passing swiftly over the little village of Goin. It was exactly five o'clock. The black outlines of the Bois de Face lay to my left, nestled along the two arms of the Moselle River. I might possibly reach those woods with a long glide if my motor failed me at the ultimate moment. I could crash in the treetops, hide in the forest until dark and possibly make my way back through the lines with a little luck. Cheery thoughts I had as I watched the menacing German territory slipping away beneath my wings!

And then I saw my balloon! The faithful fellows had not disappointed me at any rate! Conscientious and reliable men these Germans were! Up and ready for the day's work at the exact hour I had planned for them! I flattened out my glide a trifle more, so as to pass their post with the minimum noise of singing wires. A mile or two beyond them I began a wide circle with my nose well down. It was a question of seconds now and all would be over. I wondered how Chambers and Meissner and the others were getting on. Probably at this very instant they were jubilating with joy over the scene of a flaming bag of gas!

Finding the earth rapidly nearing me, I viraged sharply to the left and looked ahead. There was my target floating blandly and unsuspiciously in the first rays of the sun. The men below were undoubtedly drinking their coffee and drawing up orders for the day's work that would never be executed. I headed directly for the swinging target and set my sights dead on its center. There facing me with rare arrogance in the middle of the balloon was a huge Maltese Cross — the emblem of the Boche balloons. I shifted my rudder a bit and pointed my sights exactly at the center of the cross. Then I deliberately pressed both triggers with my right hand, while with my left I snapped on the switch.

There must be some compartment in one's brain for equalizing the conflicting emotions that crowd simultaneously upon one at such moments as this. I realized instantly that I was saved myself, for the motor picked up with a whole-souled roar the very first instant after I made the contact.   With this life-saving realization came the simultaneous impression that my whole morning's work and anguish were wasted.

I saw three or four streaks of flame flash ahead of me and enter the huge bulk of the balloon ahead. Then the flames abruptly ceased.

Flashing bullets were cutting a living circle all around me too, I noticed.   Notwithstanding the subtlety of my stalking approach, the balloon's defenders had discovered my identity and were all waiting for me.   My guns had both jammed.   This, too, I realized at the same instant.   I had had my chance, had shot my bolt, was in the very midst of a fiery furnace that beggars description and thanks to a benignant providence, was behind a lusty motor that would carry me home.

Amid all these conflicting impressions which surged upon me during that brief instant, I distinctly remember that only one poignant feeling remained in my brain.   I had failed in my mission!   With the fairest target in the world before my guns, with all the risks already run and conquered, I had failed in my mission merely because of a stupid jamming of my guns.

Automatically I had swerved to the right of the suspended gas-bag and grazed helplessly by the distended sides of the enemy Drachen.   I might almost have extended my hand and cut a hole in its sleek envelope, it occurred to me, as I swept by.   The wind had been from the east, so I knew that the balloon would stretch away from its supporting cable and leave it to the right.   More than one balloon strafer has rushed below his balloon and crashed headlong into the inconspicuous wire cable which anchors it to the ground.

I had planned out every detail with the utmost success.   The only thing I had failed in was the expected result.   Either the Boche had some material covering their Drachens that extinguished my flaming bullets, or else the gas which was contained within them was not as highly inflammable as I had been led to believe. Some three or four bullets had entered the sides of the balloon — of this I was certain. Why had they failed to set fire to it?

Later on I was to discover that flaming bullets very frequently puncture observation balloons without producing the expected blaze. The very rapidity of their flight leaves no time for the ignition of the gas. Often in the early dawn the accumulated dews and moisture in the air serve so to dampen the balloon's envelope that hundreds of incendiary bullets penetrate the envelope without doing more damage than can be repaired with a few strips of dhesive plaster.

As I doggedly flew through the fiery curtain of German bullets and set my nose for home I was conscious of a distinct feeling of admiration for the Belgian Willie Coppens. And since he had demonstrated that balloon strafing had in fact a possibility of success, I was determined to investigate this business until I too had solved its mysteries.

Then I began to laugh to myself at an occurrence that until then I had had no time to consider. As I began firing at the sausage, the German observer who had been standing in his basket under the balloon with his eyes glued to his telescope, had evidently been taken entirely by surprise. The first intimation he had of my approach was the bullets which preceded me. At the instant he dropped his telescope he dived headlong over the side of his basket with his parachute. He did not even pause to look around to see what danger threatened him.

Evidently the mother-truck began winding up the cable at the same time, for as the observer jumped for his life the balloon began to descend upon him. I caught the merest glimpse of his face as I swept past him, and there was a mingled look of terror and surprise upon his features that almost compensated me for my disappointment.

On my way homeward I flew directly towards a French observation balloon that swung on the end of its cable in my path. Without considering the consequences of my act, I sheered in and passed quite close to the Frenchman who was staring at me from his suspended basket.

Suddenly the Froggy leaped headlong from his perch and clutching his parachute rope with his two hands began a rapid descent to earth. And not until then did I realize that coming directly at him, head on from Germany as I did, he had no way of reading my cocards which were painted underneath my wings. He had decided that I was a Boche and did not care to take any chances at a jump with a blazing gas-bag about his ears.

Fortunately for me, the French gunners below could read my bright insignias from the ground and they suffered me to pass, without taking any revenge for the trick I had played upon their comrade.

Arriving at the aerodrome at five-forty-five, I found that I was the last of my little party of balloon strafers to land. The other four were standing together, looking rather sheepishly in my direction as I walked towards them.

" Well, what luck? " I enquired as I came up to them. Nobody spoke. " I thought I saw a big blaze over in your direction, Jimmy! " I went on, addressing myself to Lieutenant Meissner. " Did you get him? "

" No! " replied Jimmy disgustedly. " The balloon was not up in the air at all. I didn't get a sight of it. I didn't even see where they had hidden it."

" Did you get yours, Reed? " I asked, turning to Chambers.

" H——, no! " retorted Lieutenant Chambers emphatically. "I shot the thing full of holes, but she wouldn't drop."

The other two pilots had much the same stories. One had failed to find his balloon and the other had made an attack but it had brought no results. All had been subjected to a defensive fire that had quite reversed their opinions of the Archibald family.

"I suppose you burned yours all right, Rick?" said Reed Chambers rather enviously as we walked up to the mess together. "What do you think of us fellows anyway?"

"I think, Reed," replied I, "that we are the rottenest lot of balloonatical fakers that ever got up at two-thirty in the morning. But I am happy to discover," I added, thinking of my one puny magneto, "that none of us had to land in Germany."

CHAPTER XIX

THE CHÂTEAU-THIERRY SALIENT

THE scene of 94 Squadron's operation now changes from the Toul sector to the Château-Thierry region. On June 27th, 1918, all four of our American Fighting Squadrons were ordered to Château-Thierry. We were now four in number, for Squadron 27, commanded by Major Harold E. Hartney, and Squadron 147, commanded by Major Bonnell, had recently completed training and had moved in alongside 95 Squadron and our little Hat-in-the-Ring Squadron.

Toul is a city of some 20,000 inhabitants and would be quite the metropolis of its region, were it not for the larger city of Nancy which lies but fifteen miles east. It has certain quaint and interesting aspects, including a well preserved and ancient moat and battlements which surround the old city, a picturesque plaza in the center of the town, and several venerable old buildings dating well back into ancient history. Moreover, Toul had shops and busy streets where over-tired aviators could stroll about and make purchases and gaze upon the shifting crowds.

Our new surroundings were of rather a different character. We settled upon an old French aerodrome at Touquin, a small and miserable village some twenty-five miles south of Château-Thierry and the Marne River. The aerodrome was large and smooth and abundantly equipped with the famous French hangars which consist of steel girders with walls and roofs of canvas. They were very spacious, quite cool in summer and camouflaged admirably with the surrounding scenery.

But no provision had been made at Touquin for the pilots and officers.

All of our aeroplanes flew from Toul to Touquin, while the rest of the aerodrome impedimenta was carted rapidly away to the new quarters in lorries, trucks and trailers. The pilots of Squadrons 27 and 147 were rather new at that time; and it was thought wise to assign some of the older pilots of 94 and 95 Squadrons to the task of leading them through the air to the new field.

I was assigned to fly Major Atkinson's Nieuport and was directed to bring up the rear of the aerial procession so as to keep an eye upon those who might fall by the wayside. I found that I had more than I could handle on that occasion.

Lieutenant Buford of 95 Squadron had a reputation of scorning the use of a map in flying over France. He had been selected to lead the pilots of 27 Squadron to Touquin on that morning. I saw him leave the ground with his twenty-odd machines and disappear in the distance. When I arrived at Touquin I learned that none of Lieutenant Buford's Flight had yet put in an appearance. Late that night they all arrived safely. Upon being questioned as to their day's joy-ride, they told us that Buford's celebrated sense of direction had taken the entire Squadron directly south instead of east. After flying until their fuel had given out, they all landed upon an aerodrome which at that moment fortunately appeared below them. Here they learned they were at Lyons, in the south of France, instead of Touquin! After filling up with petrol and securing maps, they again set off and eventually arrived at their proper destination. Buford later had several very remarkable recurrences of this erratic homing instinct of his.

Many instances occurred that illustrate how easily a pilot can be lost in the air, notwithstanding a clear sky and a brilliant sun shining in its proper position. A few days before we left Toul I took Lieutenant Tittman out for his first trip over the lines. Reed Chambers accompanied us and we cautioned Tittman to keep close alongside us and in case of a battle to stay above us and simply look on without attempting to take any part.

We had scarcely arrived over Pont-à-Mousson when we discovered a Boche photographic machine proceeding towards Nancy. Reed and I made a circumspect attack, both of us keeping one eye upon our new pilot and the other constantly searching the skies for fear some roving Fokker might pounce upon Tittman while we were engaged with the Albatros.

The consequence was we lost our Albatros and found that Tittman had in the meanwhile implicitly obeyed instructions and had at no time been in any danger. Consequently, when another enemy plane appeared a few minutes later Chambers and I rushed in to a vigorous attack, without very much concern for Tittman's safety. Again the enemy escaped, owing to

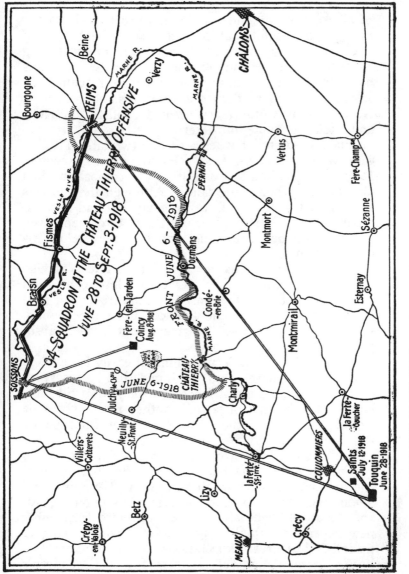

94 SQUADRON AT THE CHATEAU-THIERRY OFFENSIVE, JUNE 28 TO SEPTEMBER 3, 1918.

the misfit of our cartridges with the resultant jamming of all four of our guns. We returned to pick up our protégé and found that he had disappeared!

Upon landing with very poignant fears concerning Tittman, we were told that our balloon headquarters had telephoned in, stating that a chasse machine had just gone down in flames a short distance north of Nancy! Our worst fears seemed confirmed! Reed and I felt much like murderers.

Imagine our relief when a day or two later Tittman came walking into our mess. He told us rather shame-facedly that he had lost us during our combat and had decided to fly home and land. Although the sun was shining full in the south at noonday, Tittman flew directly east. He had flown until his petrol had given out and still had found nothing but trees below his sinking planes.

With his heart in his throat he let his Nieuport take its own place for landing. One spot looked as fatal to him as another. He crashed in the treetops, rolled through the branches and bounced upon the ground, his aeroplane in several fragments but himself absolutely unhurt.

After an hour's walk, which might easily have taken him into the Boche camp, he found that he was very near the lines and but a few kilometers from Switzerland. Had his petrol lasted another five minutes he would have landed there and have been interned by the Swiss authorities!

Undeniably there are several ways for airmen to get into trouble. Half a dozen of our group experienced motor trouble in that flight to Touquin, and among them were some of the best pilots in our squadron. But all eventually arrived, eager to learn what new experiences this change of front would bring to us and full of great expectations for the morrow.

We found delightful quarters for 94 Squadron's

officers in an old abandoned château a few miles south
of the field. It had been evacuated by its owners in
1914, when the Huns had made their first rapid advance beyond the Marne. Gorgeously furnished and
surrounded by wonderful scenery, it was by far the
finest habitation a body of pilots ever found. Our
regrets in leaving Toul were quickly banished when
we found ourselves suddenly surrounded by all this
beauty. Unfortunately enough I had but little opportunity to enjoy its comforts, for during the greater
part of our stay in this delightful spot I occupied a
cot in a nearby hospital, where a bad case of pneu-
monia was narrowly averted.

On the day of our moving from Toul I had felt a
return of the fever. Upon landing at Touquin I realized that I had a serious chill. There was nothing
for it but a report to the doctor.

From June 28th to the 2nd of July I lay by myself
in a quiet room of the hospital. And there I did a deal
of thinking. It was the first real opportunity for
thinking things over I had found since the rush of war
began. I had enlisted in the Signal Corps in New
York and the next day sailed with General Pershing
for the front. From that day to this I had been always
striving for something that had seemed mythical and
indefinite. I now determined to analyze the whole situation and try to catch up again with myself.

Aviation had always been a mystery as well as a
delight to me. The rush of an aeroplane through the
sky awoke within me every instinct of sportsmanship
and desire. With my rather intimate knowledge of
motors and engines I had always felt certain that I
should find it easy to fly. My experiences in racing
contests led me to believe that in the air, as on the
race course, I should find a great difference in individual antagonists. Some of them would be better
than I, some of them poorer: from all of them I would

be able to pick up, here and there, certain tricks and improvements which gradually might improve my own abilities. There was but one element in this game of war-aviation that troubled me.

Could I play my part in a life-and-death contest such as had been going on in the air over France for the past three or four years? Had these successful German, British and French aviators a particular gladiatorial characteristic which made it possible for them to conquer in air combats — but which might be lacking in me?

The answer to this question I did not know. I had begun my flying full of misgivings, full of a sense of my inexperience and incompetence. I had seen one cherished theory after another of mine go tumbling into space on my homeward journeys from my early combats. Through the favor of my lucky star I had survived numerous incidents — incidents that had miserably terminated other pilots' careers. And now I had actually passed through a score or more of deadly combats on aeroplanes, had been victorious in several and had escaped any injury whatsoever from the assaults of my adversaries. I wondered if I could not now begin to answer this perplexing question! Was I in that strange class of men who have plumbed the possibilities of danger in the air — who have mastered to the limits the powers of aeroplanes and aeroplane-guns, who know that they are personally superior to their antagonists for this very reason — who are therefore superior in truth because of the self-confidence that this knowledge brings them?

Cautiously and impartially I set my mind upon this problem. I felt that now was the time to make sure of myself for myself. If I could disabuse my mind of the impression that some mysterious power accounted for the successes of the famous air-fighters of the enemy service, I would be able to meet them with far greater confidence in my own merely human powers.

I reviewed the various combats in which I had taken a part. Here and there I detected mistakes that I had made — mistakes of which I should never again be guilty. Over and over again I had failed to get a victory because of a stupid jamming of my guns. Was there no way of removing this sorry impediment? I would examine every single detail of my guns myself in the future. Every cartridge that the armorers gave me would receive a strict examination and testing before I left the field. That would certainly minimize the possibilities of gun failures at critical moments.

Next, the principal fear that hampered me in the midst of a combat was the knowledge that the Nieuport's wings might give way under the stress of a necessary maneuver. Constantly I was limited in essential movements by this fear. Was there no way to strengthen these wings? Why couldn't we get the Spads that had been promised us? If I could only get a machine built according to my own designs!

I imagined how I would throw terror into the enemy formations if I could only hurl my machine about them with the headlong impetuosity that I craved to let go! I lay staring at the ceiling for some time, picturing myself in pursuit of the whole German air force who were fleeing in terror before my ideal aeroplane. Then with a shrug I pulled myself together and forced myself once more to face the realities.

My gun-jammings I could and would remedy. There was no reason why I should not have less jams than any other pilot in the service, provided I put adequate attention to the matter. The limitations of my Nieuport I must bear in mind, and endure them until the authorities found means to procure Spads for us.

Above all, I must constantly remember to remain within those limitations even if the enemy escaped me. Otherwise I should never live to continue to fight within the pilot's seat of the coveted Spad!

I thought of the insolence of the high-flying Rumplers, with a return of my craving for an aeroplane of my own design. My old friend — Number 16, of the Rising Sun Squadron! How I should love to give him a little surprise on our next meeting! I would design a fighting plane that would fly faster, that would out-climb, out-dive and out-maneuver any machine or machines that the Boches owned. And it would have a higher ceiling than the Rumpler. It was all possible. If I could only get it done!

The result of my long cogitations and self-study was a determination to begin afresh my career in the air. I convinced myself that I had fairly well solved the puzzles that had deterred me from several successes in my more immature past. Merely human qualities dominated aviators, after all. I had seen enough of the Boche tactics by now to understand that there surely was no mystery about them. Caution was one very essential element that I must never forget. With that determination I dropped to sleep, and awoke with a feeling that a great load had been lifted from my mind.

On July 4th, a day which the Americans intended to celebrate in Paris with much magnificence, I obtained permission to visit the Capital. Captain Kenneth Marr and several of our pilots went in with me to see the celebration. They returned early the following day, leaving me to take my own time in rejoining my squadron.

Hardly had they gone when the impulse came to me to go down to Orly, where the American Experimental Aerodrome was located, and see for myself just what the situation was in regard to our Spad aeroplanes. I called upon the Major in charge of the Supply Depot, and there learned to my delight that he had actually begun arrangements for the immediate equipment of the Hat-in-the-Ring Squadron with the long deferred Spads. At that moment, he told me, there were three Spads on the field that were designated for our use.

With rather a short farewell to the Major, I hastened to the field. And there I found three of the coveted fighting machines that I knew had many accomplishments superior to the rival Fokkers. The nearest machine to me had the initial figure "I," painted on its sides. I asked the mechanics in charge if this machine had been tested.

"Yes, sir! All ready to go to the front!" was the reply.

"Is this one of the machines belonging to 94 Squadron?" I enquired.

"Yes, sir. There are two more over there. The others will be in here in a few days."

"Well, I am down here from 94 Squadron myself," I continued, a sudden wild hope entering my brain. "Is there any reason why this machine should not go to the Squadron to-day?"

"None that I know of, sir!" the mechanic answered, thereby forming a resolution in my mind that I very well knew might lead me to a court martial, provided my superior officers chose to take a military view of my offense.

Inside ten minutes I was strapped in the seat of the finest little Spad that ever flew French skies. I have it to this day and would not part with it for all the possessions in the world. Without seeking further permission or considering stopping to collect my articles at my hotel, I gave the signal to pull away the blocks, sped swiftly across the smooth field, and with a feeling of tremendous satisfaction I headed directly away for the Touquin aerodrome.

Not until I had landed and had begun to answer the questions of my comrades as to how I got possession of the new machine, did I begin to realize the enormity of the offense I had committed. I did not contemplate with any pleasure the questions that the Commanding Officer would hurl at me, on this subject.

But to my joy no censure was given me. On the contrary I was given this first Spad to use as my own! Within an hour my mechanics were fitting on the guns and truing up the wings. In the meantime I decided to go out for the last time on my oldtime mount, the Nieuport.

During my absence the Group had suffered two losses and had won three victories. Lieutenant Wannamaker of 27th Squadron was from my home city of Columbus, Ohio, and he, I learned, had gone out on patrol on the 3rd of July and had been shot down above Château-Thierry. For weeks we feared he had been killed, but finally we received word from the Red Cross in Switzerland that Wannamaker had merely been forced down within enemy territory and had been captured unhurt.

It was at this period of the American offensive, it will be remembered, that the final German retreat began at Château-Thierry. Our aerodrome at Touquin was located so far behind the lines that we were limited to very short patrols over enemy territory. As the Hun continued to withdraw farther and farther back it was evident that we must abandon our magnificent château at Touquin and move nearer the front. Every day the German Rumplers came over our field and blandly photographed us while our Archy batteries poured up a frantic lot of useless shells. I doubt if the enemy remained in ignorance of our change of location a single day. For as soon as we began settling at the Saints aerodrome a few miles nearer the lines, we again noticed the visits of the high-flying Rumplers.

In fact one of our Squadron pilots, who was captured at this period, later told me, after his release, that the German Intelligence Officer exhibited to him a full list of the names of all of our pilots. The officer kindly inquired after the health of Major Hartney, who had seen distinguished service with the British before joining the American Air Service, and then he asked if Rickenbacker had been formulating any new balloon plans! Since the only plan that I had ever formulated was the ridiculous failure of our balloon attack of the week previous, I naturally felt somewhat aggrieved at this officer's low humor. But it astonished me to learn of the precise information possessed by the enemy in regard to our movements and personnel.

My feelings were somewhat restored by hearing of the opinion this same officer expressed as to the efficiency of the American air fighters. Before one can appreciate the significance of his remark it is necessary to understand the character of the famous German fighting squadrons who now confronted us.

CHAPTER XX

THE DEATH OF QUENTIN ROOSEVELT

THE German advance, beginning late in June, had resulted in forcing a deep salient in the lines between Soissons and Rheims. These two cities lie on an east-and-west line, both are situated on the Vesle River, and but twenty-odd miles separate them. Rheims, to the east, had withstood the assaults of the Hun, but Soissons and the important highways and railroads centering there were now held by the Germans.

Straight south from Soissons the trenches now ran — south for twenty miles, until the banks of the Marne River were reached; then they curved northwards and east, the belligerents facing each other from opposite sides of the river almost to Epernay — a city almost directly south of Rheims.

Thus the salient which now most threatened Paris and the region south of the Marne was approximately twenty miles deep and twenty miles wide. It included Château-Thierry which lay on the north bank of the Marne. Our aerodrome at Touquin lay south another twenty miles from Château-Thierry. In that position we were then south even of the city of Paris itself.

With full knowledge of the increasing strength of the American army in France, and having decided to stake all upon one last effort before the arrival of our troops in their entirety, the Hun commanders had then even stripped the able-bodied men from their munition factories throughout Germany, in order to secure a victory at the front before it became too late. The loss of these factory workers spelled an ultimate failure in the supply of munitions of war necessary to a long campaign. If this last desperate thrust failed, the Boches must admit themselves defeated.

The subsequent breakdown of the German Army was the natural climax to this desperate strategy. This last drive for Paris and Amiens must be the last. Every ounce of energy was therefore expended. Every division and every squadron of aviators that could be spared from other sections of the front were hurriedly concentrated upon these two districts — that of Château-Thierry and the St. Quentin-to-Amiens district.

When the orders came to 94 Squadron to shift from Toul to this new Château-Thierry sector the German fighting squadrons had already left the vicinity of Verdun-St. Mihiel-Pont-à-Mousson. Only the regular photographing and observing machines were still abroad there for our entertainment. Arrived at our new quarters, we found a very different situation. Our entertainment here promised to be fast and furious enough to suit the most ambitious airman.

It was quickly discovered by our own Intelligence Officers that the best of the German fighting squadrons were now patrolling our skies. Captured prisoners, the markings on the planes we shot down, the photographs and observations of our airmen and other sources which are employed to gain this information — all told the same story. On the aerodrome at Coincy, a large field just north of Château-Thierry, was located the distinguished Richthofen Squadron, then commanded by Captain Reinhardt. Its machines were distinguishable by their scarlet noses and by the extraordinary skilfulness of their pilots. It was now included in Jagstaffel No. 1, which comprised four Flights of seven machines each.

Jagstaffel No. 2 was a scarcely inferior aggregation of German aces under command of Captain Loerser, himself a victor over forty-two aerial antagonists. The aeroplanes of his squadron were also Fokkers. Instead of the scarlet markings on nose and wings, No. 2 Jagstaffel had the belly of each fusilage painted a bright yellow. These machines occupied the same field with the Richthofen Circus.

The third famous fighting squadron of the Germans, Jagstaffel No. 3, was at that time under command of Captain Bettenge, an air fighter celebrated in Hunland not only for his twenty-five victories but for his great success as a trainer of adroit air-fighters. This squadron occupied an aerodrome back of St. Quentin. While usually engaged with British antagonists further north, this squadron frequently made its appearance opposite us during the hottest days of fighting in our sector.

Thus it became evident to us that we American aviators were at last to meet the very choicest personnel of the enemy air forces. Not only would these experienced pilots be mounted upon superior machines, but they had been trained to fly in such close formation that they need fear no attack until they themselves were ready to accept combat. And they had consolidated here in such numbers that every time we crossed the lines we found the sky full of them. 94 Squadron at that time had 17 pilots and 24 aeroplanes available. Squadrons No. 95, No. 27 and No. 145 had approximately the same number each. No other American fighting squadrons were then assisting us in the defense of this sector.

Without desiring to make any reflection upon the French airmen who were stationed near us in this sector, it is necessary to show that the state of French morale was at that time notoriously bad. Indeed it would have been strange after four years of severe warfare to have found that personnel in France had not suffered enormously, as in the other fighting countries. After the loss of the eager volunteer for aviation, it became necessary to press into that service men who much preferred the infantry, cavalry or artillery. As was to be expected, the resultant air force of France did not measure up to its former prestige.

Consequently the few American squadrons who were suddenly plunged into the thick of this ferocious conflict at Château-Thierry found that they were overwhelmingly outnumbered, poorly supported and lamentably equipped, both in machines and experience.

When therefore I later learned that the Intelligence Office of the enemy Air Force had complimented the American pilots by saying that " they fought more like Indians than soldiers," and that " they upset all our training by dashing in single-handed against our formations "— I felt a great glow of pride and confidence in the bravery our boys exhibited throughout that trying campaign.

The losses in our group during the four weeks we occupied this sector at Château-Thierry amounted to 36 pilots, who were either captured or killed. Among the latter class was Quentin Roosevelt, who fell in flames on July 14th, 1918. Our victories during this same period were 38, two more than the number we had lost!

Quentin Roosevelt's death was a sad blow to the whole group. As President Roosevelt's son he had rather a difficult task to fit himself in with the democratic style of living which is necessary in the intimate life of an aviation camp. Every one who met him for the first time expected him to have the airs and superciliousness of a spoiled boy. This notion was quickly lost after the first glimpse one had of Quentin. Gay, hearty and absolutely square in everything he said or did, Quentin Roosevelt was one of the most popular fellows in the group. We loved him purely for his own natural self.

He was reckless to such a degree that his commanding officers had to caution him repeatedly about the senselessness of his lack of caution. His bravery was so notorious that we all knew he would either achieve some great spectacular success or be killed in the attempt. Even the pilots in his own Flight would beg him to conserve himself and wait for a fair opportunity for a victory. But Quentin would merely laugh away all serious advice. His very next flight over enemy lines would involve him in a fresh predicament from which pure luck on more than a few occasions extricated him.

A few days before his death Quentin Roosevelt went over the lines with his formation, and they came home without him. Later he arrived and laughingly announced that he had shot down his first Hun machine. Upon being questioned about the combat, he admitted that he had been lost after striking off by himself to investigate a large formation of enemy machines, which he had discovered in the distance. Resolving to be prudent in the matter, he reversed his direction after discovering they numbered over twenty to his one. He flew about alone for a while, then discovering, as he supposed, his own formation ahead of him he overtook them, dropped in behind and waited patiently for something to turn up.

It came about fifteen minutes later.

His formation continued almost straight ahead during all this time, he following quietly along in the last position. Quentin had no idea where they were headed and didn't care. He had violated his duty once by leaving them and now he intended blindly to follow the leader. Meditating thus, he failed to notice that the leader had dipped a signal and had begun to virage to the left. Quentin awoke just in time to see the aeroplane ahead of him suddenly stick his nose up and begin a virage. Then to his horror he discovered that he had been following an enemy patrol all the time! Every machine ahead of him wore a huge black maltese cross on its wings and tail! They were as unconscious of his identity as he had been of theirs.

Quentin fired one long burst as he in turn completed the virage and rejoined the formation. The aeroplane immediately preceding him dropped at once and within a second or two burst into flames. Quentin put down his nose and streaked it for home before the astonished Huns had time to notice what had happened. He was not even pursued!

It was this style of Indian warfare that had moved the German Intelligence Office to state that their training was indeed hopeless against the Americans' recklessness. German formation flying was admirable until an American joined it and maneuvered in concert with it for fifteen minutes before shooting it up! One can imagine the disgust of the methodical Boches as they digested this latest trick of the Yank!

Lieutenant Quentin Roosevelt met his death during an unusually severe dog-fight in the air. He left the aerodrome with his formation of five planes and proceeded across the lines east of Château-Thierry. The sky was thick with enemy formations as usual. Both our own and the enemy's aeroplanes were largely engaged at that time in strafing trenches and the main highways upon which columns of troops were continually advancing to occupy the lines. One did not have to seek far to find a fight.

Within ten minutes after crossing the trenches the little formation from 95 Squadron took on a Fokker formation of seven machines. They were both at a low altitude and evidently both were intent upon discovering a favorable ground target covered with marching men. The five Americans accepted the Hun challenge for a combat and dropped all other business for the time being.

During the rapid circling about, in which both groups were endeavoring to break up the formation of the antagonist, Quentin discovered the approach of another flight of red-nosed Fokkers, coming from above and behind. He withdrew by himself and flew ahead to meet the newcomers, climbing as he flew. The others were utterly unconscious of his departure, since Quentin flew in the last rear position on one of the wings.

It was a cloudy day and the aeroplanes were up near to and occasionally lost in the obscurity of the clouds. Suddenly Lieutenant Buford, the leader of Quentin's formation, saw a Nieuport falling through the clouds from above him. It was out of control as it swept by him. Without realizing whose machine it was,

Buford knew that an enemy force was above him. He already had more than his hands full in the present company. Signalling his pilots to follow him, he broke off the contest and re-crossed the lines. Then he discovered the absence of Quentin Roosevelt!

That same night a wireless message came from the Germans saying that Quentin had been shot down by Sergeant Thom of the Richthofen Circus. Thom at that time had a record of twenty-four planes to his credit. The additional information was received that Quentin had been buried with military honors. No honors, however, could have compensated our group for the loss of that boy. The news was flashed throughout the world that Quentin Roosevelt was dead! Occasional press reports came to us that some imaginative reporter had stated that perhaps he was not in reality killed, but was merely a prisoner; thereby selling several more papers while unnecessarily distressing a bereaved family with utterly false hopes.

A story came to my attention later which deserves a drastic reply. New York newspapers gave wide publicity to a statement made by a certain non-combatant named Hungerford who claimed to have been employed on the Château-Thierry sector of the front at this time. He not only attempted to describe the fight in which Quentin Roosevelt lost his life, but even intimated that had Quentin's comrades not fled, thereby leaving Quentin alone against desperate odds, the whole German formation might have been destroyed. He stated that he saw the fight and that Quentin before his sad death actually shot down two of the enemy planes.

This whole story is absolute piffle. Nobody saw Quentin's last fight except the Huns who shot him down. The fight itself occurred ten miles back of the German lines over Fère-en-Tarden. Quentin did not shoot down two enemy planes nor did his comrades

desert him in time of trouble. It will be very un-
healthful for Mr. Hungerford to meet the members
of 95 Squadron upon their return to New York. A
more gallant lot of boys never came to France, as this
non-combatant gentleman will discover when he meets
them.

During all this time I had been practically out of the
fighting at the front. I had made but two flights over
the lines at Château-Thierry, one on my old Nieuport
and the second on my Spad. On neither expedition
did I meet an enemy aeroplane, nor was I anxious to
do so until I had quite mastered the tricks and wiles
of my new Spad.

On July 10th I became suddenly aware of a sharp
pain in my right ear. It grew worse and I decided to
have the Squadron doctor look me over. He sent
me to Paris by the next train to have the ear-drum
lanced. An abscess had formed which might prove
dangerous.

Thus I was again forced to fret and turn upon a
hospital bed for several days while my Squadron was
going through with the most severe trials in its short
experience. Doug Campbell was away, leaving Jimmy
Meissner, Reed Chambers, Alan Winslow and Thorn
Taylor the principal stars of our organization. I
used to lie in my bed and wonder how many of these
old comrades would greet me when I returned to my
aerodrome!

On July 15th, while lying half asleep on my bed in
the hospital, I was suddenly startled by a tremendous
explosion outside my windows. The nurses soon came
by with frightened expressions on their faces. I asked
one what it was.

"It was one of the long-distance shells the Boches
are again firing into Paris!" she said. "They began that when they were about to start their great offensive of March 21st. For some time they have

not been shooting into Paris. Now that it begins again it is certain that they are commencing another drive!"

The young Frenchwoman was right. The very next day we heard that the long anticipated drive from Château-Thierry had begun. The heavy artillery barrage had started at midnight and the offensive upon which the Germans were founding all their hopes was now on.

It was in fact the beginning of the end of the war! Nobody then realized it, of course; but General Foch, who possessed exact information of just when and where the Huns would strike, had prepared for it by crowding in immense quantities of artillery from Château-Thierry to Rheims, from Rheims on eastward to the Argonne Forest. Just two hours in advance of the first German shell he began such a terrific barrage over the lines that the enemy forces were completely disorganized. They were never again to threaten Paris or the allied armies!

And then the Second Division of the American Army began their great drive at the top of the Château-Thierry salient at Soissons — while the French began to pinch in the line at Rheims. All that great area of twenty miles by twenty was crammed with German troops, German artillery, German supplies. It must be moved at express speed to the rear or all would be captured.

Our Squadrons at this great period did tremendous work in strafing the main highways leading to the Germans' rear. One of the pilots of 27 Squadron, "Red" Miller, of Baltimore, who was shot down and captured while on one of these highway-strafing expeditions, later described to me the extraordinary scenes he passed through while being taken to the rear under guard. It was Red Miller, in fact, who had been confronted with the complete list of names of all our squadrons by the German Intelligence Office. They questioned him immediately about his name, his squadron and many other details which they were foolish enough to think they could tempt out of him. Miller of course had an enjoyable half-hour stuffing them with the most marvelous stories that a Baltimore education could invent.

In his march to the prison camps that night, Miller was conducted up the main highway from Château-Thierry to the north. Two Boche cavalrymen rode on horseback and he trotted along on foot between them. American shells were falling thick upon this road and at every burst Miller and his conductors expected to be hurled among the dead and dying who filled the ditches.

The road was literally jammed with horses, lorries, guns and men. All were hurrying northwards. Along the sides of the roads hundreds of Boche soldiers were detailed to drag from the roadway those men, trucks, horses and guns which had been struck by American shrapnel and which lay there obstructing the traffic. Ropes were hastily attached to these obstructions and they were pulled out of the way and dumped by the roadside.

Another gang of soldiers worked side by side with these men, filling as quickly as possible the holes in the highway made by these exploding shells. Everything was hurry, noise, dust and confusion.

In a nearby hospital lay Lieutenant Norton, a dear friend and neighbor of mine from Columbus, Ohio. Norton had been wounded and had fallen within the German lines. He was taken to the nearest hospital at Fère-en-Tarden where he received good treatment until the day of the American drive. He was abandoned with all the other wounded by the fleeing Germans. When the Americans reached this hospital, three days later, Norton had died from neglect!

An amusing as well as heroic exploit of Miller's during this fearful march of his to the rear is well worth recording here.

Red was so mortified by his capture, so exhausted by his continuous trot between his two captors and so scared by the constant shelling of the road over which they were passing that he resolved to break away from his two captors and risk their bullets rather than continue indefinitely in his present plight.

It was getting dark as they passed a small piece of woods to the right. Red suddenly stopped and bent over to lace up his boots. The two horsemen shot a glance at him, then seeing he was innocently engaged, drew up their horses and waited for him. As soon as the right-hand horse had passed him Red straightened up and jumped for the nearest trees. He dashed through the brush in the darkness, scratching his face and tearing his clothes, but did not hear that a single shot had been fired at him.

He stopped and was peering about for a suitable tree in which to spend the night, hoping that by morning the country would be cleared of Huns, when an electric torch was flashed into his face! He threw up his hands and surrendered, finding that he had stumbled full into a camp of Hun artillery!

When his captors again recovered him Red fully expected to be shot for attempting to escape. Imagine his surprise when they begged him not to tell anybody about his escapade! They feared they would receive a worse punishment than he because of their carelessness in permitting him to escape!

CHAPTER XXI

THE FLYING CIRCUS SCORES HEAVILY

IT was not until July 31st that I was able to mount my Spad and again take my place in fighting formations. Even then I started out with much apprehension, for the doctors had told me that it was highly improbable that I should ever be able to fly again, owing to the condition of my ear.

To my delight I found that no ill resulted from this trial flight and I put my machine through all sorts of acrobatics, and landed with the satisfaction of knowing that I had fooled the doctors and was as good as new, in spite of my punctured ear.

That was a day of terrible losses to our group. Every squadron lost heavily, but the severest loss to the group was borne by Squadron 27.

Lieutenant John McArthur of Buffalo, New York, had up to that date destroyed five enemy machines in combat and promised to be one of the greatest fighting airmen in the American Army. Every one who knew him admired him immensely, and the pilots who had flown over the lines with him looked upon Jack McArthur almost with reverence. He was cautious, quick, a clever pilot and a dead shot. His judgment was good and he had every attribute that spells success. His example had made a wonderful organization out of the new pilots of No. 27.

Early in the morning of July 31st, McArthur led out his crack formation of six planes to try a strafing expedition upon the aerodrome and hangars of the Richthofen Circus, which had just moved back from Coincy and now occupied the aerodrome north of Fismes.

From this expedition only one of the formation ever returned.

Not until weeks later did we hear any news of this missing five. Then came a letter from one of them telling us what had occurred. They had reached their objective without mishap, and had strafed the hangars and billets of the Richthofen crowd until their ammunition was gone.

Whether or not any of the enemy machines came up to fight them, we did not learn. But the Richthofen aerodrome was twenty miles inside the lines and our aerodrome was thirty miles this side of the lines. When the strafers turned their noses homewards they found a forty mile wind against them. They had already been out over an hour and could hardly hope to reach the home field against this gale, before their fuel would be exhausted. They might easily reach some nearer aerodrome on our side of the lines, however, and towards this object they set their minds.

Half-way to the lines they encountered several formations of enemy planes who were fully aware of their predicament and were waiting for them to come out. Up and down, back and forth, McArthur led his little formation, seeking for a place to break through the enemy's ranks. Finding the Boche pilots too adroit for him, he finally resolved to break through, regardless of the tremendous odds against him.

McArthur led the attack, and like Horatius of old, he embraced all the spears in his own breast, to enable his comrades to pass through them. He fell, killed in air, and one of his pilots fell beside him. But even this heroic sacrifice was in vain.

The remaining three pilots of his formation passed the encircling enemy machines only to find that this protracted maneuvering had quite exhausted their fuel. One by one their motors spluttered and died. The entire formation dropped to earth, some landing safely, others crashing in shell holes, all of them finding themselves behind the German lines.

Squadron 94's greatest loss on that fatal day was Alan Winslow, the Chicago boy who had the honor of bringing down the first enemy machine conquered by the pilots of the Hat-in-the-Ring Squadron. Winslow was a gallant lad and one of the most popular men in the squadron.

Late that evening he was seen by another member of his flight diving down upon a Fokker with which he had taken on a combat. The two machines continued downwards until the dusky ground swallowed both of them from view. The rest of Winslow's flight returned home and long did we sit up waiting for news of old Alan that night.

The pilots stood about under the stars pooping up Very lights into the clear sky, hoping that he might see the signal from afar and come roaring in. To every war pilot there is an extraordinary pathos about the flashes of these distant signal lights at night. I never see these bright balls of fire cut through the night sky without feeling a clutch at my heart — without remembering the anguish with which I have watched and waited and hoped for the return of some dear comrade in answer to their signal.

They rush from the mouth of the pistol with a noise like that of a child's popgun. The silvery ball climbs upward two or three hundred feet with a soft roar; there it gracefully curves in its trajectory and begins slowly to fall, shedding a powerful light upon the surrounding landscape and casting its beckoning signal for a score of miles around. On any fine night as one flies homeward from the lines these Very lights strike the eye from every aerodrome, both friendly and hostile. To a member of the mess they denote a warm welcome from his comrades. To a stranger comes the significant intimation that yonder some member of an expectant family is — still missing!

A month later one of the members of our Squadron met in London Alan Winslow's brother, Paul Winslow, a member of the most famous of Great Britain's fighting Squadrons, No. 56.   Asked if any news had been received of Alan, Paul Winslow replied simply, " He went West! "

Upon returning to the Squadron, however, a letter was found awaiting him from Alan Winslow himself! He wrote from a German hospital, stating that he had been wounded in the combat, had received a bullet in the left arm which had shattered it.   The arm was amputated above the elbow and he was quite contented to find himself so well out of the occurrence!

The sorrows, the surprises — the joys of war-flying are legion!

The next day after the fall of Alan Winslow, a formation was sent out from our Squadron under the leadership of Lieutenant Loomis to protect a photographing expedition of three French Breguet machines. Although far from being in condition, I resolved to tag along behind them in my Spad and see what happened.   I got to an altitude of 15,000 feet, which was about 5,000 feet higher than the others, and from this front row in the gallery I had a wonderful view of an amazingly interesting little scrap.

The Breguets had not proceeded very far into Germany before a Fokker formation appeared upon the scene.   Of course the Fokkers saw the Nieuports, but they also saw the Breguets; and the German pilots knew that those Breguets with their photographs were the important targets for their flaming bullets.   I sat above them and followed them in the various maneuvers to get in between Lewis and his convoy.

Back and forth they circled, all the members of both formations keeping always in their proper posi-

tions. Although the Fokkers were seven to the Nieuports' five, the former did not appear very desirous of
forcing a way through them to get at close quarters
with the Frenchmen. Thus maneuvering, the whole
circus passed further and further along into Germany, until they gradually neared the landscape which
the French machines wished to photograph. This objective was the city of Fismes, the railroads and highways leading into it and the positions of any batteries
of artillery that might be concealed from the naked
eye, but which could scarcely escape revealment by the
powerful lenses of the cameras.

Plenty of other aeroplane formations were in the
vicinity. I discerned hostile planes and friendly
planes, American, British and French. It was evident that the Fokkers below desired to attract to their
aid one or more of their adjacent squadrons before attempting to force a battle with 94's Nieuports. Lieutenant Loomis, on his part, had no desire to press matters. His instructions were to defend the Breguets,
not to take on any combats that happened to offer
themselves. If the Fokkers refused to come in and
attack them, Lieutenant Loomis's Formation would
have no fighting to do.

I watched the distant enemy formations with considerable interest, ready to fly in and give warning
should any of them make a move to attack Loomis.
But they apparently had their hands full watching out
for their own safety, for the further we moved into
German territory the thicker did we find the sky filled
with cruising aeroplanes. Only a little rumpus was
needed to start one of the choicest dog-fights that ever
was seen.

With much amusement I noticed that our Frenchmen were now over Fismes and had begun taking their
photographs. Evidently the Fokker leader discovered
their industry at the same moment I did, for with a

curt dip to his wings he started his flight on a head-long dive in the direction of the Breguets.

But Loomis was then ready and anxious for the fight. Enough photographs had been taken to relieve him of the responsibility of spoiling the fun of the Frenchmen. Quickly he reversed his direction, all his flight falling neatly into position, and leaving the Froggies in the lurch, he swept forward to engage with the Fokkers. The latter seemed rather startled for a moment, wavered a bit in their course, and in the next instant the fight was on.

The Americans had the advantage from the first, for Loomis had kept his Nieuports at a good altitude above the Breguets and the Fokkers had tried to attack them from below. Loomis dived steadily at the tail of the nearest Fokker. This latter had no course open but to try and outdive him. Another Fokker got on Loomis's tail and another Nieuport followed on his tail. Soon the whole menagerie was streaming along in this fashion, every machine pouring streams of tracer bullets into the machine ahead of him. It was a splendid spectacle to witness, but I knew it would be of short duration.

One Fokker had already dropped towards earth and two of our bright colored Nieuports were streaking it for home in the wake of the disappearing Breguets. Either these two pilots had wounds or engine trouble or else considered the wisest policy was to get out of this hurricane of flaming bullets. I looked for Loomis. There he was, way down below, with three Fokkers on his tail. He was vainly attempting to reform his scattered formation and but two of his machines remained. Even as I watched them I saw several other enemy machines drawing nearer them from the north. It was high time to get down to their aid.

As I dropped down to their vicinity I saw Loomis fire three or four short bursts at his antagonists and then, swerving away to the south, he put on the sauce and rapidly drew away from their pursuit. His pilots had fortunately observed his departure and hastened to overtake him. The Fokkers kept up a short pursuit, then seeing me above them feared they were getting into another ambush, and the next moment were diving with all speed to the protection of their own landing field. I was frankly glad to let them go, for after three weeks' absence I felt little inclined to take on anything against odds.

Turning back to join my fellows, I was startled to discover that Loomis was very plainly sinking to earth. His propeller was slowly turning and I knew instinctively that he had been struck in some vital part of the engine. I overtook him and quickly measured the distance that separated him from the distant trenches. He was only seven or eight thousand feet above the ground and the lines were some six miles distant. Evidently he was fully aware of the tightness of his predicament, for he was nursing along his powerless aeroplane and sailing on as flat a level as the Nieuport could possibly maintain.

Generally speaking an aeroplane can sail along for a mile without losing more than a thousand feet altitude. Thus Loomis could make eight miles without engine power provided he were eight thousand feet above ground. Provided also that no contrary wind was blowing him backwards during this time — and also providing that no rifle and machine-gun bullets were able to terminate his progress as he drew nearer and nearer to the ground.

I flew above him, absolutely powerless to do more than wish him luck. Archy took up the chase with malevolent delight and sprayed both of us impartially with shrapnel.

I lost all interest in the angry bursts about me, in the complete fascination of Loomis's struggle for the lines. He was holding on to every inch of his altitude, with the skill of a Cape Cod skipper. At times I felt certain that he was holding her up too much. He must lose speed and headway with too great a curb on the bridle.

The ground drew closer and closer to his hanging wheels. I saw the rear trenches of the Germans pass below him. I believed he was doomed to strike the next trench, three hundred yards ahead. I wondered if I could possibly render any assistance by flying down and spraying bullets behind him until he had a chance to run to safety. No! Such a plan was foolish! There would be a hundred machine-guns turned upon him the instant he crashed, a thousand rifles would be shooting at him from concealed positions. I could not possibly do him any good.

The second line of German trenches appeared below the sinking Nieuport and I held my breath as the dainty little bird neatly skimmed over them. With rare good fortune the way ahead seemed comparatively smooth. Loomis might coast along the intervening space and roll smack into the front line trench of the Huns. There was no doubt about it. He couldn't possibly make another rod!

Just at that moment his Nieuport hit the ground, bounded up, struck again some thirty feet ahead and with another bound actually hopped over the narrow front line trench and rolled along some thirty or forty yards across No Man's Land! I yelled a little to myself in my excitement, as I saw Loomis throw himself from the still moving machine. In a trice he was streaking it for the American trenches, with Boche bullets accelerating his speed by lifting his heels just ahead of little clouds of dust.

Loomis is very fast on his feet — even in flying costume. He covered that hundred yards in something under ten seconds. He left my aeroplane far in the rear and I had to hurry up to see his finish at the bottom of the front-line American trench.

The doughboys covered his last dash with a splendid fusillade of bullets directed into the German trenches. Both sides were standing up and exposing themselves to enemy fire in the excitement of Loomis's homerun.

I saw him tumble safely into the deepest part of the trench and lie there, probably panting for breath, for apparently he hadn't received a scratch. As I considered this was the end of the morning's entertainment, I put on the gas and pushed on for home.

I walked into the Adjutant's office and made out a report of what I had seen. An hour later we were delighted to receive a telephone call from Loomis himself, which instantly relieved our anxiety about his condition. He was entirely well in body, he reported, but had not yet fully recovered his breath!

Then came another telephone call from the French headquarters, thanking 94 for bringing down one Fokker aeroplane, whose destruction they would be happy to confirm, and repeating their thanks for the protection Loomis's formation had given their photographers. Very valuable photographs had been obtained, it appeared, both of enemy positions and of the movements of their troops. Within an hour after snapping the photographs the completed pictures were in their commanding officer's hands!

CHAPTER XXII

OUR SPADS ARRIVE

BY August 8th, 1918, our whole Squadron was fitted out with the machines which we had so long coveted. The delight of the pilots can be imagined. In the meantime we had lost a number of pilots on the flimsy Nieuports, not by reason of their breaking up in air but because the pilots who handled them feared to put them into essential maneuvers which they were unable to stand. Consequently our pilots on Nieuports could not always obtain a favorable position over an enemy nor safely escape from a dangerous situation. The Spads were staunch and strong and could easily outdive the Nieuports. And our antagonists opposite the Château-Thierry sector were, as I have indicated, the very best of the German airmen. How greatly our new Spads increased our efficiency will be seen from the results which followed.

By the eighth of August our victorious doughboys had pushed back the Hun from the deep Château-Thierry salient of twenty miles square, and the lines now ran along the Vesle River, directly from Soissons to Rheims. This long advance left our aerodrome at Touquin far in the rear. So far in fact, that it was necessary for our aeroplanes to come down near the lines and refill with gasoline before continuing our two hours' patrol over enemy territory.

The old Richthofen aerodrome at Coincy was now in our hands. We established our filling station on this aerodrome. It lay then but eight miles south of the German front trenches.

At three o'clock on the afternoon of the 8th, I received orders to take every available plane from our Squadron and hurry out to the front to protect two French machines which were detailed to take photographs of an important position across the lines. Accordingly I collected all the pilots and we made an immediate departure from the field. Eleven machines were in the Flight. The others were not available, by reason of repairs then under way.

My ear was again troubling me and I was in despair over my physical condition. The pain was continuous. I was determined to stick it out without report-

ing it to the doctor, for I had the impression that
a second appearance at a Paris hospital would end
my active service at the front.   The cook smuggled
hot salt bags to me at night and I slept with these over
my ear.   But during the day, and especially while in
the air I felt constant pain from this source.

The two Frenchmen met our formation at Coincy
where we all alighted and refilled our tanks.   After
ten minutes' delay we again took off, three of my
Spads failing to get away owing to minor troubles with
their motors.   This left me with eight machines besides the two Frenchmen who were to photograph —
and not to fight.

At 3,000 feet over the field I collected the formation and fired a red Very light from my pistol as a
signal to forge ahead.   I had arranged the formation
with the two Frenchmen in the center, with one of my
Flights on their right, one on their left and one immediately behind them.   I myself flew a thousand
yards above them.   I anticipated strong opposition
upon reaching the lines, but felt that we were posted in
a solid position.   Only the front center was left un-
protected and little trouble might be expected from
this quarter as the Frenchmen each had two guns pointing to the front.

Just as we crossed the lines, all the machines flying along in beautiful formation, I noticed a group
of five Fokkers back of Soissons.   They were to the
west of us, the sun was in the west, and from their
maneuvers I knew that they had sighted us and were
flying for a position in the sun.   Once concealed by
the sun's glare, they hoped to approach us and take us
by surprise.

Keeping one eye upon them and climbing still higher
so as to keep well up to their level, I continued to lead
my flotilla straight on towards the objective.   Reaching Vailly we began to circle about, while the French

Spads snapped their cameras. One complete circuit we made and had started upon the second in order to make duplicates of all the exposures, when I observed three of the Fokkers leave their formation and begin a perpendicular dive upon the photographers. Even as I put down my own nose to intercept them, I was conscious, of a feeling of intense surprise and admiration at this exhibition of bravery on the part of the three Huns. They were coming boldly in to attack almost four times their number,— and we were still in excellent formation. It would be quite impossible for the three Fokkers to reach the Frenchmen without running the gauntlet of fire from at least twice their number of Spads. Evidently these three Heinies were pilots of the first quality!

As I descended in an oblique to meet the Fokkers, I noticed another Fokker formation of five coming straight at us from our rear. So this was the prearranged tactics of their sudden attack! I veered away slightly and looked over the situation. There was no time to lose! We must get rid of these three knights, who had come a-tilting at us with the evident intention of breaking up our formation, just in time for the onslaught of the reinforcements who were coming rapidly to their support.

The very first maneuver made by the three Fokkers verified my suspicions. The first Heinie came directly at one of the nearest French Spads, diving disdainfully through the fire of our nearest protection squad. As he approached within firing distance of the Frenchman he suddenly did a brilliant renversement and doubled back on his tracks. Busy as I was at that moment, I couldn't help but admire the daring pilot for his cleverness and coolness. He zoomed up a short distance, turned over on his wing and this time came down diagonally for a real attack. Our Spads were all firing upon him.

The Fokker was intent upon the French photographing machine. He did not pay us the compliment of even noticing our presence. I was in exactly the right position to meet his coming and at the proper moment I pulled my machine straight up on her tail, trained my sights along the line of his dive and began firing.

My bullets cut a straight streak of fire up and down his path and as the Fokker entered this path I saw my flaming bullets rip through his machine from stem to stern. By controling my Spad to keep pace with the Fokker, I let go at least a hundred rounds before I saw that my bullets were finally missing him. He must have been literally riddled with bullets.

He fell away and dropped, but did not burst into flames. I cast one glance at his two companions and saw that they were being cared for by other members of my Flights. Reed Chambers was having a merry set-to with one of them, while the other was at some distance away endeavoring to rejoin his Flight.

Chambers had set upon his antagonist with such energy that the Fritz had altered his original intention of taking a shot at the Frenchmen. The latter were still under the protection of one of my small formations and were making their way homewards. Suddenly Reed obtained a favorable position under his Fokker, and with a short burst the enemy machine fell over onto its wing and began drifting down out of control. Two of the daring Fokker pilots had more than met their match but had put up one of the most brilliant attacks I had ever witnessed.

In the meantime I was in considerable difficulty myself. From the time of my first shots I had stalled my motor and was now drifting through air with a dead propeller while watching the proceedings above me. I was an easy victim in this condition should the five Fokkers detect me without power, and the sole method of restarting my motor was a long dive that would force my propeller to revolve through sheer pressure of the air against it. I lost no time in tipping over on my wing, and then heading vertically downwards, let my machine rip through the atmosphere for a 1500-foot fall before switching on my spark.

The engine mercifully started and I again pointed up my nose and climbed with all speed to overtake my fellows. The end of the two vanquished Fokkers I had had no opportunity to observe.

My instructions to my Spads had been to stick closely to the French two-seater machines and to protect them across the lines, no matter what happened to any individuals who might be cut off. For some unknown reason the Fokkers above me did not take advantage of my isolation and made no effort to get me as I flew along in the rear of my formations. Reed Chambers had already caught up with them and they were all well over our lines.

The French machines dropped down to our field at Coincy, while the Spads of 94 continued on their way homewards. Landing beside the French photographers I inquired as to the success of the expedition and learned that they had actually snapped thirty-five views of the positions they wanted, in spite of the Fokkers' attack.

Upon inspection of the one French two-seater which had been the object of my Fokker's attack, we found that the German airman was as good a shot as he was pilot. We counted a number of bullet holes in the tail of the machine, none of them fortunately having broken any of the control wires.

Our efforts to obtain confirmations of the destruction of the two Fokkers shot down by Chambers and myself were disappointing. Our troops were advancing so rapidly that none of the regiments who were along that sector on the eighth of August could be located, when a few days later we drove over to that front to make inquiries. However one can scarcely expect to get confirmations for all one's victories, since nine-tenths of our combats were necessarily fought on the German side of the lines.

My Fokker pilot may have escaped death; and now that the war is over, I most sincerely hope that he did, for he was a brave pilot and a daring fellow.

At lunchtime on August tenth we received orders for all hands to get aloft at once and form an aerial barrier in front of a small piece of woods that lay just back of our lines northwest of Fère-en-Tardenois. This wood was scarcely two miles from the enemy trenches and our natural supposition was that our Generals were filling this area with troops or guns and desired to conceal the fact from enemy espionage.

Upon landing at the Coincy field for refilling with gasoline we found that our surmises were correct. Long convoys of motor-lorries, all cleverly camouflaged to merge with the roads and fields, were rapidly passing northwards, and all were packed full of our doughboys. The road kept humming with these convoys all the afternoon. Evidently there was to be a big push on the morrow directed against Fismes from this very advantageous position so close to their front.

Just as we were getting away, Lieutenant Tytus of the 1st Aero Squadron came running up to me and told me that he was ordered to select a flight of our machines to protect him in a photographing mission over Fismes and the roads leading into it from the north. The Army authorities desired to have the fullest information as to just what the enemy was doing, before completing arrangements for the morrow's attack. He asked me if I would pick out a few pilots from my Squadron and be ready to go up with him in ten minutes.

I asked for volunteers, as this was purely a voluntary

mission. Five pilots immediately asked for the job and we drew our machines apart from the others.

Being in command of this expedition, I determined to see to it that a complete understanding existed between our Spad pilots and the pilots of the Salmson machines of No. 1 Squadron who were to do the photographing. The region to be photographed was a large one, covering several towns lying between the Vesle and the Aisne rivers and all the highways running between them. It would take some time thoroughly to cover this territory and we were certain to be attacked before completing the excursion.

I talked to the pilots for five minutes and made everybody understand that when they saw me make a virage, or circle on one wing, just ahead of them they must immediately make a dive for our lines without any delay, photographs or no photographs. With our experience of the strength of the enemy Fokkers in this sector, it would be senseless suicide for our five machines to attempt to parley with overwhelming numbers of the enemy. It would be useless to get the photographs if we could not return with them.

At 5:30 sharp we left the ground and flew away over Fismes. At that time Fismes was directly on the line. American troops held the south half of the city and German troops occupied the northern half. Fismes lays just half-way between Rheims and Soissons.

We were directly over Fismes when I detected a formation of eight red-nosed Fokkers stealing around on our left. They had evidently just left their aerodrome and were coming over to patrol the lines. Their present maneuver was as clear as crystal to me. They hoped to get behind us at a superior altitude and then come in upon our rear with the sun at their backs. It was precisely the maneuver I should have attempted in their place.

We had the advantage of them in one particular — they did not know how deep we intended going into their territory. I saw by their actions that they intended to overlook us until we were well within their grasp, and then they would suddenly discover us.

"Very well!" I said to myself, "we will go ahead and photograph until you are ready to attack!"

Affecting ignorance of their presence, I continued straight into Germany. We made a short cut from southeast to northwest and came back in the contrary direction. A few discreet circles enabled the photographers to cover fairly well the territory they wanted, without taking us more than six miles within the German lines.

As we began our second circuit the Fokkers determined to start something. They had made up their minds that we were not playing fair with them. Five of their machines came darting down upon us from a great altitude, while the remainder continued cruising the lines between us and home. I saw the attack coming and put my Spad in motion at the same instant.

Diving down behind my little formation which was tranquilly pursuing its way northwards, I passed behind the tails of the rear machines and immediately zoomed up directly in front of them, turning sharply back to the right so that they could not help seeing me. Without further thought of their possible misunderstanding of this pre-arranged signal I began climbing for altitude directly towards the approaching Fokkers. The five enemy machines had their sharp edged wings cutting the air directly towards me. It is a thrilling and a somewhat fearful sight to see the outline of a Fokker biplane descending upon one. I see them in my dreams very frequently after too hearty a supper late at night.

Beginning firing at a comparatively long range I held the Spad on its steepest course and waited to discover which side of me the Fokkers would choose to pass. Soon they began firing too and the swift streaks of fire formed a living path along which we both traveled. I felt deep down in my heart that they would not stop to take me on. Their object was to get the two-seater which had the damaging photographs. They would swerve to my right at the last instant in order to place me between them and my formation. My Spads must be well together and headed downwards towards the lines by now. I had no time to look around, for I was lying back, half upon my back, the earth well under my tail and the sun under my engine, which prevented it from shining full into my eyes. Almost instinctively I prepared to flatten out and immediately swing over to the right. The enemy must move in that direction!

As we whizzed past each other I ceased firing and flattened out my course. The enemy machines had passed me and I now had the upper ceiling. They had fortunately continued on down after the Salmson, just as I had expected them to do. Now the other Spads in my flight must look after them. Evidently none of the five had been injured by my fire any more than they had injured me. We each of us had presented a very small target subject to injury.

As I eased off my motor I heard the crackling of machine-gun fire below me. I first cast another glance at the distant Fokker formation above me, then looked down over the sides of my office. Surely the five Fokkers could not have reached my Spads so soon! They should have been diving for the lines long ago!

As I looked down I discovered a regular dog-fight was in progress. Certainly those were Spad machines which were turning and twisting about the encircling Fokkers, and the Spads in fact seemed to outnumber the Fokkers. Something strange about the color of the Spads' wings first struck my attention, and then I discovered that this fight was between a French squadron of Spads and another formation of Fokkers that had evidently arrived at the same spot at the same time. Without my being aware of it, two different groups of aeroplanes had been watching our little party all this while and had all concentrated below me to meet the diving Fokkers!

The Salmson and my five Spads were well below me in about the position I expected to find them. The Spads had instantly obeyed my signal and had begun diving even as they headed around to the rear. They were well out of the mêlée.

Considerably chagrined over my lack of caution and thanking my lucky stars again that the new arrivals which had stolen in from an unobserved quarter were part friendly instead of all hostile, I turned about and vindictively charged into the midst of the combat.

A Fokker had just zoomed up ahead of a diving Spad, letting the Frenchman proceed below him at headlong speed, when I arrived upon his tail. With my first burst the Fokker turned over and fell earthwards out of control. Still too angry with myself to think of caution, I was badly scared a moment later by the spectacle of flaming bullets streaking past my face. I dropped over onto my wing, kicked my rudder crosswise, and fell a hundred yards in a vrille. No more bullets coming in my direction, I hastily pulled my Spad into position and cleaved the air for home! I wanted to get off by myself and think this over! Never again would I venture into hostile skies without twisting my neck in all directions every moment of the flight!

That night after an examination of my machine I called to my mechanics and directed them to bring me the painter's paints and brush. With painstaking care I took the brush and drew little circles around three holes in my wings where German bullets had passed through.

" Cover these holes as neatly as possible," I directed the mechanics, " and then have the painter put a small maltese cross over each patch. These are little souvenirs that will remind me of something next time I am over the lines! "

CHAPTER XXIII

BACK CLOSE TO VERDUN

ONE of the extraordinary things about life at the front is the commonplace way in which extraordinary things happen to one. And though one may wonder and be greatly perplexed over it, there are no intervals for giving due thought to the matter. Thus a day or two after my last experiences, while I was refilling my tank at Coincy preparatory to another flip over the lines, I met two American doughboys there who told me that my brother was in camp but a few miles north of me.

My brother had been at the front with the Signal Corps for three or four months, and though I had repeatedly tried to find his address I had not been able up to this time to locate him.

I immediately obtained permission to take an afternoon off; and borrowing a motor car from one of the officers there, I set off to the north in quest of my brother's camp.

The roads to the north had but a fortnight ago been in full possession of the enemy troops. Signs along the way pointed out the next village in unmistakable fashion. All were in quaint German script. The Huns had whitewashed the most conspicuous corner at the approach to every village and crossroads, and there upon a white background was painted in high black letters the name of the present locality. A few yards further on was an equally glaring sign pointing out the next point of topographical interest in every direction.   The distance in kilometres to each place was indicated with correspondingly large numerals. Any motor driver could pick up his directions without any slackening of speed.

The highway I was traversing led to Fère-en-Tardenois and had been badly worn by the retreating enemy artillery and wagons.   American shells had landed at precise intervals along the line of their retreat.   Hurried replacements of surface had evidently been made by the Germans in order to permit the continued use of this road.   And now our own doughboys were busily at work repairing these same roads, so that our own artillery might go on in pursuit of the fleeing Boches.

As my car approached these groups of busy workers my chauffeur blew them a long blast of warning. They withdrew to the edge of the road and watched me pass, with an expression of mingled irony and respect.   I tried to assume the haughty mien of a Major General while under their brief scrutiny and was beginning to feel highly pleased with myself when I suddenly heard one of the doughboys call out, " Hullo, Rick! "

I looked around, stopping the car by simply cutting off the spark.   An undersized doughboy had dropped his shovel and was running forward to overtake me. As he came up, I recognized him as an old friend of mine from my home town.

" Gee Whiz! Rick," he said, " where the dickens are you going? "

" Oh, up the road a ways to see my brother," I replied, " I just heard he was at the next village.   How are you, Bob?   When did you get over here to La Belle France? "

" 'Bout a month ago.   Hell of a way to come to

break rock, isn't it? Well, so long! I've got to get back on the job!"

He squeezed my hand and hurried back. I never saw him again.

As I proceeded onwards along my way, I continued to marvel at this peculiar coincidence. For months I had been making new friends, had been completely immersed in this new life — had seen nothing of my old friends. And now within a single hour I had found myself bumped suddenly alongside my own brother and against an old schoolboy friend! Within another hour we would all be flung widely apart — perhaps all three of us would be among those reported missing. I began speculating which would be the first! War is a funny thing.

After a very brief visit with my brother I returned home, passing through Fère-en-Tardenois and southwards along the same roads I had so recently traversed. Even in the short interval of my passing a marvelous amount of work had been accomplished. Huge roadrollers were crushing down the gravel, and several miles of the surface had been smoothed. When a people really want a good road built they can finish it in an incredibly short space of time.

Along both sides of the highway were piled heterogeneous masses of materials that had been abandoned by the enemy. Our salvage squads were scouring the adjoining fields and woods, collecting and bringing to the roadsides all the valuable articles for transportation to the rear. Other squads were picking up the dead, searching their blood-drenched clothing for data of identification and stretching them out in methodical rows, duly numbering each corpse and preparing it for the last rites.

Rows upon rows of three-inch shells were stacked up within convenient reach of the army lorries. Their willow and straw baskets, each containing a single

German shell, formed a regular row six feet high and fifty feet long. Then came a space filled with huge twelve-inch shells all standing upright upon their bases. Next were stacked boxes of machine-gun ammunition, hundreds and hundreds of them, occasionally interspersed with stray boxes of rockets, signal flares, Very lights and huge piles of rifles, of machine-guns and of empty brass shells of various sizes. The value of an average German city lay spread along that road — all worthless to the former owners — all constructed for the purpose of killing their fellow men!

I had an unusual experience in the air the following day. It is worth narrating, simply to illustrate the extent to which the Flight Leader of a squadron feels himself morally bound to go.

Six of my Spads were following me in a morning's patrol over the enemy's lines in the vicinity of Rheims. We were well along towards the front when we discovered a number of aeroplanes far above us and somewhat behind our side of the lines. While we made a circle or two, all the while steadily climbing for higher altitude, we observed the darting machines above us exchanging shots at one another. Suddenly the fracas developed into a regular free-for-all.

Reaching a slightly higher altitude at a distance of a mile or two to the east of the mêlée, I collected my formation and headed about for the attack. Just then I noticed that one side had evidently been victorious. Seven aeroplanes remained together in compact formation. The others had streaked it away, each man for himself.

As we drew nearer we saw that the seven conquerors were in fact, enemy machines. There was no doubt about it. They were Fokkers. Their opponents, whether American, French or British, had been scattered and had fled. The Fokkers had undoubtedly seen our approach and had very wisely decided to keep their formation together rather than separate to pursue their former antagonists. They were climbing to keep my squad ever a little below them, while they decided upon their next move.

We were seven and they were seven. It was a lovely morning with clear visibility and all my pilots, I knew, were keen for a fight. I looked over the skies and discovered no reason why we shouldn't take them on at any terms they might require. Accordingly I set our course a little steeper and continued straight on towards them.

The Spad is a better climber than the Fokker. Evidently the Boche pilots opposite us knew this fact. Suddenly the last four in their formation left their line of flight and began to draw away in the direction of Soissons — still climbing. The three Fokkers in front continued towards us for another minute or two. When we were separated by less than a quarter of a mile the three Heinies decided that they had done enough for their country, and putting down their noses, they began a steep dive for their lines.

To follow them was so obvious a thing to do that I began at once to speculate upon what this maneuver meant to them. The four rear Fokkers were well away by now, but the moment we began to dive after the three ahead of us they would doubtless be prompt to turn and select a choice position behind our tails. Very well! We would bank upon this expectation of theirs and make our plans accordingly!

We were at about 17,000 feet altitude. The lines were almost directly under us. Following the three retreating Fokkers at our original level, we soon saw them disappear well back into Germany. Now for the wily four that were probably still climbing for altitude! Arriving over Fismes I altered our course and pointed it towards Soissons, and as we flew we gained an additional thousand feet. Exactly upon the sched-

uled time we perceived approaching us the four Fokkers who were now satisfied that they had us at a disadvantage and might either attack or escape, as they
desired.   They were, however, at precisely the same altitude at which we were now flying.

Wigwagging my wings as a signal for the attack,
I sheered slightly to the north of them to cut off their
retreat.   They either did not see my maneuver or else
they thought we were friendly aeroplanes, for they
came on dead ahead like a flock of silly geese.   At two
hundred yards I began firing.

Not until we were within fifty yards of each other
did the Huns show any signs of breaking.   I had
singled out the flight leader and had him nicely within
my sights, when he suddenly piqued downwards, the
rest of his formation immediately following him.   At
the same instant one of my guns — the one having a
double feed — hopelessly jammed.   And after a burst
of twenty shots or so from the other gun it likewise
failed me!   There was no time to pull away for repairs!

Both my guns were useless.   For an instant I considered the advisability of withdrawing while I tried
to free the jam.   But the opportunity was too good
to lose.   The pilots behind me would be thrown into
some confusion when I signalled them to carry on
without me.   And moreover the enemy pilots would
quickly discover my trouble and would realize that
the flight leader was out of the fight.   I made up my
mind to go through with the fracas without guns and
trust to luck to see the finish.   The next instant we
were ahead of the quartet and were engaged in a furious dog-fight.

Every man was for himself.   The Huns were excellent pilots and seemed to be experienced fighters.
Time and again I darted into a good position behind or
below a tempting target, with the sole result of com-

pelling the Fritz o alter his course and get out of
his position of supposed danger. If he had known
I was unarmed he would have had me at his mercy.
As it was I would no sooner get into a favorable position behind him than he would double about and the
next moment I found myself compelled to look sharp
to my own safety.

In this manner the whole revolving circus went
tumbling across the heavens — always dropping lower
and steadily traveling deeper into the German lines.
Two of my pilots had abandoned the scrap and turned
homewards. Engines or guns had failed them.
When at last we had fought down to 3,000 feet and
were some four miles behind their lines, I observed
two flights of enemy machines coming up from the
rear to their rescue. We had none of us secured a single victory — but neither had the Huns. Personally I
began to feel a great longing for home. I dashed
out ahead of the foremost Spad and frantically wigwagging him to attention I turned my little 'bus towards our lines. With a feeling of great relief I saw
that all four were following me and that the enemy
reinforcements were not in any position to dispute our
progress.

On the way homeward I struggled with my jammed
guns — but to no result. Despite every precaution
these weapons will fail a pilot when most needed. I
had gone through with a nerve-racking scrap, piquing
upon deadly opponents with a harmless machine. My
whole safety had depended upon their not knowing
it.

This sort of an experience serves to bring home to
an aspiring pilot the responsibilities of the Flight
Leader. I considered this fact somewhat seriously as
I flew homewards that night and later made out my
report. I wanted to be Squadron Commander, as
every other pilot desires this promotion. Yet on this

day I began to have an inkling of what it meant to be saddled with such a responsibility.

This whole period of what we called the "Château-Thierry" show became somewhat chaotic to me. Briefly, it lasted from July 2nd to September 3rd, 1918. I had missed much of it in the hospital. The little flying I had done over the lines had not been especially satisfactory. And now I began to feel a recurrence of my ear trouble. The constant twisting of my neck in air, turning my head from side to side to watch constantly all the points of the compass had affected in some mysterious way my former malady. On August 18th I suffered actual agony and was unable to get out of bed.

This was a sad day for our happy mess. Two of our pilots, one the same Lieutenant Smyth that had made so many patrols with me, the other an equally popular fellow, Lieutenant Alexander B. Bruce, of Lawrence, Massachusetts — these two pilots while patrolling over the enemy's lines at a very high altitude had collided. With wings torn asunder both machines had dropped like plummets to the distant ground below. The news came in to us while I was in bed. I had actually just been dreaming that Smyth was up with me fighting Fokkers. And I had dreamed that he had just been shot down in flames!

When Captain Marr came in to see how I was getting along, he told me about this horrible catastrophe. Smyth had appealed to me in many ways. He had told me that he had been in the French Ambulance Service since early in the war. He had transferred to our aviation when we entered the war. His father had died while he was with us and he had vainly attempted to get home to see his mother in New York who was then critically ill. But mothers are not considered by those in authority — his application was denied.

Bruce I had not known so well, as he had been with us but a few days. But the whole frightful episode really constituted a considerable shock to the nerves of our squadron. Lieutenant Green who had been leader of this formation came in a few minutes later and confirmed the sad intelligence we had received by telephone from the French artillery battery which had witnessed the collision in mid-air.

The fighters on the front can never understand why the authorities back home deny them necessary arms and ammunition. We air-fighters cannot understand why we cannot have parachutes fitted on our aeroplanes to give the doomed pilot one possible means of escape from this terrible death. Pilots sometimes laugh over the comic end of a comrade shot down in course of a combat. It is a callousness made possible by the continuous horrors of war. If he dies from an attack by an enemy it is taken as a matter of course. But to be killed through a stupid and preventable mistake puts the matter in a very different light.

For the past six months the German airmen had been saving their lives by aeroplane parachutes. A parachute is a very cheap contrivance compared to the cost of training an aviator. Lufbery and a score of other American aviators might have been saved to their country if this matter of aeroplane equipment had been left to experienced pilots.

During the following week Paris surgeons operated upon my troublesome ear at the hospital. It has never bothered me since. As soon as I was able to get about I maneuvered for my speedy return to the front; for I had heard that the Americans were about to begin a tremendous drive on the St. Mihiel salient, near Verdun, and that our air force would be of great importance in its success.

And it was during this week in the Paris hospital

that it was first suggested to me that I should write a book of my experiences in the air.   I began this work then and there, and from that time on I kept a more complete diary of my day's work.   Naturally I did not know that the bulk of my victories were to come. Nor did I know that I should ever live to receive the command of the best Air Squadron in the American service.

One of the prizes offered by the Duchesse Tally-rand for shooting down enemy machines had come to me.   I had more victories to my credit than any other American pilot in our service, though several American aviators then in the French Squadrons exceeded my score.   Later Frank Luke, who in my opinion was the greatest fighting pilot in the war, passed me when he shot down in flames thirteen balloons in six days! A record that has never been equaled by any other pilot!

On September third I learned that 94 Squadron had moved back to the Verdun sector.   That indicated to me that plans were ripening for the St. Mihiel offensive by the Americans.   I obtained permission to leave the hospital as cured and hastened to our Aviation Headquarters to obtain my orders to return to the front. There I was told that General Mitchell's motorcar was in Paris ready to be sent to his headquarters — and would I care to drive it back?   The quickness of my acceptance can be imagined!

My Squadron was already at home on the famous old highway that had saved Verdun.   About fifteen miles south of Verdun at a little town named Erize-la-Petite the aerodrome covered the crest of a hill that two years before had been in the possession of the Germans.   Number 95 Squadron was there, together with 27 Squadron and 147 Squadron.   The lines of the enemy ran south from Verdun along the Meuse until they reached St. Mihiel, scarcely twelve miles straight east from us. The crump — crump — of the guns was constantly in our ears.

This aerodrome, which had been constructed and used by the French escadrilles, was now to be occupied by our little group until the end of the war. During the coming month of September I was to win four more victories in the air and then to be given the greatest honor that has ever come to any pilot — the command of the Squadron that he truly believes to be the finest in the whole world, his own!

CHAPTER XXIV

THE ST. MIHIEL DRIVE

ALTHOUGH we did not know it at the time, we were now on the last laps of the war. Every taxi-driver or waiter in Paris could have told one just where the Americans were concentrating for their great attack on the St. Mihiel salient. The number of guns, the number of troops and just where they were located, how many aeroplanes we had and similar topics of war interest were discussed by every man on the streets.

Consequently I was much amused when I was arrested at the outskirts of Bar-le-Duc by a suspicious member of our Military Police — " the M. P.," as he is called at the front — and very closely questioned as to my character and identity. He informed me later that every person entering or leaving Bar-le-Duc was given the same searching examination. Spies were abroad and he was taking no chances of letting information leak out as to what was going on. I assured him I would not tell a soul and was permitted to drive on.

These extraordinary precautions always seemed more or less ridiculous to men who had been close to the firing lines during the war. The nearer one gets to the lines the simpler appears the matter of espionage. Doubtless scores of Germans crossed the lines every night, arrayed themselves in the uniform of dead American or French soldiers and mingled freely and unsuspected with our troops until they desired to return to their own side. As there are hundreds of our soldiers wandering about looking for their regiments a few extra wanderers create no suspicion. Yet if one of these should venture to Bar-le-Duc or any other city far away from the actual scene of activities — Heaven help him.

At the aerodrome I was welcomed by my old friends with a heartiness known only to flying squadrons. A peculiar and lasting friendship is created between boys who fight in the air. No other fraternity upon earth is like it.

Jimmy Meissner I found was now in command of No. 147 Squadron. Al Grant of Austin, Texas, had command of 27, succeeding Major Hartney, who had been promoted to the command of the whole group at this aerodrome. 95 Squadron was still under Major Peterson who, with his galaxy of " stout fellows," including Bill Taylor, Sumner Sewell, Ted Curtis, Harold Buddy, Jack Mitchell and Benny Holden, led the four squadrons in their number of victories. This squadron rivalry led to great efforts upon the part of all our fighting flyers. Later, principally through the extraordinary prowess of Frank Luke, his Squadron, the 27th, for a time led our group in the number of its victories. But before the end of the war the highest score came to the Squadron which knew all along that they could win it — old 94, with its Hat-in-the-Ring. My squadron did a famous lot of fighting during the month of October. It passed the other squadrons of our group as well as all the other American squadrons at the front.

At dinner that night — the night of my arrival — word came to us that the Big Show was to start at five o'clock the following morning.

Precisely at five o'clock I was awakened by the thundering of thousands of colossal guns. It was September 12, 1918. The St. Mihiel Drive was on!

Leaping out of bed I put my head outside the tent. We had received orders to be over the lines at daybreak in large formations. It was an exciting moment in my life as I realized that the great American attack upon which so many hopes had been fastened was actually on. I suppose every American in the world wanted to be in that great attack. The very sound of the guns thrilled one and filled one with excitement The good reputation of America seemed bound up in the outcome of that attack.

Dressing with great haste I ran over through the rain to the mess hall. There I found groups of the fellows all standing about impatiently awaiting the chance to get away. But the weather was certainly too bad to attempt any flight to the lines. We were compelled to wait until daylight to see the true state of the heavens.

About noon word came to us that the attack was progressing quite favorably. None of our machines had been able to get up. It was still raining but the visibility was getting better. We could see that the clouds were nearly a thousand feet above the ground.

Taking Reed Chambers one side, I proposed to him that despite the rain we try a short flip over the lines to see for ourselves what it was like. He agreed and while the others were at lunch we climbed into our machines and made off. At 600 feet above ground we found that we were just under the clouds and still had quite a long view of the landscape.

Flying straight east to St. Mihiel, we crossed the Meuse River and turned down its valley towards Verdun. Many fires were burning under us as we flew, most of them well on the German side of the river. Villages, haystacks, ammunition dumps and supplies were being set ablaze by the retreating Huns.

We proceeded as far as Verdun. Then turning east we continued flying at our low altitude and passed over Fresnes and Vigneulles.

Vigneulles was the objective point of the American forces. It lies east of Verdun some fifteen miles and about the same distance north of St. Mihiel. One American army was pushing towards it from a point just south of Verdun while the other attack was made from the opposite side of the salient. Like irresistible pincers, the two forces were drawing nearer and nearer to this objective point. The German troops who were still inside the salient would soon be caught inside the pincers.

As Reed and I turned south from Vigneulles we saw that the main highway running north to Metz was black with hurrying men and vehicles. Guns, stores and ammunition were being hauled away to safety with all possible speed. We continued on south through the very heart of the St. Mihiel salient, flying always low above the roadway which connected Vigneulles with St. Mihiel. Here, likewise, we found the Germans in full cry to the rear.

One especially attractive target presented itself to us as we flew along this road. A whole battery of Boche three-inch guns was coming towards us on the double. They covered fully half a mile of the roadway.

Dipping down at the head of the column I sprinkled a few bullets over the leading teams. Horses fell right and left. One driver leaped from his seat and started running for the ditch. Half-way across the road he threw up his arms and rolled over upon his face.   He had stepped full in front of my stream of machine-gun bullets!

All down the line we continued our fire — now tilting our aeroplanes down for a short burst, then zooming back up for a little altitude in which to repeat the performance.   The whole column was thrown into the wildest confusion.   Horses plunged and broke away.   Some were killed and fell in their tracks. Most of the drivers and gunners had taken to the trees before we reached them.   Our little visit must have cost them an hour's delay.

Passing over St. Mihiel, we hastened on to our aerodrome.   There we immediately telephoned headquarters information of what we had seen and particularly of the last column of artillery we had shot up in its retreat from St. Mihiel.   This was evidently splendid news and exactly what G. H. Q. had been anxious to know, for they questioned us closely upon this subject, inquiring whether or not we were convinced that the Germans were actually quitting St. Mihiel.

I assured them that there was no question about the retreat being in full swing.   Thereupon, they told me that they would immediately begin shelling that road with our long-range guns so as further to impede the withdrawing of the enemy's supplies along this artery.

Later observations which we made over this road indicated that our gunners had made a good job of this task.   The Germans had abandoned huge quantities of guns, wagons and supplies and had only saved their own skins by taking to the woods and covering the distance to Vigneulles on foot.   The highway was utterly impassable.

That same night we were advised that the victorious Americans had taken Thiaucourt — that scene of so many of our operations back of the lines.   A stout enemy squadron had always occupied the Thiaucourt aerodrome and we had had many a combat with its members. Henceforward we would miss the menace of this opposing unit. And we were also informed that at last Montsec had fallen!

Montsec was to this sector what Vimy Ridge was to the British troops about Lens. Its high crest dominated the entire landscape. From its summit the Huns could look over the whole south country. From observation posts which we later discovered on its summit we saw that our own aerodrome had been under constant surveillance by the Hun observers! Not a machine could leave our field at Toul without being seen by these watchers atop Montsec! No wonder their photographing machines escaped us! Many and many a time we had hurried out to the lines in answer to an alerte, only to find that it was a false alarm. Now we understood why we lost them. The Huns had seen our coming and by signalling their machines had given them warning in time to evade us. They retired and landed and waited until we had returned home, then they calmly proceeded with their interrupted work!

The capture of Montsec was a remarkably fine bit of strategy, for it was neatly outflanked and pinched out with a very small loss indeed. Our infantry and Tank Corps accomplished this feat within twenty hours.

When one remembers that the French lost nearly 30,000 men killed, wounded and missing in their attack on Montsec in the fall of 1916 — and then held this dearly bought ground for only twenty minutes — one appreciates what a wonderful victory the American doughboys won.

On our trip up this same road the following day Reed Chambers and I saw the retreat of the Huns and the advance of our doughboys in full swing. The Huns were falling back northwards with an unusually strong rearguard protecting their retreat. Already they were out of reach of our guns' accurate aim, for the day was again cloudy, with occasional rains and no aeroplanes were able to regulate the gun fire..

But closely pressing them from behind came our eager doughboys fighting along like Indians. They scurried from cover to cover, always crouching low as they ran. Throwing themselves flat onto the ground they would get their rifles into action and spray the Boches with more bullets until they withdrew from sight. Then another running advance and another furious pumping of lead from the Yanks.

Reed and I flew above this scene for many miles, watching the most spectacular free show that ever man gazed upon. It was a desperate game, especially for the Huns, but I cheered and cheered as I caught the excitement of the chase, even high over their heads as I was.

In the midst of my rejoicing I suddenly heard the rat-tat-tat of a machine-gun below me and felt a few hits through my plane. I looked down in amazement and saw there behind the shell of a ruined building three Germans pointing a machine-gun at me and pumping away vindictively at my aeroplane. I tipped over my machine into a sharp virage and grasped my triggers. Before the men could lift a hand I had my stream of bullets going plump into their center. One man fell dead on the spot, his hands thrust up over his head. The other two dropped their guns and dived for a doorway. I was over the ruined village of Apremont.

Coasting along some eight or ten miles further I saw the whole country was swarming with the retreating Huns. I noted the progress of our own troops below and marked down their positions on my map. Having lost Reed during my little fracas with the machine gunners I circled westward and covered the Ver-

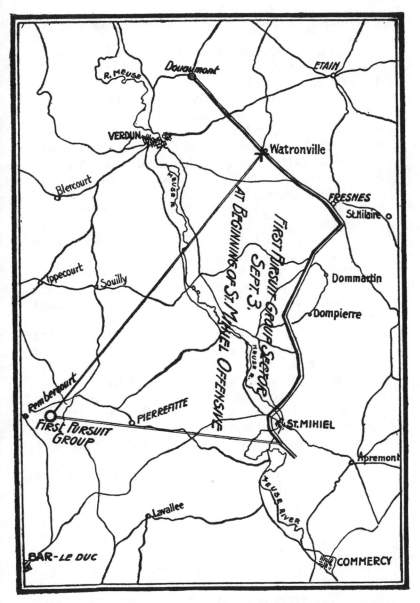

94 SQUADRON'S PATROL FROM WATRONVILLE TO ST. MIHIEL, SEPTEMBER 3 TO 26, 1918.

dun region without seeing anything either of him or of enemy aircraft. When I returned home I found the weather very bad south of the Meuse and was not surprised at the little air activity in that region.

Reed came in an hour or two later. He had landed at our old Toul aerodrome to see one of his old pals. And there he learned the grievous news that David Putnam, America's leading Ace, had just been shot down in combat. Since the death of Lufbery and Bayliss and the capture of Baer, Putnam with his twelve victories had led all the American fighting pilots. His nerve and great fighting ability were well known to all of us. He had once shot down four enemy machines in one fight.

Putnam had gone up about noon to-day with one comrade. They encountered a Fokker formation of eight planes out on patrol and immediately attacked them. Putnam was struck almost at once and his machine crashed to the ground in flames. Thus died a glorious American boy and a brilliant fighter.

The next day was an exciting one for our group. I shot down one of the von Richthofen Circus and just escaped getting downed myself. Sumner Sewell of 95 Squadron lived through one of the most extraordinary series of accidents I ever heard of, and several others had encounters that yielded a few more victories to our group.

It was a clear fine day and I took off from the field alone at about eight o'clock in the morning, with the expectation of finding the sky full of aeroplanes. Anxious to see the extent of the American advance towards Vigneulles I made for Thiaucourt and the north. Thiaucourt always gave me a shudder in former days and I usually took care to take a high path over its top. But now I spun across its abandoned aerodrome with much indifference and for the first time had a good look at its hangar arrangements.

Later, crossing the Moselle about four miles north of Pont-à-Mousson I noticed considerable anti-aircraft shelling up in the direction of Metz. I climbed higher and scanned the sky for machines.

Here they come! A large flotilla of American "Flaming Coffins" as their pilots called the Liberty machines, were coming home at 12,000 feet after a bombardment of Metz. And just behind them and a little above were four very fast moving Fokkers. I stuck up my nose and began climbing for the sun.

I continued eastward until I had gained about a thousand feet in altitude over the enemy machines, then I turned about. The Huns had followed the American machines to the lines and then had turned back westward in the direction of the Three-Fingered Lake. This was just the opportunity I had been hoping for. Now I had the sun at my back, and it was unusually brilliant this morning.

After a gradual pique with motor half open, I descended to a position within a hundred yards of the last man in their formation. The four were in diamond formation and none of them had seen my approach. At fifty yards I pressed my triggers and played my bullets straight into the pilot's seat. His machine slipped over onto its side and after one wide swoop sideways began its last long fall to earth.

No sooner did my gun begin to crackle than the leader of the flight swung up his machine in a climbing virage, the other two pilots immediately following his example. And then I received one of the biggest jolts I can remember!

We had heard that the famous Richthofen Circus had evacuated its old aerodrome in the west and had been reported in our sector. But so far none of us had met them about here. Now, as these three light Fokkers began simultaneously to come about at me I found myself staring full into three beautiful scarlet

noses headed straight in my direction. It scarcely
needed their color to tell me who they were, for the
skill with which they all came about so suddenly convinced me that this was no place for me. I had blun-
dered single-handed into the Richthofen crowd!

I did my best to get away in a dignified manner, but
a sudden spurt of fire past my nose convinced me that
I would be very lucky if I got away with an unpunc-
tured skin. The contortions I then undertook must
have awakened the admiration of my three pursuers!
At odd moments I would try to admire their extraordinary adroitness in handling their machines, for the
heavens seemed quite crowded with those three dancing
Fokkers. No matter where I turned there were always at least two of them there before me!

I need no more living proof of the flying ability of
that celebrated German Squadron of fighting pilots.
They whipped their machines about me with incredible
cleverness. I was looking for an opening for a quick
getaway and they seemed only desirous of keeping me
twisting my head off to follow their movements, so I
had this slight advantage of them there. At last an
opportunity came to try to outrun them, and with
motor full open and nose straight down I looked back
and saw them fading away in my rear.

I returned to my aerodrome quite elated with my
first victory over this crack fighting squadron.

But Lieutenant Sumner Sewell's experience completely eclipsed mine.

Sumner was tranquilly following along at the rear
end of his formation, composed of the 95 boys, when
he was startled by a sudden series of shocks in his
aeroplane. He was over the enemy's lines and some
16,000 feet up in the air. He glanced behind him and
found a Fokker immediately upon his tail. The Heinie
was deliberately riddling Sumner's Spad with flaming
bullets!

The rest of the formation actually drew away from
Sewell without knowing that he had been attacked!

Sewell turned his machine about in a quick renversement, but just as he did so he felt his heart go
into his mouth. The enemy's incendiary bullets had
set fire to his fuel tank! With a sudden puff of flame
all the rear part of his machine burst into a furious
blaze. And he was almost three miles above ground!

Sumner instinctively put down his nose so that the
flames would be swept by the wind to the rear and
away from his person. Anybody but a Hun would
have taken pity on a fellow being in such a plight and
would have turned away his eyes from so frightful a spectacle. But this Fokker Hun was built of
sterner stuff. Instead of turning away to attack the
rest of the 95 formation, Fritz stuck steadfastly on
Sumner's tail, firing steadily at him as he descended!

One can imagine the mental torture Sumner Sewell
endured during the next few minutes! It takes some
time to fall three miles even at the top speed of a 220
H.P. motor. The downward motion kept the blaze
away from him, but a backward glance informed him
that the fire was eating up the entire length of his
fusilage and that at any moment he would be flung out
into space. And the same glance assured him that
his merciless enemy was leaving nothing to Providence,
but was determined to execute him himself. Streaks
of flaming bullets passed his head, through his wings
and around him on every side, as the Fokker pilot continued his target practise with poor Sewell as his mark.
In spite of himself he was compelled to try a little
dodging to escape from so malignant an enemy.

Perhaps this very necessity saved Sewell's life. At
any rate it provided a counter-irritant which took his
mind off his frightful danger of burning alive. He
executed a sudden maneuver when he was but a thousand feet above ground which moved him out of the

range of the German. When he again looked around he discovered that the Hun had abandoned the chase, apparently satisfied that the Yank was doomed. And to his utter amazement he also discovered that the flames were now extinguished!

Sumner crashed a few hundred yards on the right side of No Man's Land. His skeleton of a Spad struck a shell hole, executed a somersault and came to rest at the bottom of another shell hole. Sumner crawled out of the wreckage and looked about him, too bewildered to realize that he was alive and on solid ground. Just at that instant a dull thud at his elbow brought him back to life.

He looked at the object at his feet — then at the wreck of his machine. There was no doubt about it. The substance which had made that thud was one of the wheels from his own machine!

The German had shot one of his wheels completely away. The fabric which covered the spokes had evidently caused it to swoop this way and that, and Sumner in his falling aeroplane had beaten it to earth!

Upon investigation, Lieutenant Sewell discovered that his fuel tank had a hole in its side large enough to admit his fist. An explosive bullet had torn out so large a hole that the gasoline had rapidly run out and his last maneuver had completely emptied his tank.

Such are the fortunes of war!

CHAPTER XXV

AMERICAN ACE OF ACES

ON September 15th the weather was ideal for flying. I left the aerodrome at 8:30 in the morning on a voluntary patrol, taking the nearest air route to the lines.

I had reached an altitude of 16,000 feet by the time I had reached the trenches. The visibility was unusually good. I could see for miles and miles in every direction. I was flying alone, with no idea as to whether other planes of our own were cruising about this sector or not. But barely had I reached a position over No Man's Land when I noticed a formation of six enemy Fokkers at about my altitude coming towards me from the direction of Conflans.

I turned and began the usual tactics of climbing into the sun. I noticed the Fokkers alter their direction and still climbing move eastward towards the Moselle. I did not see how they could help seeing me, as scarcely half a mile separated us. However, they did not attack nor did they indicate that they suspected my presence beyond continuing steadily their climb for elevation. Three complete circles they made on their side of the lines. I did the same on my side.

Just at this moment I discovered four Spad machines far below the enemy planes and some three miles inside the German lines. I decided at once they must belong to the American Second Fighting Group, at that time occupying the aerodrome at Souilly. They appeared to be engaged in bombing the roads and strafing enemy infantry from a low altitude. The Spads of the Second Pursuit Group had but recently been equipped with bomb racks for carrying small bombs.

The leader of the Fokker Formation saw the Spads at about the same moment I did. I saw him dip his wings and stick down his nose. Immediately the six Fokkers began a headlong pique directly down at the Spads. Almost like one of the formation I followed suit.

Inside the first thousand feet I found I was rapidly overtaking the enemy machines. By the time we had reached 5,000 feet I was in a position to open fire upon the rear man. Not once had any of them looked around. Either they had forgotten me in their anxiety to get at their prey or else had considered I would not attempt to take them all on single-handed. At all events I was given ample time to get my man dead into my sights before firing.

I fired one long burst. I saw my tracer bullets go straight home into the pilot's seat. There came a sudden burst of fire from his fuel tank and the Fokker continued onwards in its mad flight — now a fiery furnace. He crashed a mile inside his own lines.

His five companions did not stay to offer battle. I still held the upper hand and even got in a few bursts at the next nearest machine before he threw himself into a vrille and escaped me. The sight of one of their members falling in flames evidently quite discouraged them. Abandoning all their designs on the unsuspecting Spads below they dived away for Germany and left me the field.

I returned to my field, secured a car and drove immediately up to the lines to our Balloon Section. I wanted to get my victories confirmed — both this one of to-day and the Fokker that I had brought down yesterday in the same sector. For no matter how many pilots may have witnessed the bringing down of an enemy plane, official confirmation of their testimony must be obtained from outside witnesses on the ground. Often these are quite impossible to get. In such a case the victory is not credited to the pilot.

Upon the tragic death of Major Lufbery, who at that time was the leading American Ace, with 18 victories, the title of American Ace of Aces fell to Lieutenant Paul Frank Baer of Fort Wayne, Ind., a member of the Lafayette Escadrille 103. Baer then had 9 victories and had never been wounded.

Baer is a particularly modest and lovable boy, and curiously enough he is one of the few fighting pilots

I have met who felt a real repugnance in his task of shooting down enemy aviators.

When Lufbery fell, Baer's Commanding Officer, Major William Thaw, called him into the office and talked seriously with him regarding the opportunity before him as America's leading Ace. He advised Baer to be cautious and he would go far. Two days later Baer was shot down and slightly wounded behind the German lines!

Thereafter, Lieutenant Frank Bayliss of New Bedford, Mass., a member of the crack French Escadrille of the Cigognes, Spad 3, held the American title until he was killed in action on June 12th, 1918. Bayliss had 13 victories to his credit.

Then David Putnam, another Massachusetts boy, took the lead with 12 victories over enemy aeroplanes. Putnam, as I have said, was, like Lufbery, shot down in flames but a day or two before my last victory.

Lieutenant Tobin of San Antonio, Texas, and a member of the Third Pursuit Group (of which Major William Thaw was the Commanding Officer), now had six official victories. He led the list. I for my part had five victories confirmed. But upon receiving confirmation for the two Fokkers I had vanquished yesterday and to-day, I would have my seven and would lead Tobin by one. So it was with some little interest and impatience that I set off to try to find ground witnesses of my last two battles above St. Mihiel.

Mingled with this natural desire to become the leading fighting Ace of America was a haunting superstition that did not leave my mind until the very end of the war. It was that the very possession of this title — Ace of Aces — brought with it the unavoidable doom that had overtaken all its previous holders. I wanted it and yet I feared to learn that it was mine! In later days I began to feel that this superstition was almost the heaviest burden that I carried with me into the air. Perhaps it served to redouble my caution and sharpened my fighting senses. But never was I able to forget that the life of a title-holder is short.

Eating my sandwiches in the car that day I soon ran through St. Mihiel and made my way on the main road east to Apremont and then north to Thiaucourt. I knew that there had been a balloon up near there both days and felt certain that their observers must have seen my two combats overhead.

Unfortunately the road from Apremont to Thiaucourt was closed, owing to the great number of shell-holes and trenches which criss-crossed it. After being lost for two hours in the forest which lies between St. Mihiel and Vigneulles, I was finally able to extricate myself and found I had emerged just south of Vigneulles. I was about one mile south of our trenches. And standing there with map in hand wondering where to go next to find our balloons, I got an unexpected clue.

A sudden flare of flames struck my sight off to the right. Running around the trees I caught a view of one of our balloons between me and Thiaucourt completely immersed in flames! Half-way down was a graceful little parachute, beneath which swung the observer as he settled slowly to Mother Earth!

And as I gazed I saw a second balloon two or three miles further east towards Pont-à-Mousson perform the same maneuver. Another of our observers was making the same perilous jump! A sly Heinie had slipped across our lines and had made a successful attack upon the two balloons and had made a clean getaway. I saw him climbing up away from the furious gale of anti-aircraft fire which our gunners were speeding after him. I am afraid my sympathies were almost entirely with the airman as I watched the murderous bursting of Archy all around his machine.

At any rate I realized exactly how he was feeling, with his mixture of satisfaction over the success of his undertaking and of panic over the deadly mess of shrapnel about him.

In half an hour I arrived at the balloon site and found them already preparing to go aloft with a second balloon. And at my first question they smiled and told me they had seen my Fokker of this morning's combat crash in flames. They readily signed the necessary papers to this effect, thus constituting the required confirmation for my last victory. But for the victory of yesterday that I claimed they told me none of the officers were present who had been there on duty at that time. I must go to the 3rd Balloon Company just north of Pont-à-Mousson and there I would find the men I wanted to see.

After watching the new balloon get safely launched with a fresh observer in the basket, a process which consumed some ten or fifteen minutes, I retraced my steps and made my way back to my motor. The observer whom I had seen descending under his parachute had in the meantime made his return to his company headquarters. He was unhurt and quite enthusiastic over the splendid landing he had made in the trees. Incidentally I learned that but two or three such forced descents by parachute from a flaming balloon are permitted any one observer. These jumps are not always so simple and frequently very serious if not fatal injuries are received in the parachute jump. Seldom does one officer care to risk himself in a balloon basket after his third jump. And this fear for his own safety limits very naturally his service and bravery in that trying business. The American record in this perilous profession is held, I believe, by Lieutenant Phelps of New York, who made five successive jumps from a flaming balloon.

On my way to the 3rd Balloon Company I stopped

to enquire the road from a group of infantry officers whom I met just north of Pont-à-Mousson. As soon as I stated my business, they unanimously exclaimed that they had all seen my flight above them yesterday and had seen my victim crash near them. After getting them to describe the exact time and place and some of the incidents of the fight I found that it was indeed my combat they had witnessed. This was a piece of real luck for me. It ended my researches on the spot. As they were very kindly signing their confirmation I was thinking to myself, " Eddie! You are the American Ace of Aces! " And so I was for the minute.

Returning home, I lost no time in putting in my reports. Reed Chambers came up to me and hit me a thump on the back.

" Well, Rick! " he said, " how does it feel? "

" Very fine for the moment, Reed," I replied seriously, " but any other fellow can have the title any time he wants it, so far as I ar concerned."

I really meant what I was s_ying. A fortnight later when Frank Luke began his marvelous balloon strafing he passed my score in a single jump. Luke, as I have said, was on the same aerodrome with me, being a member of 27 Squadron. His rapid success even brought 27 Squadron ahead of 95 Squadron for a few days.

The following day I witnessed a typical expedition of Luke's from our own aerodrome. Just about dusk on September 16th Luke left the Major's headquarters and walked over to his machine. As he came out of the door he pointed out the two German observation balloons to the east of our field, both of which could be plainly seen with the naked eye. They were suspended in the sky about two miles back of the Boche lines and were perhaps four miles apart.

" Keep your eyes on these two balloons," said Frank as he passed us. " You will see that first one there go up in flames exactly at 7:15 and the other will do likewise at 7:19."

We had little idea he would really get either of them, but we all gathered together out in the open as the time grew near and kept our eyes glued to the distant specks in the sky. Suddenly Major Hartney exclaimed, "There goes the first one!" It was true! A tremendous flare of flame lighted up the horizon. We all glanced at our watches. It was exactly on the dot!

The intensity of our gaze towards the location of the second Hun balloon may be imagined. It had grown too dusk to distinguish the balloon itself, but we well knew the exact point in the horizon where it hung. Not a word was spoken as we alternately glanced at the second-hands of our watches and then at the eastern skyline. Almost upon the second our watching group yelled simultaneously. A small blaze first lit up the point at which we were gazing. Almost instantaneously another gigantic burst of flames announced to us that the second balloon had been destroyed! It was a most spectacular exhibition.

We all stood by on the aerodrome in front of Luke's hangar until fifteen minutes later we heard through the darkness the hum of his returning motor. His mechanics were shooting up red Very lights with their pistols to indicate to him the location of our field. With one short circle above the aerodrome he shut off his motor and made a perfect landing just in front of our group. Laughing and hugely pleased with his success, Luke jumped out and came running over to us to receive our heartiest congratulations. Within a half hour's absence from the field Frank Luke had destroyed a hundred thousand dollars' worth of enemy property! He had returned absolutely unscratched.

A most extraordinary incident had happened just

before Luke had left the ground. Lieutenant Jeffers of my Squadron had been out on patrol with the others during the afternoon and did not return with them. I was becoming somewhat anxious about him when I saw a homing aeroplane coming from the lines towards our field. It was soon revealed as a Spad and was evidently intending to land at our field, but its course appeared to be very peculiar. I watched it gliding steeply down with engine cut off. Instead of making for the field, the pilot, whoever he was, seemed bent upon investigating the valley to the north of us before coming in. If this was Jeff he was taking a foolish chance, since he had already been out longer than the usual fuel supply could last him.

Straight down at the north hillside the Spad continued its way. I ran out to see what Jeff was trying to do. I had a premonition that everything was not right with him.

Just as his machine reached the skyline I saw him make a sudden effort to redress the plane. It was too late. He slid off a little on his right wing, causing his nose to turn back towards the field — and then he crashed in the fringe of bushes below the edge of the hill. I hurried over to him.

Imagine my surprise when I met him walking towards me, no bones broken, but wearing a most sheepish expression on his face. I asked him what in the world was the matter.

"Well," he replied, "I might as well admit the truth! I went to sleep coming home, and didn't wake up until I was about ten feet above the ground. I didn't have time to switch on my engine or even flatten out! I'm afraid I finished the little 'bus!'"

Extraordinary as this tale seemed, it was nevertheless true. Jeffers had set his course for home at a high elevation over the lines and cutting off his engine had drifted smoothly along. The soft air and monot-

onous luxury of motion had lulled him to sleep. Subconsciously his hand controlled the joystick or else the
splendid equilibrium of the Spad had kept it upon an
even keel without control. Like the true old coach-
horse it was, it kept the stable door in sight and made
directly for it. Jeff's awakening might have been in
another world, however, if he had not miraculously
opened his eyes in the very nick of time!

The next day, September 18th, our group suffered
a loss that made us feel much vindictiveness as well as
sorrow. Lieutenant Heinrichs and Lieutenant John
Mitchell, both of 95 Squadron, were out together on
patrol when they encountered six Fokker machines.
They immediately began an attack.

Mitchell fired one burst from each gun and then
found them both hopelessly jammed. He signaled to
Heinrichs that he was out of the battle and started for
home. But at the same moment Heinrichs received a
bullet through his engine which suddenly put it out
of action. He was surrounded by enemy planes and
some miles back of the German lines. He broke
through the enemy line and began his slow descent.
Although it was evident he could not possibly reach
our lines, the furious Huns continued swooping upon
him, firing again and again as he coasted down.

Ten different bullets struck his body in five different attacks. He was perfectly defenseless agai st any
of them. He did not lose consciousness, although
one bullet shattered his jawbone and bespattered his
goggles so that he could not see through the blood.
Just before he reached the ground he managed to push
up his goggles with his unwounded arm. The other
was hanging limp and worthless by his side.

He saw he was fairly into a piece of woodland and
some distance within the German lines. He swung
away and landed between the trees, turning his machine over as he crashed, but escaping further injury

himself. Within an hour or two he was picked up and taken to a hospital in Metz.

After the signing of the Armistice we saw Heinrichs again at the Toul Hospital. He was a mere shell of himself. Scarcely recognizable even by his old comrades, a first glance at his shrunken form indicated that he had been horribly neglected by his captors. His story quickly confirmed this suspicion.

For the several weeks that he had lain in the Metz hospital he told us that the Germans had not reset either his jaw or his broken arm. In fact he had received no medical attention whatsoever. The food given him was bad and infrequent. It was a marvel that he had survived this frightful suffering!

In all fairness to the Hun I think it is his due to say that such an experience as Heinrichs suffered rarely came to my attention. In the large hospital in which he was confined there were but six nurses and two doctors. They had to care for several scores of wounded. Their natural inclination was to care first for their own people. But how any people calling themselves human could have permitted Heinrichs' suffering to go uncared for during all those weeks passes all understanding. Stories of this kind which occasionally came to our ears served to steel our hearts against any mercy towards the enemy pilots in our vicinity.

And thus does chivalry give way before the horrors of war — even in aviation!

CHAPTER XXVI

CAPTAIN OF THE HAT-IN-THE-RING SQUADRON

THE Three-Fingered Lake is a body of water well known to the American pilots who have flown over the St. Mihiel front. It lies four or five miles directly north of Vigneulles and is quite the largest body of water to be seen in this region. The Germans have held it well within their lines ever since the beginning of the war.

At the conclusion of the American drive around St. Mihiel, which terminated victoriously twenty-two hours after it began, the lines were pushed north of Vigneulles until they actually touched the southern arm of Three-Fingered Lake. Our resistless doughboys, pushing in from both directions, met each other in the outskirts of Vigneulles at two o'clock in the morning. Some fifteen thousand Boches and scores of guns were captured within the territory that had thus been pinched out.

With this lake barrier on the very edge of their lines, the Huns had adroitly selected two vantage points on their end of the water from which to hoist their observation balloons. From this position their observers had a splendid view of our lines and noted every movement in our rear. They made themselves a tremendous nuisance to the operations of our Staff Officers.

Frank Luke, the star Balloon Strafer of our group, was, as I have said, a member of the 27th Squadron. On the evening of September 18th he announced that he was going up to get those two balloons that swung above the Three-Fingered Lake. His pal, Lieutenant Wehrner, of the same squadron accompanied Luke as usual.

There was a curious friendship between Luke and Wehrner. Luke was an excitable, highstrung boy, and his impetuous courage was always getting him into trouble. He was extremely daring and perfectly blind and indifferent to the enormous risks he ran. His superior officers and his friends would plead with him to be more cautious, but he was deaf to their entreaties. He attacked like a whirlwind, with absolute coolness but with never a thought of his own safety.

We all predicted that Frank Luke would be the great-est air-fighter in the world if he would only learn to save himself unwise risks. Luke came from Phoenix, Arizona.

Wehrner's nature, on the other hand, was quite different. He had just one passion, and that was his love for Luke. He followed him about the aerodrome constantly. When Luke went up, Wehrner usually managed to go along with him. On these trips Wehrner acted as an escort or guard, despite Luke's objections. On several occasions he had saved Luke's life. Luke would come back to the aerodrome and excitedly tell every one about it, but no word would Wehrner say on the subject. In fact Wehrner never spoke except in monosyllables on any subject. After a successful combat he would put in the briefest possible report and sign his name. None of us ever heard him describe how he brought the enemy machine down.

Wehrner hovered in the air above Luke while the latter went in for the balloon. If hostile aeroplanes came up, Wehrner intercepted them and warded off the attack until Luke had finished his operations. These two pilots made an admirable pair for this work and over a score of victories were chalked up for 27 Squadron through the activities of this team.

On the evening of the 18th, Luke and Wehrner set off at five o'clock. It was just getting dark. They flew together at a medium level until they reached the lake. There they separated, Luke diving straight at the balloon which lay to the west, Wehrner staying aloft to guard the sky against a surprise attack from Hun aeroplanes.

Luke's balloon rose out of the swampy land that borders the upper western edge of Three-Fingered Lake. The enemy defenses saw his approach and began a murderous fire through which Luke calmly dived as usual. Three separate times he dived and fired, dived and fired. Constantly surrounded with a hail of bullets and shrapnel, flaming onions and incendiary bullets, Luke returned to the attack the third time and finally completed his errand of destruction. The huge gas-bag burst into flames. Luke zoomed up over the balloon and looked about for his friend. He was not in view at the moment, but another sight struck Luke's searching eyes. A formation of six Fokkers was bearing down upon him from out of Germany. Perhaps Wehrner had fired the red signal light which had been the warning agreed upon, and he had failed to see it in the midst of all that Archy fire. At any rate he was in for it now.

The German Fokkers were to the west of him. The second balloon was to the east. With characteristic foolhardiness Luke determined to withdraw by way of the other balloon and take one burst at it before the Huns reached him. He accordingly continued straight on east, thus permitting the pursuing formation of Fokkers to cut him off at the south.

With his first dive Luke shot down the second balloon. It burst into towering flames, which were seen for miles around. Again he passed through a living stream of missiles fired at him from the ground, and escaped unhurt!

As he began his flight towards home he discovered that he was completely cut off by the six Fokkers. He must shoot his way through single-handed. To make it worse, three more Fokkers were rapidly coming upon him from the north. And then Luke saw his pal, Wehrner.

Wehrner had all this time been patrolling the line to the north of Luke's balloons. He had seen the six Fokkers, but had supposed that Luke would keep ahead of them and abandon his attempt at the second enemy balloon. He therefore fired his signal light, which was observed by our balloon observers but not by

Luke, and immediately set off to patrol a parallel course between the enemy planes and Luke's road home. When he saw Luke dart off to the second balloon, Wehrner realized at once that Luke had not seen his signal and was unaware of the second flight of Fokkers coming directly upon him. He quickly sheered off and went forward to meet them.

What Luke saw was the aeroplane of his devoted pal receiving a direct fire from all three of the approaching Fokker pilots. The next instant it fell over in the air and slowly began to fall. Even as it hesitated in its flight, a burst of flames issued from the Spad's tank. Wehrner was shot down in flames while trying to save his comrade! It was a deliberate sacrifice of himself for his friend!

Completely consumed with fury, Luke, instead of seeking safety in flight, turned back and hurled himself upon the three Fokkers. He was at a distinct disadvantage, for they had the superiority both in altitude and position, not to mention numbers. But regardless as ever of what the chances were, Luke climbed upwards at them, firing as he advanced.

Picking out the pilot on the left, Luke kept doggedly on his track firing at him until he suddenly saw him burst into flame. The other two machines were in the meantime on Luke's tail and their tracer bullets were flashing unnoticed by his head. But as soon as he saw the end of his first enemy he made a quick renversement on number two and, firing as he came about, he shot down the second enemy machine with the first burst. The third piqued for Germany and Luke had to let him go.

All this fighting had consumed less time than it takes to tell it. The two Fokkers had fallen in flames within ten seconds of each other. With rage still in his heart Luke looked about him to discover where the six enemy machines had gone. They had apparently been satisfied to leave him with their three comrades, for they were now disappearing back towards the east. And just ahead of them Luke discerned fleecy white clouds of Archy smoke breaking north of Verdun. This indicated that our batteries were firing at enemy aeroplanes in that sector.

As he approached Verdun Luke found that five French Spads were hurrying up to attack an L. V. G. machine of the Huns, the same target at which our Archy had been firing. The six Fokkers had seen them coming and had gone to intercept them. Like a rocket Luke set his own Spad down at the L. V. G. It was a two-seater machine and was evidently taking photographs at a low altitude.

Our Archy ceased firing as Luke drew near. He hurled himself directly down at the German observer, firing both guns as he dove. The enemy machine fell into a vrille and crashed just a few hundred yards from our old Verdun aerodrome. In less than twenty minutes Lieutenant Luke had shot down two balloons, two fighting Fokkers and one enemy photographing machine — a feat that is almost unequaled in the history of this war!

Luke's first question when he arrived at our field was, " Has Wehrner come back? "

He knew the answer before he asked the question, but he was hoping against hope that he might find himself mistaken. But Wehrner had indeed been killed. The joy of Luke over his marvelous victories vanished instantly. He was told that with these five victories he had a total of eleven, thus passing me and making Luke the American Ace of Aces. But this fact did not interest him. He said he would like to go up to the front in a car and see if anything had been heard from Wehrner.

The following morning Major Hartney, Commanding Officer of our Group, took Luke and myself up to

Verdun to make inquiries. Shortly after lunch the officer in charge of confirmations came to us and told Lieutenant Luke that not only had his five victories of yesterday been officially confirmed, but that three old victories had likewise been that morning confirmed, making Luke's total fourteen instead of eleven. And these fourteen victories had been gained by Frank Luke in *eight days!* The history of war aviation, I believe, has not a similar record. Not even the famous Guynemer, Fonck, Ball, Bishop or the noted German Ace of Aces, Baron von Richthofen, ever won fourteen victories in a single fortnight at the front. Any air-craft, whether balloon or aeroplane, counts as one victory, and only one, with all the armies.

In my estimation there has never during the four years of war been an aviator at the front who possessed the confidence, ability and courage that Frank Luke had shown during that remarkable two weeks.

In order to do this boy honor and show him that every officer in the Group appreciated his wonderful work, he was given a complimentary dinner that night by the Squadrons. Many interesting speeches were made. When it came Luke's turn to respond he got up laughing, said he was having a bully time — and sat down! Major Hartney came over to him and presented him with a seven days' leave in Paris — which at that time was about the highest gift at the disposal of commanding officers at the front.

Among all the delightful entertainers who came over to the front from the United States to help cheer up the fighting men, none except our own Elsie Janis, who is an honorary member of our Squadron, were quite so highly appreciated by our fellows as the Margaret Mayo' Y. M. C. A. troup, which gave us an entertainment just a night or two after this. The players included such well known talent as Elizabeth Brice, Lois Meredith, Bill Morrisey, Tommy Gray and

Mr. Walker — all of New York. After a hurried preparation, we cleaned up one of the hangars, prepared a stage and made a dressing room by hanging a curtain over a truck and trailer. After a merry dinner in 94's mess hall everybody crowded into the "theater," and the way the boys laughed and shouted there, during the performance, must have sounded hysterical to the actors; but to my mind this hysteria was only an outlet for the pent-up emotion and an indication of the tension and strain under which we had so long been living. At any rate it was the best show I have ever seen at the front, barring always the one evening Miss Janis appeared on our aerodrome for an entertainment.

The night of September 24th, Major Marr returned from Paris and announced that he had received orders to return to America. Shortly afterward Major Hartney handed me an order promoting me to the Command of the 94 Squadron!

My pride and pleasure at receiving this great honor I cannot put into words. I had been with 94 since its first day at the front. I was a member of this, the very first organization to go over the lines. I had seen my old friends disappear and be replaced by other pilots whom I had learned to admire and respect. And many of these had in turn disappeared!

Now but three members of the original organization were left — Reed Chambers, Thorn Taylor and myself. And I had been given the honor of leading this distinguished Squadron! It had had Lufbery, Jimmy Hall and Dave Peterson as members. And it led all the rest in number of victories over the Huns.

But did it? I walked over to the Operations Office and took a look at the records. I had a suspicion that Frank Luke's wonderful run of the past few days had put 27 Squadron ahead of us.

My suspicions were quite correct. The sober fact

was that this presumptuous young 27 had suddenly taken a spurt, thanks to their brilliant Luke, and now led the Hat-in-the-Ring Squadron by six victories! I hurried over to 94 quarters and called together all my pilots.

The half hour we had together that evening firmly fixed a resolve in the aspirations of 94's members. No other American Squadron at the front would ever again be permitted to approach so near our margin of supremacy. From that hour every man in 94 Squadron, I believe, felt that the honor of his Squadron was at stake in this matter of bringing down Huns. At all events, within a week my pilots had overtaken 27's lead and never again did any American Squadron even threaten to overtop our lead.

After a talk that night with the pilots, I went over and called the mechanics to a caucus. We had half an hour's talk together and I outlined to them just what our pilots proposed to do with their help. And they understood that it was only by their wholesouled help that their Squadron's success would be possible. How nobly these boys responded to our appeal was well proved in the weeks that followed. Rarely indeed was a dud motor found in 94 Squadron henceforward. Never did a squadron of pilots receive more faithful attendance from their helpers in the hangar than was given us by these enthusiastic air mechanics of the Hat-in-the-Ring Squadron. I honestly believe that they felt the disgrace of being second more keenly than did we pilots.

Finally, I had a long and serious conference with myself that night. After I had gone to bed I lay awake for several hours, thinking over the situation. I was compelled to believe that I had been chosen Squadron Commander because, first, I had been more successful than the other pilots in bringing down enemy aeroplanes; and second, because I had the power to make a good leader over other pilots. That last proposition caused me infinite thought. Just how and wherein could I do the best by my followers?

I suppose every squadron leader has this same problem to decide, and I cannot help but believe that on his decision as to how he shall lead his pilots depends in a great measure the extent of his success — and his popularity.

To my mind there was but one procedure. I should never ask any pilot under me to go on a mission that I myself would not undertake. I would lead them by example as well as precept. I would accompany the new pilots and watch their errors and help them to feel more confidence by sharing their dangers. Above all, I would work harder than ever I did as mere pilot. There was no question about that. My days of loafing were over!

To avoid the red-tape business at the aerodrome — the making out of reports, ordering materials and seeing that they came in on time, looking after details of the mess, the hangars and the comfort of the enlisted men — all this work must be put under competent men, if I expected to stay in the air and lead patrols. Accordingly I gave this important matter my attention early next morning. And the success of my appointments was such that from that day to this I have never spent more than thirty minutes a day upon the ground business connected with 94's operations.

Full of this early enthusiasm I went up on a lone patrol the very first morning of my new responsibility, to see how much I had changed for the better or the worse.

Within half an hour I returned to the aerodrome with two more victories to my credit — the first double-header I had so far won!

CHAPTER XXVII

AN EVENTFUL "D" DAY

SEPTEMBER 25th, 1918, was my first day as Captain of 94 Squadron. Early that forenoon I started for the lines alone, flew over Verdun and Fort Douaumont, then turned east towards Etain. Almost immediately I picked up a pair of L. V. G. two-seater machines below me. They were coming out of Germany and were certainly bent upon an expedition over our lines. Five Fokker machines were above them and somewhat behind, acting as protection for the photographers until the lines were reached.

Climbing for the sun for all I was worth, I soon had the satisfaction of realizing that I had escaped their notice and was now well in their rear. I shut down my motor, put down my head and made a bee line for the nearest Fokker.

I was not observed by the enemy until it was too late for him to escape. I had him exactly in my sights when I pulled both triggers for a long burst. He made a sudden attempt to pull away, but my bullets were already ripping through his fusilage and he must have been killed instantly. His machine fell wildly away and crashed just south of Etain.

It had been my intention to zoom violently upwards and protect myself against the expected attack from the four remaining Fokkers as soon as I had finished the first man. But when I saw the effect of my attack upon the four dumbfounded Boches I instantly changed my tactics and plunged straight on through their formation to attack the photographing L. V. G.'s ahead. For the Heinies were so surprised by finding a Spad in their midst and seeing one of their number suddenly drop that the remaining three viraged to

right and left.   Their one idea was to escape and save
their own skins.   Though they did not actually pique
for home, they cleared a space large enough for me to
slip through and continue my dive upon the two-seaters
before they could recover their formation.

The two-seaters had seen my attack and had already
put down their heads to escape.   I plunged along after
them, getting the rear machine in my sights as I drew
nearer to him.   A glance back over my shoulder
showed me that the four Fokkers had not yet re-
formed their line and were even now circling about
with the purpose of again solidifying their formation.
I had a few seconds yet before they could begin their
attack.

The two L. V. G. machines began to draw apart.
Both observers in the rear seats were firing at me, although the range was still too long for accurate shooting.   I dove more steeply, passed out of the gunner's view under the nearest machine and zoomed
quickly up at him from below.   But the victory was
not to be an easy one.   The pilot suddenly kicked his
tail around, giving the gunner another good aim at
me.   I had to postpone shooting until I had more
time for my own aiming.   And in the meantime the
second photographing machine had stolen up behind
me and I saw tracer bullets go whizzing and streaking
past my face.   I zoomed up diagonally out of range,
made a renversement and came directly back at my
first target.

Several times we repeated these maneuvers, the four
Fokkers still wrangling among themselves about their
formation.   And all the time we were getting farther
and farther back into Germany.   I decided upon one
bold attack and if this failed I would get back to my
own lines before it was too late.

Watching my two adversaries closely, I suddenly
found an opening between them.   They were flying

parallel to each other and not fifty yards apart. Dropping down in a sideslip until I had one machine between me and the other I straightened out smartly, leveled my Spad and began firing. The nearest Boche passed directly through my line of fire and just as I ceased firing I had the infinite satisfaction of seeing him gush forth flames. Turning over and over as he fell the L. V. G. started a blazing path to earth just as the Fokker escort came tearing up to the rescue. I put on the gas and piqued for my own lines.

Pleased as I was over this double-header, the effect it might have upon my pilots was far more gratifying to me.

Arriving at the aerodrome at 9:30 I immediately jumped into a motorcar, called to Lieutenant Chambers to come with me and we set off at once to get official confirmation for this double victory. We took the main road to Verdun, passed through the town and gained the hills beyond the Meuse, towards Etain. Taking the road up to Fort de Tavannes we passed over that bloody battlefield of 1916 where so many thousand German troops fell before French fire in the memorable Battle for Verdun. At the very crest of the hill we were halted by a French poilu, who told us the rest of the road was in full view of the Germans and that we must go no farther.

We asked him as to whether he had seen my combat overhead this morning. He replied in the affirmative and added that the officers in the adjacent fort too had witnessed the whole fight through their field glasses. We thanked him and leaving our car under his care took our way on foot to the Fort.

Two or three hundred yards of shell-holes sprinkled th· ground between us and the Fort. We made our way through them, gained admittance to the interior of the Fort and in our best Pidgin French stated our errand to M. le Commandant. He immediately wrote

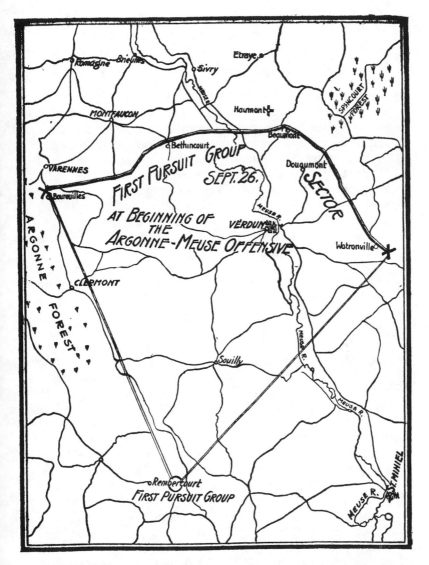

94 SQUADRON'S PATROL OF THE FRONT LINES FROM BOUREUILLES TO WATRONVILLE.

out full particulars of the combat I had had with the
L. V. G., signed it and congratulated me upon my victory with a warm shake of the hand.   Having no further business at this place, we made our adieus and
hastened back to our car.

Plunging through the shallowest shell-holes we had
traversed about half the distance to our car, which
stood boldly out on the top of the road, when a shrill
whining noise made us pause and listen.   The next
instant a heavy explosion announced that a shell had
landed about fifty yards short of us.   Simultaneously
with the shower of gravel and dirt which headed our
way we dropped unceremoniously on our faces in the
bottom of the deepest shell-hole in our vicinity.

The Huns had spotted our car and were actually
trying to get its range!

Two or three times we crawled out of our hole,
only to duck back at the signal of the next coming
shell.   After six or eight shots the Boche gunners
evidently considered their target too small, for they
ceased firing long enough for us to make a bolt across
the intervening holes and throw ourselves into the
waiting automobile.   I most fervently wished that
I had turned the car around before leaving it, and I
shall never forget the frightful length of time it took
me to get our car backed around and headed in the
right direction.   We lost no time in getting down that
hill.

Next day was to be an important one for us and
for the whole American Army.   Officially it was designated as "D" day and the "Zero hour," by the same
code, was set for four o'clock in the morning.   At that
moment the artillery barrage would begin and forty
thousand doughboys who were posted along the front
line trenches from the Meuse to the Argonne Forest
would go over the top.   It was the 26th day of September, 1918.

Precisely at four o'clock I was awakened by my
orderly who informed me that the weather was good.
Hastily getting out of doors, I looked over the dark
sky, wondering as I did so how many of our boys it
would claim before this day's work was done! For
we had an important part to play in this day's operations. Headquarters had sent us orders to attack all
the enemy observation balloons along that entire front
this morning and to continue the attacks until the
infantry's operations were completed. Accordingly
every fighting squadron had been assigned certain of
these balloons for attack and it was our duty to see
that they were destroyed. The safety of thousands of
our attacking soldiers depended upon our success in
eliminating these all-watching eyes of the enemy. Incidentally, it was the first balloon strafing party that
94 Squadron had been given since I had been made
its leader and I desired to make a good showing on
this first expedition.

Just here it may be well to point out the difficulties
of balloon strafing, which make this undertaking so
unattractive to the new pilot.

German " Archy " is terrifying at first acquaintance.
Pilots affect a scorn for it, and indeed at high altitudes
the probabilities of a hit are small. But when attacking a balloon which hangs only 1,500 feet above
the guns (and this altitude is of course known precisely to the anti-aircraft gunner) Archy becomes far
more dangerous.

So when a pilot begins his first balloon attacking
expeditions, he knows that he runs a gauntlet of fire
that may be very deadly. His natural impulse is to
make a nervous plunge into the zone of danger, fire
his bullets, and get away. Few victories are won with
this method of attack.

The experienced balloon strafers, particularly such
daring airmen as Coolidge and Luke, do not consider

the risks or terrors about them. They proceed in the attack as calmly as though they were sailing through a stormless sky. Regardless of flaming missiles from the ground, they pass through the defensive barrage of fire, and often return again and again, to attack the target, until it finally bursts into flame from their incendiary bullets.

The office charts informed me that day would break this morning at six o'clock. Consequently we must be ready to leave the ground in our machines at 5:20, permitting us thirty minutes in which to reach our objectives, and ten minutes in which to locate our individual balloons. For it is essential to strike at these well defended targets just at the edge of dawn. Then the balloons are just starting aloft, and our attacking aeroplanes are but scantily visible from below. Moreover enemy aeroplanes are not apt to be about so early in the morning, unless the enemy has some inkling of what is going on.

I routed out five of my best pilots, Lieutenants Cook, Chambers, Taylor, Coolidge and Palmer; and as we gathered together for an early breakfast, we went over again all the details of our pre-arranged plans. We had two balloons assigned to our Squadron, and three of us were delegated to each balloon. Both lay along the Meuse between Brabant and Dun. Every one of us had noted down the exact location of his target on the evening before. It would be difficult perhaps to find them before daylight if they were still in their nests, but we were to hang about the vicinity until we did find them, if it took all day. With every man fully posted on his course and objective, we put on our coats and walked over to the hangars.

I was the last to leave the field, getting off the ground at exactly 5:20. It was still dark and we had to have the searchlights turned onto the field for a moment to see the ground while we took off. As soon as we lifted into the darkness the lights were extinguished. And then I saw the most marvelous sight that my eyes have ever seen.

A terrific barrage of artillery fire was going on ahead of me. Through the darkness the whole western horizon was illumined with one mass of sudden flashes. The big guns were belching out their shells with such rapidity that there appeared to be millions of them shooting at the same time. Looking back I saw the same scene in my rear. From Lunéville on the east to Rheims on the west there was not one spot of darkness along the whole front. The French were attacking along both our flanks at the same time with us in order to help demoralize the weakening Boche. The picture made me think of a giant switchboard which emitted thousands of electric flashes as invisible hands manipulated the plugs.

So fascinated did I become over this extraordinary fireworks display that I was startled upon peering over the side of my machine to discover the city of Verdun below my aeroplane's wings. Fastening my course above the dim outline of the Meuse River I followed its windings down stream, occasionally cutting across little peninsulas which I recognized along the way. Every inch of this route was as familiar to me as was the path around the corner of my old home. I knew exactly the point in the Meuse Valley where I would leave the river and turn left to strike the spot where my balloon lay last night. I did not know what course the other pilots had taken. Perhaps they had already —

Just as these thoughts were going through my mind I saw directly ahead of me the long snaky flashes of enemy tracer bullets from the ground piercing the sky. There was the location of my balloon and either Cook or Chambers was already attacking it. The enemy had discovered them and were putting up the usual hail of flaming projectiles around the balloon site.

But even as the flaming bullets continued streaming upwards I saw a gigantic flame burst out in their midst! One of the boys had destroyed his gas-bag!

Even before the glare of the first had died I saw our second enemy balloon go up in flames. My pilots had succeeded beyond my fondest expectations. Undoubtedly the enemy would soon be swinging new balloons up in their places, but we must wait awhile for that. I resolved to divert my course and fly further to the north where I knew of the nest of another German observation balloon near Damvillers.

Dawn was just breaking as I headed more to the east and tried to pick out the location of Damvillers. I was piercing the gloom with my eyes when again — straight in front of my revolving propeller I saw another gush of flame which announced the doom of another enemy balloon — the very one I had determined to attack. While I was still jubilating over the extraordinary good luck that had attended us in this morning's expedition, I glanced off to my right and was almost startled out of my senses to discover that a German Fokker was flying alongside me not a hundred yards away! Not expecting any of the enemy aeroplanes to be abroad at this early hour, I was naturally upset for the moment. The next instant I saw that he had headed for me and was coming straight at my machine. We both began firing at the same time. It was still so dark that our four streams of flaming bullets cut brilliant lines of fire through the air. For a moment it looked as though our two machines were tied together with four ropes of fire. All my ammunition was of the incendiary variety for use against gas-bags. The Hun's ammunition was part tracer, part incendiary and part regular chunks of lead.

As we drew nearer and nearer I began to wonder whether this was to be a collision or whether he

would get out of my way.   He settled the question by
tipping down his head to dive under me.   I instantly
made a renversement which put me close behind him
and in a most favorable position for careful aim.
Training my sights into the center of his fusilage I
pulled both triggers.   With one long burst the fight
was over.   The Fokker fell over onto one wing and
dropped aimlessly to earth.   It was too dark to see
the crash, and moreover I had all thoughts of my victory dissipated by a sudden ugly jerk to my motor
which immediately developed into a violent vibration.
As I turned back towards Verdun, which was the nearest point to our lines, I had recurring visions of crashing down into Germany to find myself a prisoner.
This would be a nice ending to our glorious balloon
expedition!

Throttling down to reduce the pounding I was able
just to maintain headway.   If my motor failed completely I was most certainly doomed, for I was less
than a thousand feet above ground and could glide but
a few hundred yards without power.   Providence was
again with me, for I cleared the lines and made our
Verdun aerodrome where one flight of the 27th Squadron was housed.   I landed without damage and hastily
climbed out of my machine to investigate the cause of
my trouble.

Imagine my surprise when I discovered that one
blade of my propeller had been shot in two by my late
adversary!   He had evidently put several holes
through it when he made his head-on-attack.   And
utterly unconscious of the damage I had received, I
had reversed my direction and shot him down before
the weakened blade gave way!   The heavy jolting of
my engine was now clear to me — only half of the
propeller caught the air.

Lieutenant Jerry Vasconcelles of Denver, Colorado,
was in charge of the Verdun field on which I had

landed. He soon came out and joined me as I was staring at my broken propeller. And then I learned that he had just landed himself from a balloon expedition. A few questions followed and then we shook hands spontaneously. He had shot down the Damvillers balloon himself — the same one for which I had been headed. And as he was returning he had seen me shoot down my Fokker! This was extremely lucky for both of us, for we were able each to verify the other's victory for him, although of course corroboration from ground witnesses was necessary to make these victories official.

His mechanics placed a new propeller on my Spad, and none the worse for its recent rough usage the little 'bus took me rapidly home. I landed at 8:30 on my own field. And there I heard great news. Our Group had that morning shot down ten German balloons! My victory over the Fokker made it eleven victories to be credited us for this hour's work. And we had not lost a single pilot!

As the jubilant and famished pilots crowded into the mess hall one could not hear a word through all the excited chatter. Each one had some strange and fearful adventure to relate about his morning's experiences. But the tale which aroused howls of laughter was the droll story told by Lieutenant White of the 147th Squadron.

White had searched long and earnestly for the balloon that he desired to attack. He thought himself hopelessly lost in the darkness, when off to one side he distinguished the dark outline of what he thought was his balloon. Immediately redressing his machine he tipped downwards and began plugging furious streams of flaming bullets into his target. He made a miscalculation in his distance and before he could swerve away from the dark mass ahead of him his machine had plunged straight through it!

And then he discovered that he had been piquing upon a round puff of black smoke that had just been made by a German Archy!

CHAPTER XXVIII

FRANK LUKE STRAFES HIS LAST BALLOON

NEITHER side could afford to leave its lines undefended by observation balloons for a longer period than was necessary for replacements. Our onslaught of the early morning had destroyed so many of the Huns' Drachen, however, that it was quite impossible for them to get new balloons up at once, along their entire sector.

That same afternoon I flew along their lines to see what progress they were making in replacements of their observation posts. The only balloon I could discover in our sector was one which lifted its head just behind the town of Sivry-sur-Meuse. I made a note of its position and decided to try to bring it down early next morning.

Accordingly I was up again at the same hour the following day and again found the sky promised clear weather. Leaving the field at 5:30, I again took a course over Verdun in order to pick up the Meuse River there and follow it as a guide.

On this occasion I caught a grand view of No Man's Land as seen from the air by night. It was not yet daylight when I reached the lines and there I caught a longitudinal view of the span of ground that separated the two opposing armies. For upon both sides of this span of ground a horizontal line of flashes could be seen issuing from the mouths of rival guns. The German batteries were drawn up along their front scarcely a mile back of their line. And

on our side a vastly more crowded line of flashes indicated the overwhelming superiority in numbers of
guns that the American artillerymen were using to
belabor the already vanquished Huns. So far as my
eye could reach, this dark space lay outlined between
the two lines of living fire. It was a most spectacular
sight. I followed down its course for a few miles,
then turned again to the north and tried to find the
Meuse River.

After ten minutes' flight into Germany, I realized
I had crossed the river before I began to turn north
and that I must be some distance inside the enemy's
lines. I dropped down still lower as I saw the outlines of a town in front of me and circling above it
I discovered that I had penetrated some 25 miles inside Hunland and was now over the village of Stenay.
I had overshot Sivry by about twenty miles.

I lost no time in heading about towards France.
Opening up the throttle, I first struck west and followed
this course until I had the Meuse River again under
my nose. Then turning up the river, I flew just above
the road which follows along its banks. It was now
getting light enough to distinguish objects on the
ground below.

This Meuse River highway is a lovely drive to take
in the daytime, for it passes through a fertile and
picturesque country. The little city of Dun-sur-
Meuse stands out on a small cliff which juts into a
bend of the river, making a most charming picture of
what a medieval town should look like. I passed directly down Main Street over Dun-sur-Meuse and
again picked up the broad highway that clung to the
bank of the river. Occasional vehicles were now
abroad below me. Day had broken and the Huns were
up and ready for work.

It occurred to me that I might as well fly a bit lower
and entertain the passing Huns with a little bullet-

dodging as we met each other. My morning's work was spoiled anyway. It was becoming too late to take on a balloon now. Perhaps I might meet a general in his automobile and it would be fun to see him jump for the ditch and throw himself down on his face at the bottom. If I was fortunate enough to get him that would surely be helping along the war!

Ahead of me I saw a truck moving slowly in the same direction I was going. " Here goes for the first one! " I said to myself. I tipped down the nose of my machine and reached for my triggers.

As my nose went down something appeared over my top wing which took away my breath for an instant. There directly in my path was a huge enemy observation balloon! It was swaying in the breeze and the cable which held it to earth ran straight down until it reached the moving truck ahead of me. Then it became clear as daylight to me. The Huns were towing a new balloon up the road to its position for observation! They had just received a replacement from the supply station of Dun-sur-Meuse, and after filling it with gas were now getting it forward as rapidly as possible. It was just the target I had been searching for!

Forgetting the truck and crew, I flattened out instantly and began firing at the swaying monster in the air. So close to it had I come before I saw it that I had only time to fire a burst of fifty shots when I was forced to make a vertical virage, to avoid crashing through it. I was then but four or five hundred feet above ground.

Just as I began the virage I heard the rat-tat-tat-tat of a machine-gun fire from the truck on the road beneath me. And mingled with this drum fire I heard the sound of an explosion in the fusilage just behind my ear! One of their explosive bullets had come very close to my head and had exploded against a longeron or wire in the tail of the aeroplane! There was nothing I could do about that however, except to fly along as steadily as possible until I reached a place of safety and could make an investigation of the damage received. I cleared the side of the gas-bag and then as I passed I turned and looked behind me.

The enemy balloon was just at the point of exploding and the observer had already leaped from his basket and was still dropping through air with his parachute not yet opened. It was a very short distance to Mother Earth, and sometimes a parachute needs two or three hundred feet fall in which to fully open and check the swiftness of the falling body. I wondered whether this poor chap had any chance for his life in that short distance and just what bones he was likely to break when he landed. And then came a great burst of fire, as the whole interior of the big balloon became suddenly ignited. I couldn't resist one shout of exultation at the magnificent display of fireworks I had thus set off, hoping in the meantime that its dull glare would reach the eyes of some of our own balloon observers across the lines who would thus be in a position to give me the confirmation of my eleventh victory.

Again I decided to pay a call at Jerry Vasconcelle's field at Verdun and there get out and ascertain the extent of the damage in the tail of my Spad. Jerry welcomed me with some amusement and wanted to know whether this dropping in on him was to be a daily occurrence. Yesterday it had been a broken prop and to-day a broken tail. Before answering him I got out, and together we made a minute examination of my machine.

A neat row of bullet holes ran back down the tail of my machine. They were as nicely spaced as if they had been put in by careful measurement. The first hole was about four inches back of the pad on which my head rests when I am in the seat. The others were directly back of it at regular intervals. One, the explosive bullet, had struck the longeron that runs the length of the fusilage, and this had made the sharp explosion that I had heard at the time. The gunners on the truck had done an excellent bit of shooting!

None of the holes were in a vital part of the machine. I took off the field after a short inspection and soon covered the fifteen or sixteen miles that lay between the Verdun field and our own.

Upon landing I found very bad news awaiting me.

On the previous afternoon Lieutenant Sherry and Lieutenant Nutt, both of 94 Squadron, had gone out on patrol and had failed to come in. Long after dark their mechanics remained on the field pooping up Very lights, in the hope that they might still be searching about, trying to find their way. At last we abandoned all hope ourselves and waited for the morning's news from outside sources.

Now it had arrived and to my great joy it was in the form of a telephone call from old " Madam " Sherry himself. But his next message informed us that Nutt had been killed in combat! And Sherry himself had been through an experience that might easily have turned one's hair gray. Just before lunch time Sherry came in by automobile and told us the story of his experiences.

He and Nutt had attacked an overwhelming formation of eight Fokker machines. They had stolen up on the Heinies and counted upon getting one or two victims before the others were aware of their presence. But the attack failed and suddenly both American pilots were having the fight of their lives. The Hun pilots were not only skilful and experienced, but they worked together with such nicety that Sherry and Nutt were unable either to hold their own or to escape.

Soon each was fighting a separate battle against four enemy machines. Sherry saw Nutt go crashing down and later learned that he had been shot through the heart and killed in air. A moment later Sherry's machine received several bullets in the motor which put it immediately out of commission. Dropping swiftly to earth, Sherry saw that the Hun pilots were not taking any chances but were determined to kill him as he fell.

He was two miles and more in the air when he began his forced descent. All the way down the enemy pilots pursued him, firing through his machine continuously as it glided smoothly towards earth. Only by miracles a dozen times repeated did he escape death from their bullets. He saw the lines below him and made desperate efforts to glide his machine to our side of the fence despite the furious attempts of the Boches to prevent this escape. At last he crashed in one of the million shell-holes that covered No Man's Land of last week. His machine turned over and broke into a score of fragments, Sherry being thrown some yards away where he landed unhurt at the bottom of another shell-hole.

While he was still pinching himself to make sure he was actually unhurt he discovered his implacable enemies piquing upon him with their Fokkers and firing long bursts of bullets into his shell-hole with their machine-guns!

Sherry clung as closely to the sides of his hole as he could and watched the dirt fly up all around him as the Fokkers made dive after dive at him. It must have been like watching a file of executioners leveling their guns at one and firing dozens of rounds without hitting one. Except that in Sherry's case, it was machine-guns that were doing the firing!

Finally the Fokkers made off for Germany. Crawling out of his hole, Sherry discovered that a formation of Spads had come to his rescue and had chased the Germans homewards. And then he began to wonder on which side of the trenches he had fallen. For he had been too busy dodging Fokkers to know where his crippled machine was taking him.

One can imagine Sherry's joy when he heard a doughboy in perfectly good United States yell from a neighboring shell-hole: —

"Hey, guy! Where the h—'s your gas-mask?"

Madam didn't care for the moment whether he had a gas-mask or not, so glad was he to learn that he had fallen among friends and was still in the land of the living.

He quickly tumbled into the next shell-hole, where he found his new friend. The latter informed him that he was still in No Man's Land, that the German infantry were but a hundred yards away and that gas shells had been coming across that space all the afternoon. He even gave Madam his own gas-mask and his pistol, saying he guessed he was more used to gas than an aviator would be! He advised Sherry to lay low where he was until nightfall, when he would see him back into our lines. And thus Lieutenant Sherry spent the next few hours reviewing the strange episodes that flavor the career of an aviator.

Sherry finished his story with a grim recital of what had occurred when they went out next morning to recover Nutt's body. It too had fallen in No Man's Land, but the Americans had advanced a few hundred yards during the night and now covered the spot where Nutt's body lay. Sherry accompanied a squad of doughboys out to the spot where Nutt's smashed machine had lain during the night. They found poor Nutt, as I have said, with several bullets through the heart.

They extricated the body from the wreckage and were beginning to dig a grave when a shot from a hidden Hun sniper struck one of the burial party in the foot. The others jumped to their guns and disappeared through the trees. They soon returned with a look of savage satisfaction on their faces, although Sherry had not heard a shot fired. While they continued their work he strolled off in the direction from which they had returned.

Behind a trench dugout he found the German sniper who had had the yellowness to fire upon a burial party. The man's head was crushed flat with the butts of the doughboys' guns! * * * * *

" Frank Luke, the marvelous balloon strafer of the 27th, did not return last night! "

So reads the last entry in my flight diary of September 29, 1918. Re-reading that line brings back to me the common anxiety of the whole Group over the extraordinary and prolonged absence of their most popular member. For Luke's very mischievousness and irresponsibility made every one of us feel that he must be cared for and nursed back into a more disciplined way of fighting — and flying — and living. His escapades were the talk of the camp and the despair of his superior officers. Fully a month after his disappearance his commanding officer, Alfred Grant, Captain of the 27th Squadron, told me that if Luke ever did come back he would court-martial him first and then recommend him for the Legion of Honor!

In a word, Luke mingled with his disdain for bullets a very similar distaste for the orders of his superior officers. When imperative orders were given him to come immediately home after a patrol Luke would unconcernedly land at some French aerodrome miles away, spend the night there and arrive home after dark the next night. But as he almost invariably landed with one or two more enemy balloons to his credit, which he had destroyed on the way home, he was usually let off with a reprimand and a caution not to repeat the offense.

As blandly indifferent to reprimands as to orders, Luke failed to return again the following night. This studied disobedience to orders could not be ignored, and thus Captain Grant had stated that if Luke ever did return he must be disciplined for his insubordination. The night of September 27th Luke spent the night with the French Cigognes on the Toul aerodrome.

The last we had heard from Luke was that at six o'clock on the night of September 28th he left the French field where he had spent the night, and flying low over one of the American Balloon Headquarters he circled over their heads until he had attracted the attention of the officers, then dropped them a brief note which he had written in his aeroplane. As may well be imagined, Luke was a prime favorite with our Balloon Staff. All the officers of that organization worshiped the boy for his daring and his wonderful successes against the balloon department of their foes. They appreciated the value of balloon observation to the enemy and knew the difficulties and dangers in attacking these well-defended posts.

Running out and picking up the streamer and sheet of paper which fell near their office they unfolded the latter and read:

" Look out for enemy balloon at D-2 and D-4 positions.— Luke."

Already Luke's machine was disappearing in the direction of the first balloon which lay just beyond the Meuse. It was too dark to make out its dim outline at this distance, but as they all gathered about the front of their " office " they glued their eyes to the spot where they knew it hung. For Luke had notified them several times previously as to his intended victims and every time they had been rewarded for their watching.

Two minutes later a great red glow lit up the northwestern horizon and before the last of it died away the second German balloon had likewise burst into flames! Their intrepid hero had again fulfilled his promise! They hastened into their headquarters and called up our operations officer and announced Frank Luke's last two victories. Then we waited for Luke to make his dramatic appearance.

But Luke never came! That night and the next day we rather maligned him for his continued absence, supposing naturally enough that he had returned to his French friends for the night. But when no news of him came to us, when repeated inquiries elicited no information as to his movements after he had brought down his last balloon, every man in the Group became aware that we had lost the greatest airman in our army. From that day to this not one word of reliable information has reached us concerning Luke's disappearance. Not a trace of his machine was ever found! Not a single clue to his death and burial was ever obtained from the Germans! Like Guynemer, the miraculous airman of France, Frank Luke was swallowed by the skies and no mortal traces of him remain!

CHAPTER XXIX

A NIGHT-MISSION

AVIATORS are conscious of an antagonistic feeling towards them in the minds of the infantrymen in the trenches who, covered with mud and trench insects, frequently overworked and underslept and always facing imminent death from enemy's bullets, find an ironic pleasure in contrasting their hard lot with the life of ease and excitement led by the young officers of the flying corps.

To see an aeroplane cavorting about over their heads fills them with bitterness at the thought that these well dressed men are getting paid for that pleasant sport, while they are forced to work like beasts of burden in the rain. Infantry officers have told me that rarely have they seen an American aeroplane over them when it was needed to chase away enemy machines, and that Huns repeatedly came over them at low altitudes strafing the troops with machine-gun fire, to their great injury and demoralization.

It is not difficult to understand this bitterness under the circumstances. Much of this feeling might be cleared away, however, if the infantrymen realized that while enemy machines are strafing them, our airmen are retaliating probably twofold upon the enemy troops beyond the lines. Every day our machines were engaged in this hazardous work of trench strafing. Much of the success of our infantry advances was due to the cooperation of our air forces behind the front and beyond the vision of our doughboys in the trenches. Admitting as they do the disastrous effect of aeroplane attacks upon their own lines, they can easily imagine how terrified their enemy infantrymen became at the daily appearance of our fighting planes in their midst.

As to the comparative risks of injury in these two arms of warfare, I believe even the most skeptical doughboy would admit after reflection that an airman's daily duties surround him every moment with the possibilities of death. Comfort and dress, entertainments and good food are all in our favor, of course. But I have yet to meet a pilot of any nation at war who does not try to balance this advantage with a whole-souled admiration and praise of his less fortunate brother-in-arms, who does so much more than his share of the " dirty work."

Much of this jealousy and misunderstanding is due

to the fact that the man on the ground can never see and never know anything of the things the airman is doing for him. It is a pity that such must be the case, for, while rivalry between different branches of the Army may be beneficial, bitterness is not.

While sitting at dinner about sundown on the evening of September 30th, discussing the latest victory claimed that afternoon by Lieutenant Kaye and Lieutenant Reed Chambers who had destroyed a Fokker aeroplane over Romaigne, an orderly brought me a note from the C. O. of the Group, requesting me to select two volunteers for a most important mission and report at Headquarters with them forthwith. It was then 6:30 and quite dark.

We were naturally excited at this sudden summons and I wondered what extraordinary necessity called for aeroplanes at this late hour. I selected Ham Coolidge and Wierd Cook out of the men who volunteered for this unknown mission, and setting off with our flying kit in our hands we hastened over to Major Hartney's office.

There to our great surprise we found General Mitchell impatiently pacing the floor while awaiting our coming. He immediately welcomed us and began at once to explain the object of our hurried summons.

Our troops were at that time engaged in the attack on Montfaucon and were advancing up the ten-mile valley that runs between the edge of the Argonne Forest and the Meuse River. Montfaucon occupied the crest of the loftiest hill in this valley and was situated almost in its exact center. From this favorable spot the Crown Prince of Germany had viewed the battles for Verdun and the country to the south during those fierce days of 1916. Later I visited the massive headquarters of the Crown Prince and marveled at the extensive view of the surrounding landscape one obtained from this site.

For four days our doughboys had flung themselves courageously upon the well prepared defenses of the enemy along this valley. Costly gains were made and valuable territory was slowly yielded to our victorious troops by the Germans. Between the old line and the new line from Grand Pré to the Meuse two different American Divisions named the defile through which they had separately fought, "Death" Valley. From their superior heights beyond the Meuse the enemy artillery swept their roads with a pitiless hail of shrapnel. An occasional rush was made by isolated regiments of our men, which gained them the shelter of intervening hills. And thus just under the crest of Montfaucon our aeroplanes had discovered a body of several thousand American doughboys who had been marooned for thirty-six hours, entirely without food or ammunition, except the small supply they had carried in with them. A thick curtain artillery fire had been placed behind them by the enemy, cutting all the roads in several places and rendering even a retreat difficult.

Major Hartney had already discussed with our Group Captains the advisability of carrying food to these troops by aeroplane on the morrow. The Army Headquarters expected confidently that they would be able to break through to the relief of these starving troops during the night. If this failed we should devote ourselves to their victualing by aeroplane, beginning at daybreak.

And now General Mitchell had motored over to impart to us some startling news. The Army Intelligence Bureau had reported that eleven troop trains had left Metz at noon carrying to the Montfaucon front the famous Prussian Guard for an attack upon our entrapped doughboys. Immediate confirmation of this fact was desired, and late as it was, aeroplanes were the only means of obtaining this confirmation and they must be sent. Owing to the darkness the flight would be an extremely hazardous one and only experienced pilots should be permitted to go. The searchlight would throw its beam up into the night during the entire time we were away and we should be able to see its signal for many miles within Germany. It was imperative that the aviators should know the location of all the railway lines leading to the front from Metz and likewise necessary that they should succeed with their mission and return safely with the desired information. He would not order any individual to go, but would be pleased to have two volunteers.

I replied that every man in the 94th Squadron was anxious to go. I had selected Coolidge and Cook as two of my best men and both were not only familiar with the enemy railroad lines but could find their way home if anybody could.

"Very well," said the General. "Strike the main railroad line on the Meuse, follow it up as far as Stenay and from there go to Montmédy and on to Metz. Note carefully every moving thing on that route if you have to fly as low as the treetops. Locate the time and the place of every train, how many cars it has, which way it is headed and the nature of its load, if you can. I will wait here until you return."

Three would be better than two, I thought to myself as I accompanied Cook and Coolidge out to their machines. I saw them off and then ordered the mechanics to run out my Spad. A few minutes later I taxied down the field, turned and headed for our row of signal lights. The motor roared as I opened up my throttle and sped swiftly back for a take-off. The tail lifted, the wheels skimmed the ground, then cleared it, and slightly elevating the controls I saw the ground lights disappearing under my lower wing.

Above all was blackness. Away to the north fitful flashes of fire dotted the ground. Over my head our aerodrome searchlight cut a yellow slice of ever widening sky, until it lost itself among the stars. Several other searchlights were also playing about the heavens. I noted carefully the angle ours made with the horizon so that I should recognize it from any distance.

" How are those boys faring to-night, I wonder? " thought I to myself as I flew at a 500-foot level over the marooned doughboys' heads. For I had left Verdun to my right and was on a route straight over Montfaucon. I must have passed over the marching thousands who were advancing under cover of the night to get a favorable position for the next day's work. On the roads below me I saw occasional lights where bridges were being stealthily repaired and shell-holes refilled with earth and rock by our engineers. So congested were these roads and so badly torn by the enemy's fire that our supplies could not be brought up fast enough to keep our front line going. Our own artillery was well advanced but had no shells to fire! Even during the pauses in the enemy's barrage no food could be taken to those regiments that were cut off, because the roads had been almost obliterated by the bursting shells of the enemy.

Later on I heard of the herculean efforts made by our Engineer Corps to repair these roads by night. Enlisted men were sent up from miles behind the lines to assist in this emergency. Even one elderly Colonel, who happened along and discovered the situation, took the post of an able-bodied Military policeman and ordered the younger man to work on the roads. And all through the night the German shells continued to drop in their midst, undoing their frantic construction and killing many of the workers in the process.

Against this point the Prussian Guards were coming for an attack! I wondered how Headquarters got that information and how the Huns knew we were in such a bad situation in Death Valley! Aeroplanes,

probably, had brought the information to both sides.
Grimly I assured myself that aeroplanes would prevent some of the Prussians from ever reaching their
objective, if we should discover their coming this night.

Turning east I soon discerned the Meuse River shining in the starlight, and following its course at three
or four hundred feet above its surface I flew on deeper
and deeper into hostile territory. Barring motor
failure, I had little to fear. No enemy searchlights
appeared ahead of me and so far as I know not a bullet
was fired at me. There is a distinctive sound to the
Hispano-Suiza motor that should have betrayed its
nationality to any attentive Hun ear familiar with aeroplane engines, but despite this fact and the low altitude at which I was compelled to fly to find my way,
my passing seemed to arouse no interest. Soon I
passed the wide lagoons of Mouzay and realized that
I was almost forty miles behind our lines. And there
between me and the next town of Stenay I saw the
glare of an engine box on the tracks ahead of me.
Dropping still lower down, I prepared to count the
coaches as they passed under me when I discovered it
was only a short freight train which was proceeding
away from the front instead of towards it. Paying no
further attention to its progress, I continued along over
the tracks until I reached the station at Stenay. Back
and forth over the sidings and switches I flew, one
eye upon the dusky ground and one in the direction of
the enemy aerodrome which I well knew occupied the
hilltop just east of the town. No unusual aggregation
of railroad cars were on the tracks and no activity
whatever in railroad circles appeared doing in Stenay
this night. Picking up the main line to Montmédy,
I cast one more glance behind me at the Fokker aerodrome and faded away into the night unpursued.

Over Montmédy ten minutes later I found one train
going towards Stenay and one towards Metz, but

neither was a troop train. No other coaches whatever
occupied the sidings. I began to think that Intelligence Bureaus might sometimes be mistaken, and in
spite of myself I felt a little disappointed. For I had
an extra supply of machine-gun ammunition with me
and had pictured to myself the amount of damage one
small aeroplane might do to the gentlemen of the
Prussian Guard inside the windows of their troop
trains. All the way along the main line from Montmédy to Metz I hoped rather than feared that I would
meet the expected guests of the evening. But I was
doomed to disappointment. The nearer to Metz I got
the more I realized that if their trains had left Metz
at noon, as advertised, they must certainly have reached
or passed Montmédy by now. I was absolutely positive that not a single coach had slipped under me unnoticed, for most of the way along I had flown scarcely
high enough to clear the telegraph wires that occasionally crossed the tracks.

Glancing at my compass I swung off to the right and
left the tracks. It was quite evident that the Prussian
Guards scare was a false alarm. In five minutes I
should be over Verdun.

Ten minutes passed — and then twenty, and still
no Verdun. If I had been misled by my compass and
had kept too far to the west — even so I should have
crossed the Meuse long ago. I leaned over and shook
the compass. It whirled a few times, then settled
itself in exactly the opposite direction! Again I shook
it and again it pointed to a new direction. Never have
I seen a compass — except those captured from Boche
machines — that even pretended to disclose the direction of north! Mingled with my rage was a fear that
was getting almost panicky. I searched the horizon
for our searchlight but not one was in sight. Thinking I might be in ground mist I rose higher and circling about scanned the horizon and blackness below.

Not even the flash of a gun that might direct me to the battlefront was visible!

Three-quarters of an hour of gasoline remained to me. And a much over-rated sense of direction — and no compass. Then I thought of the north star! Glory be! There she shines! I had been going west instead of south and would have had two hundred miles or so of fast flying before striking the British lines near Ypres on my present course. Keeping the star behind my rudder I flew south for fifteen minutes, then dropping down, almost immediately found myself above a bend in a stream of water that resembled a familiar spot in the River Meuse. With a sudden return of self-confidence I followed the river until I struck Verdun — picked up our faithful searchlight and ten minutes later I landed safely below the row of lights that marked the edge of our aerodrome.

My mechanics assured me that both Coolidge and Cook had returned. Hastening to the operations office I made my report that no Hun trains were coming our way, which General Mitchell received with a simple, "Thank God!" The next day our advancing troops caught up with the marooned doughboys and sent them for a much deserved rest to the rear.

As I walked across the field to my bed I looked up and recognized my friend the North Star shining in my face. I raised my cap and waved her a salute and repeated most fervently, "Thank God!"

On the following day, which was October 1st, a large formation of 94 pilots crossed the lines and cruised about for nearly two hours in German lines without a fight. We scared up one covey of Fokkers, but were unable to get them within range.

Changing machines, I went back alone late in the afternoon and hung about the lines until it began to grow dusk. I had spotted a German balloon down on the ground back of the Three-Fingered Lake and was convinced that it would be inadequately guarded since it was not doing duty and was supposed to be hidden from view. Sure enough, when I arrived at its hiding place I found no anti-aircraft gunners there to molest me. It was too easy a job to be called a victory, for I merely poked down my nose, fired a hundred rounds or so and the job was done. The balloon caught fire without any coaxing and I calmly flew on my way homewards without molestation.

Without molestation, that is, from the enemy. I turned back across our lines at Vigneulles and there on our own side of the trenches I met the attention of two searchlights and a furious barrage of flaming projectiles from our own guns. The latter all passed well behind my tail, as I could see them plainly leaving the ground and could trace their entire progress in my direction. The American gunners had not had the long experience of the Hun Archy experts and I saw at a glance that they were all aiming directly at my machine instead of the proper distance ahead of me. Their aim was so bad that I did not even feel indignant at their over-zealousness. Later I learned that this area was forbidden to our aeroplanes and the gunners there had been ordered to shoot at everything that passed overhead after dark.

My successful expedition against the balloon was known at the aerodrome when I arrived. The glare of its fire had been seen on the field and later telephonic reports from our observing posts duly confirmed its destruction.

That night around the mess one of the boys read aloud from the Paris *Herald* that the British Independent Air Force had sent a large formation of planes over Cologne-on-the-Rhine the night before and had dropped hundreds of heavy bombs into the city.

Jimmy Meissner, the Captain of 147 Squadron was with us, paying a visit to the old Squadron that he has always considered his own. Jimmy appeared to be pondering deeply over the reading of this particular news. When it was finished he exclaimed: —

"Gee Whiz! I hope they didn't kill my aunt! She lives in Cologne!"

For a moment everybody looked at Jimmy in astonishment. Then we roared with laughter. Jimmy Meissner, with his German name and his aunt in Cologne, had shot down eight enemy aeroplanes! How many such anomalies must have amused our mess halls now that American soldiers of German ancestry found themselves fighting against the former fatherland of their grandfathers.

CHAPTER XXX

A DAY'S WORK — SIX VICTORIES

WITH the beginning of October, 94 Squadron took on a new phase of air fighting. We were taken away from the General Orders affecting the 1st Pursuit Wing and were delegated to patrol the lines at low altitude — not exceeding 2,000 feet. This meant serious business to us, for not only would we be under more severe Archy fire, but we would be an easy target for the higher Hun formations, who could pique down upon us at their own pleasure.

These new orders were intended to provide a means of defense against the low-flying enemy machines which came over our lines. Usually they were protected by fighting machines. Rarely did they attempt to penetrate to any considerable distance back of No Man's Land. They came over to follow the lines and see what we were doing on our front, leaving to their high-flying photographic machines the inspection of our rear.

On October 2nd Reed Chambers led out the first patrol under these new orders. He had five machines with him and I went along on a voluntary patrol, to see how the new scheme was going to work out. In order to act somewhat in a protective capacity, I took a higher level and followed them back and forth over their beat at 2,000 feet or more above them.

The course of this patrol was between Sivry-sur-Meuse and Romaigne. We had turned back towards the west at the end of one beat and were nearing the turning point when I observed a two-seater Hanover machine of the enemy trying to steal across our lines behind us. He was quite low and was already across the front when I first discovered him.

In order to tempt him a little more distance away from his lines I made no sign of noticing him but throttled down to my lowest speed and continued straight ahead with some climb. The pilots in Chambers' formation were below me and had evidently not seen the intruder at all as yet.

Calculating the positions of our two machines, as we drew away from each other, I decided I could now cut off the Hanover before he reached his lines, even if he saw me the moment I turned. Accordingly I piqued swiftly back, aiming at a point just behind our front, where I estimated our meeting must take place. To my surprise, however, the enemy machine did not race for home but continued ahead on his mission. Was this brazenness, good tactics mixed with abundant self-confidence or hadn't the pilot and observer seen me up above them? I wondered what manner of aviators I had to deal with, as I turned after them and the distance between us narrowed.

A victory seemed so easy that I feared some deep strategy lay behind it all. Closer and closer I stole up in their rear, yet the observer did not even look about him to see if his rear was safe. At 100 yards

I fixed my sights upon the slothful observer in his rear cockpit and prepared to fire. He had but one gun mounted upon a tournelle and this gun was not even pointing in my direction. After my first shot he would swing it around, I conjectured, and I would be compelled then to come in through his stream of bullets. Well, I had two guns to his one and he would have to face double the amount of bullets from my Spad. Now I was at fifty yards and could not miss. Taking deliberate aim I pulled both triggers. The observer fell limply over the side of his cockpit without firing a shot. My speed carried me swiftly over the Hanover, which had begun to bank over and turn for home as my first shots entered its fusilage.

Heading off the pilot, I braved his few shots and again I obtained a position in his rear and had him at my mercy. And at that very critical moment both of my guns jammed!

Infuriated at this piece of bad luck I still had the thought to realize that the enemy pilot did not know I could not shoot, so I again came up and forced him to make a turn to the east to avoid what he considered a fatal position. And at that moment I saw Reed Chambers flying directly towards me, the rest of his patrol streaming in along behind him. Reed was firing as he flew. His first bursts finished the pilot and the Hanover settled with a gradual glide down among the shell-holes that covered the ground just north of Montfaucon — a good two miles within our lines.

It was the first machine that I had brought down behind our lines — or assisted to bring down, for Reed Chambers shared this victory with me — in such condition that we were able to fly it again.

A few minutes' work with my guns cleared both jams. I had paid little attention to the rest of my pilots during this operation — and indeed had scarcely noticed where my aeroplane was taking me through the air — for I had to work with one hand holding the lever and the other pressing back the feeding mechanism of the guns, and the Spad was taking care of herself. Now after clearing out the crushed cartridges, I had just fired a few rounds into Germany, to see that the guns were both in working order, when suddenly not fifty yards in front of me I saw a whole flock of enemy Fokkers passing through a thin stratum of clouds. It was an ideal hiding place for a surprise attack, and they had been lying in wait for our Spads without noticing me until I almost bumped into them.

The next instant I was over on my wing and nose performing a double-quick spin out of their range. All eight of them were on top of me firing as they followed my gyrations. Tracer bullets went whizzing past me every second and, try as I might, I could not select an opening that would permit me to slip through them with any hope of safety. The earth was rapidly coming up to meet me and the Fokkers were as ravenously bent on my destruction as ever when I opened up my motor and dove vertically towards the ground with throttle wide open. As I did so I was conscious that other machines were coming in from behind me and that the Fokkers had suddenly left off firing their beastly flaming bullets. Glancing back I saw my own Spads had arrived in the very nick of time. Reed Chambers was in pursuit of the fleeing Huns and the whole circus was climbing southwards to gain the shelter of the low-hanging clouds.

Reed saw they would gain their protection before he could overtake them. With his usual good judgment he let them proceed until the last man was swallowed up within them, then he turned suddenly to the north and sought a place between them and their lines where they might be expected to issue out and make for home. Climbing for all I was worth, I arrived at the northern edge of the cloud-bank at the same time Reed reached there. We had made one or two circles just beneath the billowy mass of white, when out burst the leader of the Huns over our heads and one by one his formation followed him.

In a trice Reed and I were under the last Fokkers' tails. Reed took the left and I took the right and at almost the same second we both began firing. I had let go 200 rounds when I saw my man falling; and again at almost the same instant Reed ceased firing and his man too dropped out of line and began his last landing. The rest of the formation fled straight on into their own lines and we were unable to overtake them. As we turned back we saw our two victims crash almost simultaneously fully a mile back of our lines.

Before we reached the aerodrome official confirmation of our three victories had been telephoned in.

Lieutenant Cook, who was now looked upon as our most successful balloon strafer had gone out this morning with Lieutenant Crocker as helper, to get an enemy balloon that hung over the eastern edge of the town of Grand Pré. Cookie now had three balloons and was becoming quite fastidious in his methods of shooting down these disagreeable targets. He naturally insisted upon especial attention being given his ammunition and his guns, for he believed in making one straight dash through the circle of Archy and getting in one long burst of incendiary bullets into the balloon and then leaving it alone. This returning again and again through the Archy barrage for several attacks is simply a foolish method of suicide.

At 5.30 in the morning Cook and Crocker left the field and proceeded to the Argonne. Here they located Grand Pré but could not discover the balloon. Finally after arousing the whole neighborhood Cook found his gas-bag supinely resting on the ground where it was tied down into its bed. It was in a decidedly bad place for an attack, but Cook unhesitatingly stuck down his nose and began firing as he dived.

About twenty or thirty shots left his guns — and then both jammed. With a string of burning words Cookie turned around as he zoomed up over the balloon and hurled at it the small hammer or tool used by pilots for clearing gun-jams. He was so enraged over his bad luck that he did not even wait for Crocker to overtake him, but made straight for home, climbed out of his machine and marched into the Armorers' office, mad as a hornet. What language he used there neither Cook nor the Armament officer would afterwards repeat, but in the midst of his abusive descriptions of guns, ammunition, mechanics and armament officers in general, in walked Lieutenant Crocker, whom Cook had left behind him at Grand Pré!

"Congrats, Cookie!" said Crocker triumphantly. "That was certainly fine work! You got him with his truck, office and all, this time."

Cook looked at Crocker with some anger and much mortification. "Got what?" he shouted rather violently. Ordinarily Cookie was the sweetest tempered man in the outfit, barring Jimmy Meissner.

"Why, the Hun balloon!" replied Crocker, looking at him indignantly. "Didn't you see him go up in flames? He hung fire for a half minute owing to the dew and dampness on the outside, but when he started he went with one burst!"

Cook stood looking at his friend anxiously for a moment. There was no question about his seriousness and truth. Then Cookie said slowly: —

"Well, I'm d—d! That's the first time I ever heard of getting a balloon with a jam-hammer and hot language!"

The next day, October third, a carefully planned attack on an enemy balloon back of Doulcon was carried

out in the middle of the afternoon by our Squadron.
Montfaucon was still the center of operations for the
American Army. The country was extremely difficult owing to the hills and forests along the Meuse
River, all of which the Germans had amply prepared
for stubborn defense. The presence of their observation balloons added one source of benefit to them
which we knew could be destroyed. So we were sent
out in full daylight to accomplish this end.

Thorn Taylor led our formation. Practically our
whole Squadron left the aerodrome at three o'clock,
Ham Coolidge and Crocker who were selected as the
two balloon strafers for the day flying with us on the
patrol. At 3.30 precisely we were to find ourselves
over the Hun balloon at Doulcon and there these two
pilots were to make a sudden dash down at the balloon,
one behind the other. It was a new daylight dodge we
would try to put over the Germans before they suspected the object of our mission.

We expected to find enemy planes about guarding
this important observation post of the enemy and it
was necessary to take along enough machines of our
own to sweep them away from the path which our
two strafers must take to get to their balloon. Therefore, I had all the pilots set their watches exactly with
mine and gave them all instructions to cross the lines
precisely at 3.45 and fly between Coolidge and Crocker
and any hostile aircraft that might intercept them.
With every man fully schooled in his part of the game
we all took off.

Walter Avery of 95 Squadron accompanied us.
Avery was the pilot who had forced down the celebrated Hun Ace, Menckoff early in August on the
Château-Thierry front. Menckoff then had a string
of 37 victories to his credit and, strange as it may seem,
this was Avery's first air combat. Avery disabled
Menckoff's motor with one of his bullets and the Ger-

man pilot decided it wiser to drop down our side of
the lines and surrender himself rather than take the
chance of being killed trying to glide home on a crippled machine. Great was his disgust, when he landed,
to discover that his conqueror was a green American
pilot.

As the formation continued its patrol some distance
this side of our lines Coolidge and Crocker left the rest
and placed themselves a good distance the other side
of Montfaucon. We found no enemy machines in our
vicinity, but were not sure that they would not appear
as soon as we approached the Doulcon balloon.

As my watch neared the hour I crept a little nearer
the point of attack. Looking over the situation ahead
of me some four or five miles, I suddenly saw two
Spads streaking it ahead with all their speed in the direction of the balloon. I looked at my watch. It was
but 3.40. Coolidge and Crocker were each afraid that
the other would steal a march on him and were both
so anxious to get the balloon that they disobeyed
orders and had gone in several minutes ahead of
the stated time. Looking around I saw that my formation of Spads were just coming up in implicit
obedience to orders. But now, instead of protecting
our two picked men, we would arrive there only after
the ceremony was over!

As we all opened up in pursuit of the two pilots I
saw advancing to cut them off from the balloon a
formation of six Fokkers. Then one lone Spad
seemed to appear from somewhere in the clouds and
flew in to engage the Fokkers. During the brief mêlée which followed many things happened at the same
time. The lone Spad fell to earth and crashed back
in Germany. The balloon burst into flames indicating
that either Coolidge or Crocker had succeeded in reaching the mark despite the Fokkers. And at the same
moment the clouds behind me seemed to be emitting

swarms of Fokker fighting aeroplanes which hurled themselves upon our Spads.

They were behind me, for I had distanced the others somewhat and had altered my direction to go to the rescue of the unknown Spad which had just fallen. But as I had started too late to be of any assistance I again diverted my course to attack two German biplane machines which I could distinguish coming in to the fight from the direction of Dun-sur-Meuse. I wondered whether it was Coolidge or Crocker or some other who had fallen. Whoever it was, he had made a gallant fight, although if they had obeyed orders and waited for the agreed time of attack he would not have had such odds against him.

One of the biplane machines saw me coming and cravenly turned back without notifying his companion. I surprised the latter and after a very brief bit of maneuvering shot him down completely out of control. Knowing it would be extremely difficult to gain a confirmation of this victory so far behind the German lines I waited about for a few moments until I saw him crash violently into the ground. I was satisfied I had destroyed him, whether anybody else ever knew it or not. In fact this victory of mine never was confirmed.

Many twisting combats were in progress as I gained again the part of the heavens above Doulcon. Several machines had fallen but whether friend or foe I could not distinguish from this distance. The Spads were scattered all over the sky and our formation was hopelessly destroyed. I determined to call them together and take them back to our lines. Our balloon was in flames, our mission ended and we were taking unwise risks fighting ten miles within the German lines where a mishap would drop some luckless pilots prisoners in their territory.

The enemy pilots were only too willing to let us go.

As I collected my pilots about me and headed for home the Boches lost no time in widening the distance between us. I dropped back and saw that the last of the Spads had crossed the lines and were well on their way. Then, noticing something going on east of me near the city of Verdun, I made a detour to investigate it.

It was a combat between two machines that was going on just south of our front. Hastening ahead with all possible speed I arrived there at a most fortunate moment, to find that Ted Curtiss of 95 had just been forced to abandon an attack on a German L. V. G. by reason of a gun-jam. The Hun pilot was endeavoring to make his escape as I reached him from one side and a Spad that I later recognized as belonging to Ham Coolidge came in on the other.

Diving down with terrific speed I began firing at 100 yards. With my first burst I noticed the gas-tank of the enemy machine catch on fire. Ham began firing as he approached on the other side but already the two unfortunate occupants of the observing machine knew their coming doom. The L. V. G. descended rapidly, the wind fanning the flames into a fiery furnace. The two unfortunate aviators must have been burned to a crisp long before the ground was reached. When the crash did come there was a great explosion and all that remained of the aeroplane was a black cloud of smoke and dust that ascended a few yards and was scattered to the four winds.

Adjusting matters that night I found that Ham Coolidge was the hero of the day with the balloon and one Fokker to his credit besides one-half the vanquishing of the L. V. G. Thorn Taylor, Will Palmer and Crafty Sparks had each brought down a Fokker, making a total of five besides the two-seater that I had crashed back of Dun. Our lead was now safely beyond that of our next rival — 27 Squadron. And from that day it increased and has never been lessened.

Avery, as well as Eugene Scroggie, one of my pilots from Des Moines, Iowa, were missing. I had seen one Spad fall but could not tell which of these pilots was in it. But in spite of this uncertainty I felt so confident that both pilots were not dead but merely prisoners that I put off writing to their parents for weeks. At the cessation of hostilities both of these boys were turned back to us by Germany. Scroggie had been shot through the foot but was able to come back to his Squadron. Poor Avery had received a disfiguring wound in the face which had been neglected by the German surgeons. But he was immediately put under the best of our medical care after he was released from Germany, and will doubtless soon return to the States in as perfect condition as he left.

CHAPTER XXXI

" SEEING THE WAR "

IT was not until the morning of October 5th that I learned that the Hanover machine which Reed Chambers and I had shot down on October 2nd, was still lying under guard of our doughboys but a mile or so north of Montfaucon. It seemed to be in good condition and the officers there had telephoned to us to send out and bring it in to our hangars. I might say in passing that it is extremely rare to find an enemy machine within our lines that has not been cut to pieces for souvenirs by the thousand and one passers-by before it has been on the ground a single hour. It is marvelous how quickly a crowd gathers at the site of a crashed machine. Motor drivers leave their trucks on the road and dash across the fields to examine the curiosity and to see if they cannot find a suitable souvenir straight from Germany to carry away with them. From every direction soldiers and French peasants come running to the wreck. By the time the pilot gets safely landed and makes his way to the scene there is little of the enemy machine remaining.

Up to this time the American Air Force had never captured one of these two-seater Hanover machines. We were all of us anxious to fly different types of German aeroplanes, to compare them with our own, to examine what new devices they employed, to test their engines and to see towards what improvements their designers were tending. So as soon as we heard that our victim of the 2nd of October had landed without crashing and was being cared for near Montfaucon we lost no time in getting into an automobile and making our way to the front lines.

It was raining the morning we set off and no flying was likely to be possible until after midday at best. We ran west and north until we struck the eastern edge of the famous Argonne Forest at Varennes, and there we began to get graphic pictures of the results of the gigantic artillery duel that had been going on for the last fortnight between the American forces and the Germans. The roads from Varennes to Montfaucon were almost entirely remade. Along both sides of the road for as far as the eye could reach the shell-holes covered the landscape as thickly as in almost any part of No Man's Land. The soil was the familiar yellow clay. Since the rainfall the country through which we were passing resembled a desolate fever-stricken swamp.

Trees were sheared of their branches and even the trunks of large trees themselves were cut jaggedly in two by the enemy's shells. Occasionally the ugly base of a dud shell could be seen protruding six or eight inches from the tree's trunk. The nose had buried itself squarely in the tree, but for some reason the shell had failed to explode.

And along the whole way numberless strings of motor trucks were passing and repassing, some laden with ammunition, food, medical and other supplies hurrying to the front lines, dodging as they splashed through the slimy mud the slower going processions of heavy guns. Long lines of " empties " were coming against this stream, many of them not empty it is true, but filled with the wounded who were being carried back to a field hospital for amputations or other surgical operations.

Occasionally we would find ourselves blocked as the whole procession came to a halt. Somewhere up the line a big twelve-inch gun had slithered around across the road and had completely blocked all traffic. On several occasions we waited half an hour before the road was cleared and the procession again proceeded.

I do not know whether other observers have been impressed with the appearance of our American doughboys in the same way I have; but to me there seemed to be an extraordinary cheerfulness about the demeanor of these boys, whether they were coming in or going out of action. They were always smiling. Long lines of khaki-clad Americans marching two abreast, often enough preceded by several officers, likewise marching on foot through the mud at the head of the column — all were whistling, singing, smiling as they hiked along at route step. They made caustic comments as their roving eyes struck anything comic or unusual in the scenes around them. Failing such opportunities, they ragged one another or recalled such incidents as might be expected to excite hilarity and amusement. They invariably were a happy and cheerful lot. Column after column we passed going in. Column after column we met coming out.

Finally we left the main road and struck a slightly

less congested but far more disreputable road, which led us up to the crest of the hill on which stood Montfaucon. Guns of the Americans were sounding behind us now, and ahead we heard the enemy guns steadfastly replying. The town itself was nevertheless occupied by some of our troops, and a Y. M. C. A. hut had been opened within the ruins of a little shop on Main Street at about the center of the winding settlement. Here we stopped and left our car at the side of the street. A long queue of doughboys stood in line waiting to get to the rude shop window where chocolate and cigarettes were being sold as fast as the two Y. M. C. A. officers could pass them out. We entered the side door and warmed our muddy boots before a small open fire burning in the center of the floor of what had once been the kitchen. Here we ate a lunch of biscuits and chocolate while we questioned the men as to the exact location of the aeroplane we had brought down.

A mile or so nearer the enemy trenches to the north of the town the machine was lying quite unhurt, we were informed. We again took our car and made our way slowly through the narrow and desolate streets. On both sides the stone and mortar buildings had been leveled almost flat. The streets had been completely filled with the débris of bricks, beams and rubble, but enough space had been cleared through the center to permit one vehicle to pass at a time. As we reached the edge of the town we saw one substantial building on the very topmost point of the hill which, though badly battered, still stood the most conspicuous and most pretentious object in Montfaucon. We instantly recognized it from our numerous observations from the air. It was the residence of the Crown Prince through those early campaigns against Verdun of 1915–1916. More recently it had been occupied by the General commanding the German armies which had been opposing the American drive against the Argonne. And now it was in our hands!

Leaving the car we walked up to make an inspection of this celebrated headquarters. It stood upon a ledge of rock which hung over the hill-side from its very peak. Around its base was a huge mountain of reinforced concrete from six to eight feet in thickness. From within one caught a wonderful view of the whole surrounding country. The Meuse valley could be followed to a point well below Verdun and the whole of the Argonne patch of woods lay under the eye from this lofty tower.

The German Hanover machine we found just beyond the town. It was indeed in remarkably good condition. It had glided down under the control of the pilot and had made a fairly good landing, considering the rough nature of the ground. The nose had gone over at the last moment and the machine had struck its propeller on the ground, breaking it. The tail stood erect in air, resting against the upper half of a German telegraph pole. A few ribs in the wings were broken; but these could easily be repaired. Our mechanics with their truck and trailer had already arrived at the spot and were ready to take down the wings and load our prize onto their conveyance.

A newly dug grave a few yards away indicated the last resting place of the observer that my bullets had killed in air. The pilot had been sent back to one of our hospitals for treatment. A bullet had pierced his face, shattering his jaw.

While the mechanics were taking the Hanover apart for loading, we proceeded on to one of our observation posts facing the German lines, where we got a close-up view of a regular war. It was a spectacle never to be forgotten!

Through the periscopes I saw the German trenches just opposite me, behind which our shells were drop-

ping with a marvelous accuracy. They were passing
over my head with a continuous whine and the noise
and jarring "crump" of their explosions so near our
post made it necessary to shout our conversation into
one another's ears. Enemy shells were passing overhead contrariwise — mostly directed at our artillerymen far in our rear.

Our shells were creeping back nearer and nearer
to the open ditches in which the German troops were
crouching. I watched the gradual approach of this
deadly storm in complete fascination. Some gigantic
hand seemed to be tearing up the earth in huge handfuls, forming ugly yellow holes from which sprang a
whirling mass of dirt, sticks and dust. And nearer
and nearer to the line of trenches this devastating an-
nihilation was coming. To know that human beings
were lying there without a possible means of escape —
waiting there while the pitiless hailstorm of shrapnel
drew slowly closer to their hiding places — seemed
such a diabolical method of torture that I wondered
why men in the trenches did not go utterly mad with
terror.

Suddenly I noticed that our gunners had drawn back
their range to the exact line of the trenches. A first
shell fell directly into the trench in front of me, tearing
it open and gutting it completely for a space of thirty
feet. The next instant a Boche soldier sprang out
of the trench alongside this point and flinging down his
rifle proceeded to run for all he was worth back to a
safer zone in the rear trenches. Hardly had he gone
ten yards when a high explosive shell lit in front of
him. Before I saw the burst of the shell I saw him
stop with his arms flung up over his head. Next instant he was simply swept away in dust and disappeared, as the explosion took effect. Not a vestige
of him remained when the dust had settled and the
smoke had cleared away.

At five o'clock the men had our Hanover loaded on their trailer and we were ready to depart for home. Passing down the Montfaucon hill by another road, we came upon a row of concrete dugouts built into the side of the hill by the Germans, but now occupied by American troops. Doubtless the Huns had expected this occupation by their enemies and had waited for a few days to make certain that the little huts would be well filled with our troops before springing their surprise. Just as we approached this group of buildings the first German shell fell full into the middle of them! The Huns had gotten the exact range the first shot!

Lieutenant Chambers and I were cut off from our road and for a few minutes we had the panic of our lives. A motor truck a short way ahead of us, which was likewise standing still waiting for this storm to pass, got a direct hit and was blown into fragments. Reed and I waited for no more, but made a bolt for the nearest shelter we could find.

Flat on our faces at the bottom of a nearby trench we listened to the shells bursting about our ears. While not wishing any ill luck to any other poor chaps, we did most fervently hope that the Huns had not miscalculated their range by two hundred yards in our direction. A bold glance over the top of our parapet showed that the concrete buildings were already a mass of dust. Just then one shell landed not fifteen feet in front of my nose and I threw up my feet and struck the water in the bottom of my ditch as hard as possible with my face.

As suddenly as it had started the bombardment ceased. Frugal souls, these Boches are! Not a shell too few, not one too many, is their very efficient motto. But we did not trust to this motto for several more minutes; and when we did cautiously emerge from our hole, we spent several more minutes washing the clay mud from our uniforms.

One more extraordinary spectacle Reed Chambers and I witnessed on that memorable day. Not two miles further on we espied a formation of nine Fokkers pass overhead, proceeding at a very low level in the direction of our rear. The sky was still cloudy and threatening but no rain was falling. We stopped the car, to avoid being mistaken for a general and thus attracting Fokker bullets through our car. Both of us jumped out and ran to an open space where we could see in what direction the Hun pilots were directing their course. As we looked up through the trees we saw over our heads two darting Spads coming down straight at the tail of the Hun procession from a high altitude. Although we could not distinguish whether they were American or French, we knew even at that distance that the two pursuing machines were Spads.

It was probably the most exciting moment Reed or I had ever experienced. We both shouted for joy to see the clever stalking of such a superior force by the two brave Spads. Moreover, this was the first air battle that either of us had ever seen from the ground and it afforded us a panorama of the whole that is impossible to get from the center of a fight.

The two piquing Spads opened fire on their downward course when at only 3,000 feet above ground. Their aim was not good, however, and neither of the attacked machines received a vital hit. Then the scene of action became one churning mass of revolving and looping aeroplanes. The leading Fokkers had reversed directions and were attacking the Spads. These latter did not keep together, but each was carrying on a separate free-lance combat, occasionally pouring out streams of flaming bullets at any enemy machine that crossed its path.

For a good five minutes or longer the aerial tumult continued, without any further results than giving us spectators below a most beautiful exhibition of contortions and airmanship.   I was full of admiration for the two aviators who, I was now almost certain, must be Americans and must belong to our group.   At any rate they were brave fellows to stick so long against such odds.   Then we saw two machines coming our way out of control.   They were some distance away, but since they were headed towards Germany and were not being pursued it was very evident that they were Fokkers.   The two brave Spads had been victorious.

Soon both wounded Fokkers were passing directly above us.   Motors cut off and steadily losing height, one was absolutely certain to crash near us, while the other seemed still to be under the control of its pilot. They were Fokkers sure enough!   As we looked back to the scene of the recent combat we saw the Spads streaking it homewards with the balance of the Fokkers strung out behind them in a useless pursuit.   No Fokker can overtake a good Spad unless he has sufficient advantage in elevation to increase his speed by diving.   The victorious Spads lost themselves in the distant clouds; and the Fokkers, after reforming their depleted numbers, returned to their lines some distance to the east of us.

The last we saw of the two victims one had crashed nose down at less than a mile from where we stood. The other had succeeded in gliding almost two miles further, finally crashing, as we ascertained next day, in No Man's Land just north of Montfaucon.

The day was getting late and our progress home would be slow owing to the enormous traffic on the roads, so we did not take time to visit the spot of the nearest Fokker's fall.   Thus we returned joyfully homewards after a most exciting and successful day, with our captured two-seater Hanover safely following

along behind. And at mess that night, to crown our
satisfaction, we learned that the two victorious Spad
operators who had that afternoon added two more
victories to the score of 94 Squadron were sitting opposite us, grinning with complacency. They were
Lieutenant Jeffers and Lieutenant Kaye.

The following morning we received explicit orders
to bring down an enemy balloon that was hanging
above the enemy town of Maroq, about four miles inside their lines. Lieutenants Coolidge and Cook armed
their guns with special ammunition and, accompanied
by six other planes as a protective escort, we set off
early in the morning and attained undiscovered a good
position behind the balloon. Coolidge started a first
attack, with Cook following him in case he was unsuccessful. But Coolidge was not unsuccessful. His
first burst set fire to the target and Cookie was obliged
to make a sudden bank to avoid its threatening flames.
Without further molestation than the usual Archy fire
of the front, we returned to our aerodrome without
having seen a single enemy aeroplane in the sky. It
had been quite the simplest balloon strafing party in
which we had ever been engaged.

No further victories came to our Squadron, owing
to the continuous bad weather, until October 9th, when
at about five in the afternoon I had my machine pushed
out into the mud of the aerodrome and got away
through the clouds for a short survey of the lines.
No enemy machines were out, but I discovered a balloon watching our front from a point just back of
Dun-sur-Meuse. Making a wide detour to lose myself from their sight, I came back at Dun from the
rear, just as it was getting so dark that it would be
difficult for them to distinguish my machine from any
considerable distance.

But it was also too dark for me to do any observing
from balloons and the Boches had hauled their Drachen

down for the night. I passed the spot twice before I could make out the outline of the sleek gas-bag from my low height of only 200 feet above ground. Then taking a fresh start I made two attacks at it in its nest before I succeeded in setting it afire. It finally caught with sufficient glow to light up the whole country around, including several machine-gun pits and Archy batteries which I discovered were frantically firing at me. Their aim was bad, however, and I flew safely back to the hangars and landed to receive the information that the result of my patrol had been witnessed by our balloon posts south of Dun and confirmation already had been telephoned in.

It was my sixteenth official victory.

CHAPTER XXXII

A REGULAR DOG-FIGHT

ON the afternoon of October 10th the 94th Squadron received orders to destroy two very bothersome enemy balloons, one of which was located at Dun-sur-Meuse, the other at Aincreville. The time for this attack was fixed for us at 3.50 P. M. sharp. A formation of defending planes from 147 Squadron was directed to cover our left wing while a similar formation from the 27th was given the same position on our right. I was placed in command of the expedition and was to arrange all minor details.

Selecting Lieutenants Coolidge and Chambers to act as the balloon executioners, I sent orders to all the pilots who were to accompany our secret raid to assemble their formation at 3,000 feet above Montfaucon at 3.40 o'clock precisely. Then with Coolidge and Chambers ahead of us, the united force would proceed first to the Dun balloon, where we would protect the two Strafers against Hun aeroplanes while they went in to attack their objective. Then, after destroying the first, if circumstances permitted, we should proceed on to Aincreville, destroy that balloon and beat a retreat straight for home. If Coolidge and Chambers encountered any hostile aircraft they were instructed to avoid fighting, but retire immediately to the protection of our formation.

A clear afternoon made it certain that the Boche machines would be thick about us. According to our Secret Intelligence Reports the enemy had here concentrated the heaviest air force against the Americans that had ever been gathered together since the war began. Both the Richthofen Circus and the Loezer Circus were now opposed to us and we had almost daily seen the well-known red noses of the one and the yellow-bellied fusilages of the other. Also we had distinguished the Checker-Board design of the No. 3 Jagstaffel and the new scout machines which the Huns had but lately sent to the front — the Sieman-Schuckard, which was driven by a four-bladed propeller and which had a much faster climb than had the Spad. Further reports which came to us stated that the new Fokkers now arriving at the front had four instead of two guns mounted forward, two as of yore fastened along the engine top and two others attached to the top wing. Personally I have never seen one of these " Roman Candle " affairs which so startled several pilots who reported having fights with them. They may have been in use along our front, of course, but I have never met one nor seen a pilot who was certain that he had met one. It was said that when all four guns began firing their tracer bullets at an enemy machine, the exhibition resembled the setting off of Fourth of July Roman Candles, so continuous a stream of tracer bullets issued from the nozzles of the four machine-guns.

This heavy consolidation of enemy aircraft along our front was necessary to the Germans for two reasons. The retreating Hun infantry must hold the Meuse front until they had time to withdraw their troops from Belgium and the north or the latter would be cut off; secondly, the allied bombing squadrons which were now terrifying the Rhine towns were all located along this front and must be prevented from destroying those Prussian cities so dear to the heart of the Hun. General Trenchard of the British Independent Air Force proved he was right when he demonstrated that his bombing of enemy cities would necessarily withdraw from the battle front much of the enemy's air strength to defend those helpless cities against such attacks.

So it is not necessarily to be believed that Germany was actually in such fright over the appearance of the American airmen that she straightway sent all her best aviators to the Verdun region to oppose us. She really had quite other objects in view. But such a move nevertheless resulted in filling the skies opposite us with the best fighting airmen in the German service. It promised to be a busy month for us.

Fourteen of my Spads then left the ground on October 10th at 3.30 in the afternoon, with eight of 147's machines and seven of those from 27 Squadron taking their places on the right and left of us as arranged. I pushed my Spad No. 1 up several thousand feet above the flotilla to watch their progress over the lines from a superior altitude. The enormous formation below me resembled a huge crawling beetle, Coolidge and Chambers flying in exact position ahead of them to form the stingers. Thus arranged we proceeded swiftly northwest in the direction of Dun-sur-Meuse.

We arrived over the lines to be welcomed by an outlandish exhibition of Archy's fury, but despite the

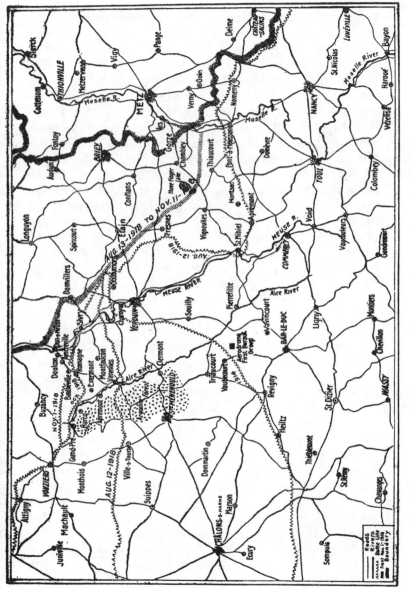

THE AMERICAN FRONT AT THE TIME OF THE ARMISTICE.

large target we made no damage was received and none of our Spads turned back. Reaching a quieter region inside German territory I looked about me. There indeed was our Dun balloon floating tranquilly in the sunshine. It was 3.40 by my watch. We had ten minutes to maneuver for position and reach our objective. I looked down at my convoy and found that 147's Formation at the left had separated themselves somewhat widely from the others. Then studying the distant horizon I detected a number of specks in the sky, which soon resolved themselves into a group of eleven Fokkers flying in beautiful formation and evidently just risen from their aerodrome at Stenay, a dozen miles beyond Dun. They were approaching from the west and must reach the detached formation of 147's pilots before the rest of my flight could reach them, unless they immediately closed up. I dived down to dip them a signal.

On my way down I glanced around me and saw approaching us from Metz in quite the opposite direction another formation of eight Fokkers. Certainly the Huns had wonderful methods of information which enabled them to bring to a threatened point this speedy relief. While I debated an instant as to which danger was the most pressing I looked below and discovered that the enemy balloon men were already engaged in pulling down their observation balloon, which was the object of our attack back of Dun-sur-Meuse. So they suspected the purpose of our little expedition! It lacked yet a minute or two of the time set for our dash at the balloon and as I viewed the situation it would not be wise for Coolidge and Chambers to take their departure from our formation until we had disposed of the advancing Fokkers from the west. Accordingly I kept my altitude and set my machine towards the rear of the Stenay Fokkers, which I immediately observed wore the red noses of the von

Richthofen Circus. They were heading in at the 147 Formation which was still separated almost a mile away from our other Spads. Lieutenant Wilbur White of New York was leading No. 147's pilots. He would have to bear the brunt of the Fokker attack.

Evidently the Fokker leader scorned to take notice of me, as his scouts passed under me and plunged ahead towards White's formation. I let them pass, dipped over sharply and with accumulated speed bore down upon the tail of the last man in the Fokker formation. It was an easy shot and I could not have missed. I was agreeably surprised, however, to see that my first shots had set fire to the Hun's fuel tank and that the machine was doomed. I was almost equally gratified the next second to see the German pilot level off his blazing machine and with a sudden leap overboard into space let the Fokker slide safely away without him. Attached to his back and sides was a rope which immediately pulled a dainty parachute from the bottom of his seat. The umbrella opened within a fifty foot drop and settled him gradually to earth within his own lines.

I was sorry I had no time to watch his spectacular descent. I truly wished him all the luck in the world. It is not a pleasure to see a burning aeroplane descending to earth bearing with it a human being who is being tortured to death. Not unmixed with my relief in witnessing his safe jump was the wonder as to why the Huns had all these humane contrivances and why our own country could not at least copy them to save American pilots from being burned to a crisp!

I turned from this extraordinary spectacle in mid-air to witness another which in all my life at the front I have never seen equaled in horror and awfulness. The picture of it has haunted my dreams during many nights since.

Upon seeing that my man was hit I had immediately

turned up to retain my superiority in height over the other Huns.   Now as I came about and saw the German pilot leap overboard with his parachute I saw that a general fight was on between the remaining ten Fokkers and the eight Spads of 147 Squadron.   The Fokker leader had taken on the rear Spad in White's Formation when White turned and saw him coming. Like a flash White zoomed up into a half turn, executed a renversement and came back at the Hun leader to protect his pilot from a certain death.   White was one of the finest pilots and best air fighters in our group.   He had won seven victories in combat.   His pilots loved him and considered him a great leader, which he most assuredly was.   White's maneuver occupied but an instant.   He came out of his swoop and made a direct plunge for the enemy machine, which was just getting in line on the rear Spad's tail.   Without firing a shot the heroic White rammed the Fokker head on while the two machines were approaching each other at the rate of 250 miles per hour!

It was a horrible yet thrilling sight.   The two machines actually telescoped each other, so violent was the impact.   Wings went through wings and at first glance both the Fokker and Spad seemed to disintegrate.   Fragments filled the air for a moment, then the two broken fusilages, bound together by the terrific collision fell swiftly down and landed in one heap on the bank of the Meuse!

For sheer nerve and bravery I believe this heroic feat was never surpassed.   No national honor too great could compensate the family of Lieutenant White for this sacrifice for his comrade pilot and his unparalleled example of heroism to his Squadron. For the most pitiable feature of Lieutenant White's self-sacrifice was the fact that this was his last flight over the lines before he was to leave for the United States on a visit to his wife and two small children.

Not many pilots enter the service with loved ones so close to them!

This extraordinary disaster ended the day's fighting for the Hun airmen. No doubt they valued their own leader as much as we did Lieutenant White, or perhaps they got a severe attack of "wind-up" at witnessing the new method of American attack. At any rate they withdrew and we immediately turned our attention to the fight which was now in progress between the Spads of 27 Squadron at our right and the Hun formation from Metz. It looked like a famous dog-fight.

As I came about and headed for the mixup I glanced below me at Dun and was amazed to see one of our Spads piquing upon the nested balloon through a hurricane of flaming projectiles. A "flaming onion" had pierced his wings and they were now ablaze. To add to his predicament, a Hun machine was behind his tail, firing as he dived. I diverted my course and started down to his rescue, but it was too late. The fire in his wings was fanned by the wind and made such progress that he was compelled to land in German territory, not far from the site of the balloon. In the meantime other things were happening so rapidly that I had little opportunity to look about me. For even as I started down to help this balloon strafer I saw another Spad passing me with two Fokkers on his tail, filling his fusilage with tracer bullets as the procession went by. A first glance had identified the occupant of the Spad as my old protégé — the famous Jimmy Meissner! For the third time since we had been flying together Providence had sent me along just in the nick of time to get Jimmy out of trouble. Twice before on the old Nieuports Jimmy had torn off his wings in too sudden a flip and his unscrupulous antagonists had been about to murder him as he wobbled along, when I happened by. Now, after a four months' interlude Jimmy comes sailing by again, smiling and good-natured as ever, with two ugly brutes on his tail trying their best to execute him.

I quickly tacked onto the procession, settling my sights into the rear machine and letting go a long burst as I came within range. The Hun fell off and dropped down out of control, the other Fokker immediately pulling away and diving steeply for home and safety.

Two other Fokkers fell in that dog-fight, neither of which I happened to see. Both Coolidge and Chambers, though they had been cheated of their balloon, brought down a Fokker apiece, which victories were later confirmed. The Spad which had dropped down into German hands after being set afire by the flaming onions belonged to Lieutenant Brotherton, like White and Meissner, a member of the 147th Squadron.

Four more victories were thus added to 94's score by this afternoon's work. We did not get the balloons but we had done the best we could. I was never in favor of attacking observation balloons in full daylight and this day's experience — the aroused suspicions of the observers, the pulling down of the balloon as strong aeroplane assistance at the same time arrived, and the fate of Lieutenant Brotherton, who tried unsuccessfully to pass through the defensive barrage — is a fair illustration, I believe, of the difficulties attending such daylight strafings. Just at dawn or just at dusk is the ideal time for surprising the Drachen.

Our captured Hanover machine, it will be recalled, had been brought back to our aerodrome and by now was in good condition to fly. We left the Hun Maltese Cross and all their markings exactly as we found them and after telephoning about to the various American aerodromes in our vicinity that they must not practise target shooting at a certain Hanover aeroplane that they might encounter while wandering over our part of the country, we took the machine up to see how it flew.   The Hanover was a staunch heavy craft and had a speed of about one hundred miles an hour when two men (a pilot and an observer) were carried. She handled well and was able to slow down to a very comfortable speed at landing.   Many of us took her up for a short flip and landed again without accident.

Then it became a popular custom to let some pilot get aloft in her and as he began to clear the ground half a dozen of us in Spads would rise after him and practise piquing down as if in an attack.   The Hanover pilot would twist and turn and endeavor to do his best to outmaneuver the encircling Spads.   Of course, the lighter fighting machines always had the best of these mock battles, but the experience was good for all of us, both in estimating the extent of the maneuverability of the enemy two-seaters and in the testing of our relative speeds and climbings.

While engaged in one of these mock combats over our field one afternoon we came down to find Captain Cooper, the official Movie Picture expert, standing below watching us.   He had his camera with him and had been attempting to grind out some movie films while we were flying overhead.   He spent the night with us and after some planning of the scenario we decided to take him up in the rear seat of a Liberty aeroplane and let him catch with his camera a real movie of an aeroplane combat in mid-air.   All the details carefully arranged, we gathered next morning on the field, put him in the rear seat of the Liberty and helped him strap in his camera so that the pressure of the wind would not carry it overboard.   Jimmy Meissner was to be his pilot.   Jimmy climbed in the front seat, warmed up his motor and when everything was ready and we other " actors " were sitting in our seats waiting for him to get away, Jimmy gave the signal, opened up his motor and began to taxi over the grass.   Several hundred feet down the field he turned back, facing the wind, which was blowing from the west.   Here he prepared for his real take-off.   His machine rushed along with ever quickening speed until the tail lifted, the wheels next skimmed the ground and the Liberty rose gradually into the air.   Just as they approached the road which skirts the west side of the aerodrome, the Liberty's engine stopped.   A line of wires ran along the roadside some fifteen feet above ground.   Jimmy saw them and attempted to zoom over them — but in vain.   The Liberty crashed full in the middle of the highway, bounded up a dozen feet and after a half somersault, stuck her nose in the ground the other side of the road and came to a rest.

We hurried over, expecting to find the occupants badly injured, as the Liberty herself appeared to be a total wreck.   But out stepped Jimmy and Captain Cooper, neither of them the worse for their experience.   And to complete our surprise, the camera, although covered with the débris of the machine, was quite unhurt!

That ended our little movie show for this day. We had no other two-seater machine on hand.   But we were delighted to find that Captain Cooper, in spite of his narrow escape, was quite determined to go through with the show.   So we went to the Supply Station for another machine and again put the Captain up for the night while awaiting its coming.

Next day, October 19th, I was directed to appear before General Patrick at Souilly to receive the American decoration, the Distinguished Service Cross, with four oak leaves.   These oak leaves represent the number of citations in Army Orders that the wearer of a decoration has received.

The usual formalities, which I have already described, attended the ceremony.   Over twenty pilots

of the American Air Service were presented with the
D. S. C. by General Patrick, after which the military
band played the National Anthem while we all stood
at attention.

I could not help thinking of the absent pilots whose
names were being read out but who did not answer,
and for whom decorations were waiting for deeds of
heroism that had ended with their death. There was
White, for whom the whole Group mourned. What
a puny recognition was a simple ribbon for heroism
such as his! There was Luke — the most intrepid air-
fighter that ever sat in an aeroplane. What possible
honor could be given him by his country that would
accord him the distinction he deserved!

One thing was certain. The reputation of these
great American airmen would live as long as the comrades who knew them survived. Perhaps none of us
would ever live to see our homeland again. I glanced
down the line of honor men who were standing immo-
bile in their tracks, listening to the last notes of " The
Star Spangled Banner "! Who will be the next to go,
I wondered, knowing only too well that with every
fresh honor that was conferred came a corresponding
degree of responsibility and obligation to continue to
serve comrade and country so long as life endured.

CHAPTER XXXIII

AN AEROPLANE MOVIE SHOW

THE new Liberty duly arrived and after a brief
rehearsal of our parts in the coming show we
again had our machines run out on the field on the
morning of October 21st and took our stations in the
line. Captain Cooper was again placed in the rear
seat of the Liberty, with Jimmy Meissner in the front

seat acting as his pilot. Jimmy was to keep his machine as near the actors as possible, always flying to the left side, so that the photographer might face the show and keep his handle turning with the least possible difficulty.

Reed Chambers sat in the front seat of the captured Hanover and piloted it. He carried two guns which would fire only tracer and flaming bullets, and with true Movie instinct Reed was prepared to do his utmost to imitate with two guns the Roman Candle effect of the latest four gun effort of the Huns whom he was supposed to represent. In the rear seat of the Hun machine sat Thorn Taylor, the villain of the play. He was dressed in villainous enough looking garments to deceive even the most particular Hun. He too had a gun, one which swung on a tournelle and which would emit a most fearsome amount of smoky and fiery projectiles when the climax of the action was reached. As a clever *pièce de résistance* Thorn carried with him, down out of sight of the camera until the proper time came, a dummy Boche pilot stuffed with straw. At the height of the tragedy 'Thorn was supposed to duck himself down out of sight behind his cockpit and heave overboard the stuffed figure, which would fall with outstretched arms and legs, head over heels to earth. This would portray the very acme of despair of the Boche aviators, who, it would be seen, preferred to hurl themselves out to deliberate death rather than longer face the furious assaults of the dashing young American air-fighters.

As to the latter — I was supposed to be *it*. In my old Spad No. 1, with the Hat-in-the-Ring insignia plainly inscribed on the sides of the fusilage and the red, white and blue markings along wings and tail sufficiently glaring to prove to the most skeptical movie fan that this was indeed a genuine United States areoplane — I was to be Jack, the Giant Killer, with an abundance of smoky and fiery stuff pouring from all my guns every time the monstrous hostile machine hove in sight. A few films of a distant formation passing through the sky had been taken early in the game so as to delude the innocent public into the belief that I was going up to demolish the whole caravan with my one resistless machine. A series of falls and vrilles would put the one Hanover out of the fighting enough times to account for a whole formation of them. Then as the last desperate encounter took place Thorn Taylor, after shooting all his spectacular ammunition well over my head, would force the dummy to commit suicide rather than longer endure the suspense of waiting.

It was a clever plot. The whole aerodrome was in raptures over the idea and everybody left off work to gather on the field to witness the contest. I doubt if the later performances will ever have a more expectant, more interested or so large an audience.

Jimmy and his camera operator got away safely this time and right behind them the comedian and tragedians of the show winged their way. Arrived at 2,000 feet over the field we pulled up our belts and began the performance. It was necessary to keep an eye on the camera, so as not to get out of its beam while pulling off our most priceless stunts, and at the same time we had to be a little careful as to the direction in which our bullets were going. Captain Cooper was thrusting his head out into the windstream, manfully trying to keep my swifter moving machine always within the eye of his camera. As I came up under the Hanover aeroplane's tail I would let off a terrific stream of flaming projectiles which are perfectly visible to the naked eye and certainly ought to be caught by a camera even in the daytime. Thorn shot as lustily under me and over me as I approached and even Reed's front guns were spitting death in a continuous stream at the imaginary enemy planes ahead of him.

Over and over we repeated the performance, the Hanover dying a dozen deaths in as many minutes. At last, our movie ammunition beginning to near exhaustion, it became necessary to stage a big hit that denoted the climax of the play. Coming about above the Hanover, while Captain Cooper was grinding industriously away not over twenty feet from its side, I came down in a swift pique, made a zoom and a renversement on the opposite side of the Hanover, and kicking my rudder over came back directly at the enemy, full into the gaping lens of the camera. Firing my last rounds of ammunition as I approached, I saw them go safely over the tops of both machines. As I drew in to the closest possible distance that remained safe for such a maneuver I threw my Spad up into a zoom, passed over the vanquished Boche and came back in a loop somewhere near my original position. As I glanced at the Hanover I saw that she was doomed! A quantity of lampblack, released by the crafty Taylor, was drifting windward, indicating that something seriously wrong had occurred with the enemy machine. Such a dense cloud of smoke would satisfy the dullest intellect that he must soon begin to suspect fire. Ah, Ha! There she comes! I knew she was afire! Sure enough several bright landing flares suddenly ignited under the Hanover's wings throwing a bright gleam earthwards but prevented from injuring the wings themselves by the tin surfaces above them. Finding longer existence on such a burning deck utterly unendurable the poor dummy gathered himself together in the arms of the stalwart Taylor and with one tremendous leap he departed the blazing furnace forever!

While Taylor kept himself resolutely hidden below decks Chambers, throwing out the last of his sack of lampblack, lifted over onto the side the doomed machine and gave a good exhibition of the falling leaf. Down — down it drifted, the daring photographer leaning far out of his cage to catch the last expiring gasps of the stricken Hanover — the last of the wicked formation of hostile machines that had dared to cross our frontiers early in the picture. And then — just as he was prepared to flash on the " good night " sign and entertain the departing audience with views of the best line of corsets to be had at reasonable prices at Moe Levy's emporium — just then the real climax of the play did appear.

We had necessarily wandered some little distance away from the vicinity of our aerodrome while firing genuine flaming bullets over each other, so that the falling missiles would not cause any injuries to property or persons below. Paying little attention as to just where we were flying so long as open country was below us, we had not noticed that we were some miles south and west of our starting place and almost immediately over the edge of a French aerodrome. Suddenly a puff of real Archy smoke in the vicinity of the Hanover told me that some enthusiastic outsider was volunteering his services in behalf of our little entertainment. Another and another shell burst before I could reverse my direction and get started to place my Spad close to the black machine wearing the Iron Cross of the Kaiser. Reed Chambers took in the situation at a glance. He pointed down the Hanover's nose and began at once to descend for a landing on the French aerodrome below us. At the same moment several French Breguets left the field and began climbing up to assist me in my dangerous task of demolishing the Hanover.

Diving down to intervene between them before any more shooting was done I succeeded in satisfying the Frenchmen that I had the affair well in hand and that the Hanover was coming down to surrender. Without further incident we all landed and got out of our machines. The French pilots, their mechanics and poilus gathered about in a curious body while I laughingly hurried over to the side of Reed's machine and explained to the assembly the meaning of this strange performance. They all laughed heartily over their mistake — all except Reed and Thorn Tayor of the Hanover crew who, from the expressions on their faces seemed to admit that the joke was on them.

Getting away again the Hanover flew home under my protection. After it had landed I climbed up through the clouds where Jimmy and the Movie man were still waiting for me. There I stunted for a while in front of the camera, giving some excellent views of an aeroplane bursting through the clouds and some close-up views of all the aerial tumbling that a Spad is capable of performing.

Next day Captain Cooper departed with his films for Paris, where he expected to turn them over to the American authorities and if permitted, take a copy of them for public exhibition in Paris and the United States. A day or two after Christmas, on my way through Paris to New York, I learned that these pictures had turned out very well and would soon be shown in the Movie palaces of the cities of America.

The captured Hanover was flown into the American Station at Orly, near Paris, a few days after the armistice was signed, and from there was shipped to America to be placed upon exhibition. Major Hartney and Laurence L. Driggs, of New York, who were visiting us at that time, flew in it from Verdun to Paris in a little less than an hour and a half. One captured Fokker machine and an escort of two Sopwith Camels and one Spad accompanied them, for the enemy machines still carried the war markings of the German air service, and inquisitive Frenchmen along the way might be tempted to try to capture them a second time.   So far as I know these were the only two enemy aeroplanes captured by the American forces during the war. The Fokker came down upon our field at Verdun just a day or two before the end of hostilities, and was turned over to 95 Squadron as their capture, since they operated this field.   The pilot had given himself up, saying he thought he was landing upon his own aerodrome at Metz.   He had become lost in the fog, and as the two aerodromes are similarly situated along the edge of a river's course, his mistake was quite probable.

Another two-seater, a Halberstadt machine, came down upon the American field at the Supply Station at Columbey-les-Belles under similar circumstances a few days before the armistice was signed.   But in this case, the "capture" was a deliberate surrender.   The two occupants climbed out of their machine and in pure New York patois informed the startled mechanics that they wished to make a bargain with them.

They were, it transpired, two Yiddish gentlemen of German extraction, who for some years had been in business in New York.   The war caught them in Germany and they were perforce thrust into the service of what had once been their mother country.   After many vicissitudes, they both entered aviation, seeking for the opportunity of flying over the lines and giving themselves up.   Now a chance had arrived.   Both of them getting permission to cross the lines in the same machine they had made straight for our headquarters at Columbey-les-Belles and now offered a perfectly good machine, valued at not less than ten thousand dollars in exchange for their freedom, and a pass back to Harlem.

It was an attractive offer, but since they were already in our custody as prisoners and the machine was regarded as a capture, their conditions were respectfully declined. The Halberstadt was likewise later sent to Orly and thence to America with the Fokker and Hanover, which had been taken in by 94 and 95 Squadrons.

The following afternoon I escaped assassination by four red-nosed Fokkers by the narrowest margin ever vouchsafed to a pilot, and at the end of the combat flew safely home with my 21st and 22nd victories to my credit. Curiously enough I had gone out over the lines alone that day with a craving desire to get a thrill. I had become "fed-up" with a continuation of eventless flights. Saying nothing to any of my fellows at the aerodrome I went off alone with an idea of shooting down a balloon that I thought might be hanging just north of Montfaucon. While I did not get a shot at the balloon I got all the thrill I needed for several days to come.

It was about five-thirty in the afternoon when I ordered out my machine and set off for Montfaucon. As I neared the Meuse valley I found the whole vicinity was covered with a thick haze — so thick in fact that the Germans had hauled down all their observation balloons. There was nothing a mile away that could be observed until another day dawned. Over to the South the sky was clearer. Our own balloons were still up. But no enemy aeroplanes would be likely to come over our front again so late in the evening.

While I was reflecting thus sadly a bright blaze struck my eye from the direction of our nearest balloon. I headed around towards this spot in the shortest possible space of time. There could be but one explanation for such a blaze. A late roving Hun must have just crossed the lines and had made a successful attack upon our balloon over Exermont! He ought to be an easy victim, I told myself, as soon as he should start to cross back into Germany since I was on his direct road to the nearest point in his lines. He was

now coming my way. Though I could not see him, I
did see the bursting Archy shells following his course
northward. He must pass considerably under me, and
no doubt would be quite alone.

Just then a series of zipping streams of fire flashed
by my face and through my fusilage and wings! I
divined rather than saw what this was without looking around. Two, or perhaps more than two enemy
machines were piquing on me from above. Utterly
absorbed in planning what I should do to catch the
other fellow I had been perfectly blind to my own surroundings. The Hun balloon strafer had a protective
formation waiting for him. They had seen me come
over and had doubtless been stalking me for many
minutes without my knowing it.

These thoughts flashed through my mind as I almost automatically zoomed up and did a climbing
chandelle to escape the tracer bullets directed at me.
I did not even stop to look at the position of my as-
sailants. Knowing they were above, I concluded instantly that they had prepared for my diving away
from them and that therefore that would be the best
thing for me to avoid. I fortunately had reasoned
correctly. As I sped upwards two red-nosed Fokkers,
my old friends of the von Richthofen Circus sped
down and passed me. But even before I had time
enough to congratulate myself upon my sagacity I
discovered that only half of them had passed me.
Two more Fokkers had remained above on the chance
that I might refuse to adopt the plan they had determined upon for me.

One glimpse of the skilful contortions of these two
upper Fokkers showed me that I was in for the fight
of my life. I lost all interest in the progress or existence of the balloon strafer that had destroyed one of
our balloons under my very nose. My one dearest
desire was to get away off by myself, where thrills

were never mentioned and were quite impossible to get. The masterly way in which the Fokkers met and even anticipated every movement I made assured me that I had four very experienced pilots with whom to deal. Zig-zagging and side-slipping helped me not one whit and I felt that I was getting a wind-up that would only sap my coolness and soon make me the easy prey of these four extremely confident Huns. The two machines that had first attacked me impudently remained below me in such a position that they invited my attack, while also preventing my escape in their direction. I made up my mind to start something before it was too late. Even though it meant getting into trouble, I decided that would be better than waiting around for them to operate upon me as they had no doubt been practising in so many rehearsals. Noting a favorable opening for an attack on the nearest man below me I suddenly tipped over at him and went hurtling down with all my speed, shooting from both guns.

I had aimed ahead of him, instead of directly at him, to compel him either to pass ahead through the path of my bullets or else dip down his nose or fall over onto his wing — in either case providing me with a fair target before he could get far away. He either preferred the former course or else did not see my bullets until it was too late. He ran straight through my line of fire and he left it with a gush of flame issuing from his fuel tank. I fully believe that several bullets passed through the pilot's body as well.

Considerably bucked up with this success I did not seize this opportunity to escape, but executed blindly a sudden loop and renversement, under the strongest impression that my two enemies above would certainly be close onto my tail and preparing to shoot. Again I had guessed correctly, for not only were they in just the position I expected to find them and just where I

myself would have been were I in their places, but
they were also startled out of their senses over my
sudden and unexpected assault upon their comrade.
It is never an encouraging sight to see a comrade's machine falling in flames. It is sufficient to make the
stoutest heart quail unless one is hemmed in and is
fighting for his very life. But however that may
be, my three neighbors did not turn to continue the
combat with me, nor did they even pause for an instant to threaten my pursuit. All three continued
their headlong dive for Germany with a faster and
heavier Spad machine following them and gaining on
them every second. My blood was up and I considered that I had been badly treated by the red-nosed
Boches. I was three miles inside their lines, other
enemy machines might very easily be about — I had
no time to look about to see — and I had just escaped from the very worst trap into which I had ever
fallen. Yet I could not resist the mad impulse of
paying back the three Huns for the scare they had so
recently given me.

Though the Spad is faster than the Fokker, the fleeing Huns'had a slight start over me and I did not immediately overtake them. One of the three gradually
fell back behind the others. The ground was getting
nearer and nearer and it was growing very much
darker as we approached the earth's surface. At
about 1,000 feet above ground I decided the nearest Fokker was within my range. I opened fire, following his gyrations as he maneuvered to avoid my
ever nearing stream of lead. After letting go at him
some 200 bullets, his machine dropped out of control
and I ceased firing. His two companions had never
slackened their pace and were now well out of sight
in the shadows. I watched my latest antagonist flutter down and finally crash and then awoke to the fact
that I was being fired at by hundreds of guns from

the ground. The gunners and riflemen were so near to me that I could distinctly see their guns pointed in my direction. I had dropped down to within a hundred yards of earth.

All the way back to the lines I was followed by machine-gun bullets and some Archy. Absolutely untouched I continued on to my field, where I put in my claim for two enemy Fokkers, and after seeing to the wounds of my faithful Spad walked over to the 94 mess for supper.

CHAPTER XXXIV

AN OVER-ZEALOUS ALLY

WAR-FLYING is much like other business — one gets accustomed to all the incidents that attend its daily routine, its risks, its thrills, its dangers, its good and bad fortune. A strange sort of fatalism fastens to the mind of an aviator who continues to run the gauntlet of Archy. He flies through bursting shells without trying to dodge them, with indeed little thought of their menace. If a bullet or shell has his name written on it there is no use trying to avoid contact with it. If it has not — why worry?

To score a fatal hit these invisible missiles of death have a great space to fill when a small aeroplane and a still smaller pilot are at a height of ten or twelve thousand feet above earth. Even when flying through the defensive fire of a balloon battery at two or three hundred feet elevation or when cruising along the trenches but fifty feet above the rifles and machine guns of the enemy we learned to disdain the furious fire that was turned upon our swift flying planes. Experience had taught us that the non-flying sharpshooter is wofully ignorant of the rapidity with which we pass his aim when we are traveling at the rate of two miles a minute — exactly 176 feet each second! It requires a second or more for him to steady his aim. How many riflemen can compute the exact point 176 feet ahead of their gun-muzzle where the bullet and the pilot's head must meet in order to bring down the prize? Not one! Occasional hits are made at random, but the percentage is ridiculously low. When tracer bullets are fired at one's aeroplane it is amusing to see how far behind the tail of the machine the streams of bullets are passing. When hundreds of Archy shells are bursting about one's vicinity one of the flying fragments may, of course, happen to take the path that coincides with that of the pilot. Upon this problem no scientist would dare to assume a position of authoritative knowledge as to the chances or percentages of possible hits. To the pilot who has actually experienced these daily strafings by Archy the whole danger resolves itself into a question as to whether or not he will permit his imagination to terrorize him into fleeing away from so appalling but so futile a menace. In other words, he knows that the actual danger is almost nil. If a flying fragment of shrapnel happens to strike him it is bad luck. There is no way to avoid it. A hundred to one no hits will be received. Thus comes the fatalism that saves the experienced airman from worry.

On Sunday, October 27th, only a fortnight before the end of the war, Hamilton Coolidge, one of the best pilots and most respected men in the American Air Service, met an annihilating death from a direct hit by an Archy shell in full flight. The shell had not yet burst when it struck the Spad in which Coolidge was sitting. The aeroplane was moving forward at its usual fast speed when the mounting shell, probably traveling at the speed of 3,000 feet per second struck squarely under the center of the aeroplane's engine.

Poor Coolidge must have been killed instantly. The Spad flew into fragments and the unfortunate pilot dropped like a stone to the ground.

Coolidge was one of the top-score aces of 94 Squadron and one of the most popular men in the service. A graduate of Groton and later of Harvard, he possessed all the qualifications of leadership and a brilliant career in any profession he might have chosen to adopt. In his work at the front he never shirked and never complained. The loss of Lieutenant Hamilton Coolidge was one of the severest that we had been called upon to suffer.

It was beginning to be a matter of constant conjecture among us as to just what day Germany would cave in and surrender. The collapse of Austria and the constant and obvious weakening of the Hun troops opposite our sector were well known to us. Hence it seemed doubly bitter that Ham Coolidge should meet death now, just as the end of the war was at hand. Especially tragic was it to all of us who knew Coolidge's fighting ability that he should be the one airman who should meet his end in this incredible manner. More than one pilot bitterly remarked that no German airman could down Ham Coolidge, so they had to kill him by a miracle!

And miracle it was, for no other American pilot, and but one or two other aviators during the whole course of the war were shot down from on high by an Archy in full flight. The shell had Hamilton's name written on it and there was no escape!

Coolidge, with his usual intrepidity was hurrying in to the assistance of a formation of American bombing machines which, after dropping their eggs on the enemy town of Grand Pré, as they started home, were in turn attacked by a large number of swifter flying Fokker machines. The Archy shells were directed at the bombers and not at the Spad of Ham Coolidge!

After having scornfully passed through hundreds of barrages which were aimed at him our unlucky ace had collided with a shell not at all intended for him!

Although I did not see this ghastly accident to poor Coolidge, I was in the midst of the same barrage of Archy on the other side of Grand Pré at the same time.

The bombing machines above mentioned had not gained their objective without considerable fighting all the way over the lines.

Thousands and thousands of German troops had been unloaded from trains during the previous night and were now hidden in Grand Pré and its neighborhood. The enemy fighting machines were out in force to defend this spot against bombing planes until these troops had an opportunity for moving and scattering themselves along their front. From every side Fokkers were piquing upon the clumsy Liberty machines which, with their criminally constructed fuel tanks, offered so easy a target to the incendiary bullets of the enemy that their unfortunate pilots called this boasted achievement of our Aviation Department their " flaming coffins." During that one brief fight over Grand Pré, I saw three of these crude machines go down in flames, an American pilot and an American gunner in each " flaming coffin " dying this frightful and needless death.

During the combats which followed I again succeeded in bringing down two of the red-nosed Fokkers. The first victim was on my tail when I first noticed him. With one backward loop I had reversed our positions and had my nose on *his* tail. One short burst from both my guns and he tumbled down through space to crash a few miles within the German lines.

The second combat occurred just a few minutes later. The last of the Liberty bombing machines had passed over the lines or had crashed in flames and I thought the day's work was over when I noticed some-

thing going on to the east of me in the region of
Bantheville. I began climbing and speeding forward
to get a look at this performance when to my surprise
I discerned that one of the Liberty machines had been
left behind and was in very evident distress. Fortunately there was but a single enemy Fokker on his
tail. The Yankee pilot was kicking his machine about
and the gunner at the rear was managing to keep his
enemy at bay when, at a favorable elevation above
them both, I found an opportunity to pique down and
catch the Fokker, unaware of my approach. The
Liberty motor, I discovered, was almost dud. It had
either been struck by a bullet or had developed some
interior trouble of its own. The pilot had all he could
do to maintain headway and avoid the maneuvers of
his enemy. Each time he banked the Liberty, it fell
downwards two or three hundred feet. The Fokker
had only to worry him enough and the American machine must drop into German territory, a captive.

As I began firing the German pilot, who had been
so intent upon the capture of his prize that he had forgotten to watch his rear, zoomed suddenly up to let
me pass under him. But that was too old a dodge to
entrap me. I began a similar zoom just a fraction
of a second before he started his and I was the first
to come out — on top. As I again prepared to open
fire I saw a curious sight. The Fokker with a red
nose had not been able to complete his loop. He had
stalled just at the moment he was upright on his tail,
and in this position he was now hanging. And more
extraordinary still, his engine had stalled and his propeller was standing absolutely still. I could see the
color and laminations of the wood, so close had I approached to my helpless victim.

On March 10th, 1918, there is the following entry
in my flight diary: "Resolved to-day that hereafter
I will never shoot at a Hun who is at a disadvantage,

regardless of what he would do if he were in my position."

Just what episode influenced me to adopt that principle and even to enter it into my diary I have forgotten. That was very early in my fighting days and I had then had but few combats in air. But with American flyers the war has always been more or less a sporting proposition and the desire for fair play — the anger it always arouses in a true American to see any violation of fair play — prevents a sportsman from looking at the matter in any other light, even though it be a case of life or death. However that may be, I do not recall a single violation of this principle by any American aviator that I should care to call my friend.

My Fokker enemy was now in a very ludicrous position. Of course he could not continue hanging on there forever with his nose pointing upwards, his tail to the ground and his propeller dead. He began falling with a tail slip. He was wondering why I didn't finish him or at least didn't begin some attack so that he might know which way to head his last dive. We were over ten thousand feet above ground, and looking down I saw that we were still two or three miles within German lines. Naturally enough the pilot will turn his nose homeward when he falls far enough to get headway for a glide. Accordingly I kept control of the situation by heading him off and firing a few shots to show him that I did not mean to let him escape.

Now the tables are turned. Instead of my Fokker friend nursing homewards to Germany a captured and crippled American machine, I am endeavoring to impress upon him that an American is desirous of escorting back to the American lines a slightly crippled but very famous Fokker with a red nose. What a triumphant entry I will make with one of Baron von

Richthofen's celebrated fighting planes! I picture the flights over our field I will make with my prize to-morrow. The Boche pilot was satisfied that I had the upper hand and he was gliding along in the proper direction with admirable docility. We should clear the lines by at least five miles. I could steer him from behind by firing a few bursts ahead, which had the effect of pushing him over in the direction I wanted him to go. It was as simple as driving a tame horse to the creek.

Over the lines we passed, the Fokker gliding steadily along ahead of me, no other aeroplanes in the sky. Under the impression that I knew this country better than my companion might know it I compelled him to steer for the Exermont field, which lay just about four miles behind our front line trench. He willingly complied, immediately heading in the desired direction and apparently quite content to play fair with me and spare me his Fokker, since I had spared him his life. Of course, I was fully aware that he might attempt to set fire to his machine as soon as he touched the ground. I should have done the same had I been in his place. But I did not intend that he should have this opportunity. With his dead engine he could not change his course once he began to settle to the ground. I would put myself immediately behind him and if he attempted to do any injury to his aeroplane I would shoot him on the spot. With this plan in mind I left him a moment when he was making his last circle over the field at about 300 feet altitude and withdrew so that I might turn and land my machine in such a position that he must come to a stop just ahead of me. And then I received one of the worst disappointments of my whole life.

A Spad aeroplane suddenly appeared from out of the sky just as I turned away from my convoy. The unknown idiot in the Spad began firing a long burst into my helpless captive. I did not suspect his presence until I heard him firing. Whipping madly back I piqued down and intervened between the malignant Spad and my protégé, even firing a short burst to warn the intruder away. The latter understood me well enough, for he left us and did not return. The marks on his machine were not familiar to me and to this day I do not know whether this interfering person was an American or a Frenchman. But whichever he was, he had absolutely ruined all my chances of a capture.

The Fokker pilot had been at the outside of his turn when this unexpected attack was received. The Spad had headed him off, compelling him to turn to the right instead of to the left in the direction of the field. Now he was so low that it would be suicide to attempt to make the field. Trees and rough ground were beneath him and the only safe course would be to pancake as flatly as possible in the rough open ground directly ahead of him. All my hopes vanished as I saw the nature of his landing place. I circled above him until after the crash. He had over-shot his mark a little and ended up against the edge of the opposite bit of woods. My red-nosed prize was scattered in pieces over the ground!

To my genuine joy I saw the pilot disentangle himself from the wreckage and walk out upon the ground. An officer on horseback and some of our doughboys were advancing on the run to make him a prisoner. He waved his thanks to me as I passed overhead and I waved back in the most friendly manner. Inwardly I was furious with him, myself and most especially with the wretched pilot of the unknown Spad. So nearly had I succeeded in capturing intact a most valuable Fokker from Germany's most famous Squadron! So near and yet —

Returning home I was somewhat mollified to learn that my belated commission as Captain had just arrived. I had been acting Captain for several weeks and had been told that my commission was on its way, but these rumors often proved unfounded. But it had arrived at last and I would this night add an extra bar to each shoulder. And then I was told of the awful loss of poor Hamilton Coolidge. Surviving six months of very active flying over enemy's lines, fighting nearly a hundred combats and escaping without a single wound while he brought down confirmed eight enemy aeroplanes, our gallant comrade had been suddenly swept away by a catastrophe that appalled us to contemplate!

Early next morning I secured a Staff car and proceeded up to the front to find the spot where lay the last remains of my dear friend. We reached Montfaucon and turned northwest around the edge of the Argonne Forest, passing on the way the wreckage of my red-nosed Fokker just outside the town of Exermont. Arrived to within a mile of our front line, sheltered all along the road by hanging curtains of burlap and moss, part of which had been left by the Huns and partly our own concoction of camouflage, we were halted by an officer who told me we could move no further without coming under shell fire from the enemy guns.

Abandoning the car at the roadside, we skirted the edge of woods that adjoined the road and made our way on foot to the flat lands just across the Aire River from the opposite town of Grand Pré. And here in the bend of the Aire, almost in full sight of the enemy, we came upon the body of Captain Coolidge. A lieutenant in infantry who had seen the whole spectacle and had marked down the spot where Ham's body had fallen, accompanied us and it was through his very kind offices that we reached the exact spot without much searching. The Chaplain of his regiment likewise accompanied us. And there, not sixty yards behind our front lines, we watched the men dig a grave. The Chaplain administered the last sad rites. Amid the continuous whines of passing shells we laid the poor mangled body of Captain Hamilton Coolidge in its last resting place. Over the grave was placed a Cross suitably engraved with his name, rank and the date of his tragic death. A wreath of flowers was laid at the foot of the cross. Then with uncovered head I took a photograph of the grave, which later was sent "back home" to the family who mourned for one of the most gallant gentlemen who ever fought in France.

CHAPTER XXXV

THE END DRAWS NEAR

OCTOBER was a month of glorious successes for 94 Squadron, having brought us thirty-nine victories with but five losses. For, besides Captain Coolidge and Lieutenant Nutt the Squadron had lost Lieutenant Saunders of Billings, Montana, shot down on the 22nd, when out after balloons with Cook and Jeffers. Cook on this occasion succeeded in setting fire to the balloon he was attacking, and Jeffers turning upon the Fokker which had just sunk Saunders, shot him down in flames sixty seconds later.

On the 29th, Lieutenant Garnsey of Grand Haven, Michigan, fell in our lines near Exermont, after having fought a brilliant combat against greatly superior numbers. Reed Chambers, after bringing down an enemy machine on the 22nd, which he attacked at the tail of a Fokker formation containing five aeroplanes, returned to the aerodrome in considerable pain from a sudden seizure of appendicitis and next day was sent to the hospital, where he had the appendix removed.

The Squadron had developed eight aces, including

Lufbery, Campbell, Coolidge, Meissner and Chambers, all of whom were now absent, and Cook, Taylor and myself, who were left to carry on to the end of the war. Meissner was absent only in the sense that he was now in command of the 147th Squadron and his victories were going to swell the score for his newly adopted squadron instead of our own.

Many others were "going strong" at the end of October and needed but the opportunity to fight their way up into the leading scores of the group. Rain and dud weather kept us on the ground much of the time and when we did get away for brief patrols we found the enemy machines were even more particular about flying in bad weather than we were. None put in an appearance and we were forced to return empty-handed so far as fighting laurels were concerned.

Our first Night Flying Squadron had been formed early in October, under command of Captain Seth Low of New York, and had its hangars on our Group aerodrome. This was not a Squadron of bomb-carrying aeroplanes, but one with which to attack bombing machines of the enemy and prevent their reaching their intended targets over our lines. The night-flying aeroplanes were the English Sopwith Camels, a light single-seater capable of extraordinary evolutions in the air and able to land upon the ground in the darkness at a very low speed. The British had inaugurated this special defense against the Hun bombers in their raids upon London. Later the same system was tried at the British front with such success that over a score of German bombers were brought down in a single month by one Squadron of Night Flying Camels.

Of course such a defense must have the cooperation, both of signaling and listening squads, to notify the Night Flyers as to just when and where an attack is threatened, and also the timely cooperation of the

Searchlight squads is essential to enable the airmen to pick up the enemy machines in the darkness while at the same time blinding with the glare the eyes of the Hun pilots. Principally by reason of the lack of this cooperation our Camel Squadron, though it made several sorties along the lines during the month of October did not meet any enemy bombers and had no combats. Time and study of this problem would doubtless have made of the Squadron 185 a valuable defense to our sector of the front, including the cities of Nancy, Toul and Columbey-les-Belles, which were repeatedly visited at night by German Gothas.

Bombs were getting heavier and more destructive. More and more machines were being devoted to this branch of aviation. But now instead of the Germans monopolizing this terror-spreading game the tables were turned and the Allies dropped ten times the amount of bombs into German cities. Even the oldest residents were moving out of the beautiful cities of the Rhine.

On the next to the last day of October I won my 25th and 26th victories, which were the last that I was to see added to my score. Two others that I had previously brought down were never confirmed. After the deplorable death of Frank Luke, who had won eighteen victories in less than six weeks of active flying at the front, there were no other American air-fighters who were rivaling me in my number of victories. But ever since I had been Captain of the 94th Squadron the spur of rivalry had been entirely supplanted in me by the necessity of illustrating to the pilots under my orders that I would ask them to do nothing that I myself would not do. So covetously did I guard this understanding with myself that I took my machine out frequently after the day's patrol was finished and spent another hour or two over the lines. The obligations that must attend leadership were a constant thought to me. Greater confidence in my leadership was given me when I noticed that my pilots appreciated my activity and my reasons for it. Never did I permit any pilot in my squadron to exceed the number of hours flying over the lines that was credited to me in the flight sheets. At the close of the war only Reed Chambers' record approached my own in number of hours spent in the air.

I allude to this fact because I am convinced after my six weeks' experience as Squadron Commander that my obedience to this principle did much to account for the wholehearted and enthusiastic support the pilots of my Squadron gave me. And only by their loyalty and enthusiasm was their Squadron to lead all the others at the front in number of victories and number of hours over enemy's lines.

With Reed Chambers' forced absence at the hospital the leadership of our First Flight was put in charge of Lieutenant Kaye. On October 30th I had been out on two patrols in the forenoon, both of which had been without unusual incident or result. When Kaye left the field with his Flight at three o'clock in the afternoon I decided to accompany him to observe his tactics as Flight Leader. This formation, composed of only four machines, two of which were piloted by new men, was to fly at only 2,000 feet elevation and was to patrol to enemy's lines between Grand Pré and Brieulles. I took my place considerably in their rear and perhaps 1,000 feet above them. In this position we reached Brieulles and made two round trips with them between our two towns without discovering any hostile aeroplanes.

As we turned west for the third trip, however, I noticed two lone Fokkers coming out of Germany at a low elevation. From their maneuvers I decided that they were stalking Lieutenant Kaye's Flight and were only waiting until they had placed themselves in a favorable position before beginning their attack. I accordingly turned my own machine away into Germany to get behind them, still keeping my altitude and trusting that they would be too intent on the larger quarry to notice me.

I had hardly begun to turn back when I saw that they had set their machines in motion for their attack. Opening up myself I put down my nose and tried to overtake them, but they had too great a start. I saw that Kaye had not seen them and in spite of the odds in our favor I feared for the two new men, who were at the end of the formation and who must assuredly bear the first diving assault of the Fokkers. Fortunately, Kaye saw them coming before they had reached firing range and he immediately turned his formation south in the direction of home. " Cook is with Kaye and those two will be able to defend the two youngsters if the Fokkers really get to close quarters," I thought to myself. I could not hope to overtake them myself, anyway, if they continued back into France. So, after a little reflection I stayed where I was, witnessing a daring attempt of the Fokkers to break up Kaye's Formation which, nevertheless, was unsuccessful. Both Fokkers attacked the rear Spad, which was piloted by Lieutenant Evitt, one of our new men. Instead of trying to maneuver them off he continued to fly straight ahead, affording them every opportunity in the world of correcting their aim and getting their bullets home. Evitt discovered upon landing that one of his right struts was severed by their bullets!

After this one attack the Fokkers turned back. I was in the meantime flying deeper into Germany, keeping one eye upon the two enemy machines to discover in which direction they would cross the lines to reach their own side. They seemed in no hurry to get back, but continued westward, heading towards Grand Pré.

Very well! This suited me perfectly. I would make a great detour, coming back out of Germany immediately over Grand Pré with the hope that if they saw me they might believe me one of their own until we got to close quarters.

But before I reached Grand Pré I noticed them coming towards me. I was then almost over the town of Emecourt and quite a little distance within their lines. They were very low, and not more than a thousand feet above ground at most. I was quite twice this heighth. Like lambs to the slaughter they came unsuspectingly on not half a mile to the east of me. Letting them pass I immediately dipped over, swung around as I fell and opening up my motor piqued with all speed on the tail of the nearest Fokker. With less than twenty rounds, all of which poured full into the center of the fusilage, I ceased firing and watched the Fokker drop helplessly to earth. As it began to revolve slowly I noticed for the first time that again I had outwitted a member of the von Richthofen crowd. The dying Fokker wore an especially brilliant nosepiece of bright red!

As my first tracer bullets began to streak past the Fokker his companion put down his nose and dived for the ground. As he was well within his own territory I did not venture to follow him at this low altitude, but at once began climbing to avoid the coming storm of Archy and machine-gun fire. Little or none of this came my way, however, and I continued homeward, passing en route over the little village of St. George, which was then about two miles inside the enemy lines. And there directly under my right wing lay in its bed a German observation balloon just at the edge of the village. On a sudden impulse I kicked over my rudder, pointed my nose at the huge target and pulled the triggers. Both guns worked perfectly. I continued my sloping dive to within a hundred feet of the sleeping Drachen, firing up and down its whole length by slightly shifting the course of my aeroplane. Not a human being was in sight! Evidently the Huns thought they were quite safe in this spot, since this balloon had not yet been run up and its location could not be known to our side. I zoomed up and climbed a few hundred feet for another attack if it should be necessary. But as I balanced my machine and looked behind me I saw the fire take effect. These flaming bullets sometimes require a long time to ignite the balloon fabric. Doubtless they travel too fast to ignite the pure gas, unmixed with air.

The towering flames soon lit up the sky with a vivid glare and keeping it behind me, I speeded homeward, with many self-satisfied chuckles at my good fortune. But too much self-satisfaction always receives a jolt. I had not gone ten miles before I received the worst kind of a scare.

It had become quite dark and I was very near to the ground. Still some distance inside the German lines, for I had kept east in the hope that another Hun balloon might be left for my last rounds of ammunition, I thought of looking at my watch to see how late it really was. I had fuel for only two hours and ten minutes. A vague sort of premonition warned me that I had been overlooking something of importance in the past few minutes. One glance at my watch and I realized exactly what had been weighing in the back of my mind. The time indicated that I had now been out exactly two hours and ten minutes.

A real terror seized me for a moment. I was not up far enough above earth to glide for any distance when my motor stopped. Even as I banked over and turned southward I wondered whether my motor would gasp and expire in the turning. I feared to climb and I feared to stay low. I gazed over the sides of my office and tried to make out the nature of the landing ground below. Throttling down to the slowest possible speed to save fuel I crept towards the lines. It was dark enough to see that suspicious Heinies below were shooting at me on the chance that I might be an enemy. Glad I was to see those flashes receding farther and farther to my rear. I had passed the lines somewhere west of Verdun and now must chance any open field I came to when the engine gave its last cough. Why didn't it stop? I wondered. It was now five or six minutes overdue. In miserable anticipation of the lot Fate had in store for me I struggled on, noting with additional gloom that the searchlight that should long ago be pointing out the way to my aerodrome had not been lighted. I could not be more than ten miles from home. Why couldn't those men attend to their business when pilots were known to be out? I took out my Very pistol and fitted in a red light. That would notify them at home that I was in trouble and in a hurry to land.

Just as I fired the second Very light I heard the motor begin its final sputtering. And then just as I felt cold chills running up my back the blessed landing lights flashed out and I saw I was almost over the field. Forgetting all my recent joy I made myself as wretched as possible the following few seconds in concluding that I could not by any possibility reach the smooth field. It seemed to work — the treatment. I had expatiated my sins of over-confidence and appeased the Goddess of Luck, for I cleared the road, landed with the wind and struck the ground with a quiet thud less than a hundred feet from the entrance to 94's hangar — right side up! But I walked over to mess with a chastened spirit.

The following morning was rainy and all the afternoon it continued to pour. Just before dusk we received orders to have our whole force over the lines at daybreak to protect an infantry advance from

Grand Pré to Buzancy. We all felt that we were to witness the last great attack of the war. And we were right.

A heavy fog of the genuine Meuse Valley variety prevented our planes leaving the ground until the middle of the forenoon. All the morning we heard the tremendous artillery duel at the north of us and very impatiently waited for a clearing of the weather. That dull morning was somewhat relieved by our receipt of newspapers stating that Turkey had surrendered unconditionally and that Austria was expected to follow suit the following day. Placing about a hundred of these journals in my plane, I set out for the lines with our patrol at 9.30 o'clock.

Arrived over the front lines near the town of Lapelle, I flew at an altitude of only a hundred feet from the ground. And there I saw our doughboys after their victorious advance of the morning crouching in every available shell-hole and lying several deep in every depression while looking forward for a snipe shot at any enemy's head that came into view. Others were posted behind woods and buildings with bayonets fixed, waiting for the word to go forward. As I passed overhead I threw overboard handfuls of morning papers to them and was amused to see how eagerly the doughboys ran out of their holes to pick them up. With utter disdain for the nearby Hun snipers, they exposed themselves gladly for the opportunity of getting the latest news from an aeroplane. I knew the news they would get would repay them for the momentary risk they ran.

Dropping half my load there I flew on over the Mozelle valley where I distributed the remainder of the papers among the men in the front line trenches along that sector. Returning then to the region of Buzancy I first caught sight of a huge supply depot burning. A closer view disclosed the fact that it was

German and German soldiers were still on the premises. They were destroying materials that they knew they would be unable to save. In other words they were contemplating a fast retreat.

A few dashes up and down the highways leading to the north quickly confirmed this impression. Every road was filled with lorries and retreating artillery. All were hurrying towards Longuyon and the German border.

All the way up the Meuse as far as Stenay I found the same mad rush for the rear. Every road was filled with retreating Heinies. They were going while the " going was good " and their very gestures seemed to indicate that for them it was indeed the " *finis de la guerre.*" I hurried home to make my report which I felt certain would be welcome to those in authority.

The following day I obtained permission to visit Paris on a three days' leave. For the first time since I had been in France I found the streets of Paris illuminated at night and gaiety unrestrained possessing the boulevards and cafés. With the Place de la Concord and the Champs Elysées crammed with captured German guns and German aeroplanes, with flags and bunting astream everywhere it looked here too that people thought it was the " *finis de la guerre.*" I am told that Paris did not go raving mad until that unforgettable night of the signing of the Armistice; but from the street scenes I saw there during those first days of November while the Huns were in full retreat from the soil of France that had so long been polluted by their feet it is difficult to imagine how any people could express greater happiness.

Personally I am glad that I was with my Squadron instead of in Paris on the night the war ended. For great as were the sights there, none of them could have expressed to an aviator such a view of the sentiment and feeling of aviation over the termination of this game of killing as was exhibited at our own aerodrome on the night the official order " Cease Firing! " came to us.

CHAPTER XXXVI

LAST VICTORY OF THE GREAT WAR

RETURNING from Paris on November 5th I found it still raining.   Almost no flying had been possible along this sector since my departure.   In fact no patrol left our field until November 8th, the same day on which we caught by wireless the information that the Boche delegates had crossed the lines between Haudry and Cheme on the La Chapelle road to sign the armistice.   Peace then was actually in sight.

For weeks there had been a feeling in the air that the end of the war was near.   To the aviators who had been flying over the lines and who had with their own eyes seen the continuous withdrawals of the Germans to the rear there was no doubt but that the Huns had lost their immoderate love for fighting and were sneaking homewards as fast as their legs would carry them.   Such a certainty of victory should have operated to produce a desire to live and let live among men who were desirous of " seeing the end of the war," that is, men who preferred to survive rather than run the risks of combat fighting now that the war was fairly over.

But it was at this very period of my leadership of the 94th Squadron that I found my pilots most infatuated with fighting.   They importuned me for permission to go out at times when a single glance at the fog and rain showed the foolishness of such a request. Not content with the collapse of the enemy forces the pilots wanted to humiliate them further with flights deep within their country where they might strafe aeroplane hangars and retreating troops for the last time. It must be done at once, they feared, or it would be too late.

On the 9th of November Lieutenant Dewitt and Captain Fauntleroy came to me after lunch and begged me to go to the door of my hut and look at the weather with them. I laughed at them but did as they requested. It was dark and windy outside, heavy low clouds driving across the sky, though for the moment no rain was falling. I took a good look around the heavens and came back to my room, the two officers following me. Here they cornered me and talked volubly for ten minutes, urging my permission to let them go over the lines and attack one last balloon which they had heard was still swinging back of the Meuse. They overcame every objection of mine with such earnestness that finally against my best judgment I acquiesced and permitted them to go. At this moment Major Kirby who had just joined 94 Squadron for a little experience in air fighting before taking command of a new group of Squadrons that was being formed, and who as yet had never flown over the lines stepped into the room and requested permission to join Dewitt and Fauntleroy in their expedition. Lieutenant Cook would go along with him, he said, and they would hunt in pairs. If they didn't take this opportunity the war might end overnight and he would never have had a whack at an enemy plane.

Full of misgivings at my own weakness I walked out to the field and watched the four pilots get away. I noted the time on my watch, noted that a heavy wind was blowing them away and would increase their difficulties in returning, blamed myself exceedingly that I had permitted them to influence me against my judgment. The next two hours were miserable ones for me.

The weather grew steadily worse, rain fell and the

wind grew stronger. When darkness fell, shortly after four o'clock, I ordered all the lights turned on the field and taking my seat at the mouth of our hangar I anxiously waited for a glimpse of the homecoming Spads. It was nearing the limit of their fuel supply and another ten minutes must either bring some word from them or I should know that by my orders four pilots had sacrificed themselves needlessly after hostilities had practically ceased. I believe that hour was the worst one I have ever endured.

Night fell and no aeroplanes appeared. The searchlights continued to throw their long fingers into the clouds, pointing the way home to any wandering scouts who might be lost in the storm. Foolish as it was to longer expect them I could not order the lights extinguished and they shone on all through the night.

The next day was Sunday and another Decorations Ceremony was scheduled to take place at our field at eleven o'clock. A number of pilots from other aerodromes were coming over to receive the Distinguished Service Cross from the hands of General Liggett for bravery and heroic exploits over enemy's lines. Several of our own Group, including myself were to be among the recipients.

The band played, generals addressed us and all the men stood at attention in front of our line of fighting planes while the dignified ceremony was performed. Two more palms were presented to me to be attached to my decoration. The Army Orders were read aloud praising me for shooting down enemy aeroplanes. How bitter such compliments were to me that morning nobody ever suspected. Not a word had come from any one of my four pilots that I had sent over the lines the day before. No explanation but one was possible. All four had been forced to descend in enemy territory — crashed, killed or captured — it little mattered so far as my culpability was concerned.

In fact a message had come in the night before that a Spad had collided in air with a French two-seater near Beaumont late that afternoon. A hurried investigation by telephone disclosed the fact that no other Spads were missing but our own — thus filling me with woful conjectures as to which one of my four pilots had thus been killed in our own lines.

At the conclusion of the presentation of decorations I walked back to the hangar and put on my coat, for it was a freezing day and we had been forced to stand for half an hour without movement in dress tunic and breeches. The field was so thick with fog that the photographers present could scarcely get light enough to snap the group of officers standing in line. No aeroplanes could possibly be out to-day or I should have flown over to Beaumont at daybreak to ascertain which of my pilots had been killed there.

I was invited to mess with 95 Squadron that noon and I fear I did not make a merry guest. The compliments I received for my newly received decorations fell on deaf ears. As soon as I decently could get away I made my adieus and walked back across the aerodrome. And about half-way across I saw an aeroplane standing in the center of the field. I looked at it idly, wondering what idiot had tried to get away in such a fog. Suddenly I stopped dead in my tracks. The Spad had a Hat-in-the-Ring painted on its fusilage — and a large number " 3 " was painted just beyond it. Number " 3 " was Fauntleroy's machine!

I fairly ran the rest of the way to my hangar where I demanded of the mechanics what news they had heard about Captain Fauntleroy. I was informed that he had just landed and had reported that Lieutenant Dewitt had crashed last night inside our lines but would be back during the course of the day. And to cap this joyful climax to a day's misery I was told five minutes later at Group Headquarters that Major

Kirby had just telep'honed in that he had shot down an enemy aeroplane across the Meuse this morning at ten o'clock, after which he had landed at an aerodrome near the front and would return to us when the fog lifted!

It was a wild afternoon we had at 94 mess upon receipt of this wonderful news. Cookie too was later heard from, he having experienced a rather more serious catastrophe the previous afternoon. He had attacked an observation balloon near Beaumont. The Hun defenses shot off one blade of his propeller and he had barely made his way back across the lines when he was compelled to land in the shell-holes which covered this area. He escaped on foot to the nearest American trench and late Sunday afternoon reached our mess.

Major Kirby's victory was quickly confirmed, later inquiries disclosing the wonderful fact that this first remarkable victory of his was in truth the last aeroplane shot down in the Great War! Our old 94 Squadron had won the first American victory over enemy aeroplanes when Alan Winslow and Douglas Campbell had dropped two biplane machines on the Toul aerodrome. 94 Squadron had been first to fly over the lines and had completed more hours flying at the front than any other American organization. It had won more victories than any other — and now, for the last word, it had the credit of bringing down the last enemy aeroplane of the war! One can imagine the celebration with which 94 Squadron would signalize the end of the war! What could Paris or any other community in the whole world offer in comparison?

And the celebration came even before we had lost the zest of our present gratitude and emotion.

The story of Major Kirby's sensational victory can be told in a paragraph. He had become lost the night before and had landed on the first field he saw. Not realizing the importance of telephoning us of his safety, he took off early next morning to come home. This time he got lost in the fog which surrounded our district. When he again emerged into clear air he found he was over Etain, a small town just north of Verdun. And there flying almost alongside of his Spad was another aeroplane which a second glance informed him was an enemy Fokker! Both pilots were so surprised for a moment that they simply gazed at each other. The Fokker pilot recovered his senses first and began a dive towards earth. Major Kirby immediately piqued on his tail, followed him down to within fifty feet of the ground firing all the way. The Fokker crashed head on, and Kirby zoomed up just in time to avoid the same fate. With his usual modesty Major Kirby insisted he had scared the pilot to his death. Thus ended the War in the Air on the American front.

While listening to these details that evening after mess, our spirits bubbling over with excitement and happiness, the telephone sounded and I stepped over and took it up, waving the room to silence. It was a message to bring my husky braves over across to the 95 Mess to celebrate the beginning of a new era. I demanded of the speaker, (it was Jack Mitchell, Captain of the 95th) what he was talking about.

" Peace has been declared! No more fighting! " he shouted. " C'est le finis de la Guerre."

Without reply I dropped the phone and turned around and faced the pilots of 94 Squadron. Not a sound was heard, every eye was upon me but no one made a movement or drew a breath. It was one of those peculiar psychological moments when instinct tells every one that something big is impending.

In the midst of this uncanny silence a sudden BOOM-BOOM of our Arch battery outside was heard. And then pandemonium broke loose. Shouting like mad, tumbling over one another in their excitement the daring pilots of the Hat-in-the-Ring

Squadron sensing the truth darted into trunks and kitbags, drew out revolvers, German Lugers, that some of them had found or bought as souvenirs from French poilus, Very pistols and shooting tools of all descriptions and burst out of doors. There the sky over our old aerodrome and indeed in every direction of the compass was aglow and shivering with bursts of fire. Searchlights were madly cavorting across the heavens, paling to dimness the thousands of colored lights that shot up from every conceivable direction. Shrill yells pierced the darkness around us, punctuated with the fierce rat-tat-tat-tat-tat of a score of machine-guns which now added their noise to the clamor. Roars of laughter and hysterical whoopings came to us from the men's quarters beside the hangars. Pistol shots were fired in salvos, filled and emptied again and again until the weapon became too hot to hold.

At the corner of our hangar I encountered a group of my pilots rolling out tanks of gasoline. Instead of attempting the impossible task of trying to stop them I helped them get it through the mud and struck the match myself and lighted it. A dancing ring of crazy lunatics joined hands and circled around the blazing pyre, similar howling and revolving circuses surrounding several other burning tanks of good United States gasoline that would never more carry fighting aeroplanes over enemy's lines. The stars were shining brightly overhead and the day's mist was gone. But at times even the stars were hidden by the thousands of rockets that darted up over our heads and exploded with their soft 'plonks, releasing varicolored lights which floated softly through this epochal night until they withered away and died. Star shells, parachute flares, and streams of Very lights continued to light our way through an aerodrome seemingly thronged with madmen. Everybody was laughing — drunk with the outgushing of their long pent-up emotions.

"*I've lived through the war!*" I heard one whirling Dervish of a pilot shouting to himself as he pirouetted alone in the center of a mud hole. Regardless of who heard the inmost secret of his soul, now that the war was over, he had retired off to one side to repeat this fact over and over to himself until he might make himself sure of its truth.

Another pilot, this one an Ace of 27 Squadron, grasped me securely by the arm and shouted almost incredulously, "*We won't be shot at any more!*" Without waiting for a reply he hastened on to another friend and repeated this important bit of information as though he were doubtful of a complete understanding on this trivial point. What sort of a new world will this be without the excitement of danger in it? How queer it will be in future to fly over the dead line of the silent Meuse — that significant boundary line that was marked by Arch shells to warn the pilot of his entrance into danger.

How can one enjoy life without this highly spiced sauce of danger? What else is there left to living now that the zest and excitement of fighting aeroplanes is gone? Thoughts such as these held me entranced for the moment and were afterwards recalled to illustrate how tightly strung were the nerves of these boys of twenty who had for continuous months been living on the very peaks of mental excitement.

In the mess hall of Mitchell's Squadron we found gathered the entire officer personnel of the Group. Orderlies were running back and forth with cups brimming with a hastily concocted punch, with which to drink to the success and personal appearance of every pilot in aviation. Songs were bellowed forth accompanied by crashing sounds from the Boche piano — the proudest of 95's souvenirs, selected from an officer's mess of an abandoned German camp. Chairs and benches were pushed back to the walls and soon the whole roomful was dancing, struggling and whooping for joy, to the imminent peril of the rather temporary walls and floor. Some unfortunate pilot fell and in a trice everybody in the room was forming a pyramid on top of him. The appearance of the C. O. of the Group brought the living mass to its feet in a score of rousing cheers to the best C. O. in France. Major Hartney was hoisted upon the piano, while a hundred voices shouted, " SPEECH — SPEECH ! " No sooner did he open his lips than a whirlwind of sound from outside made him pause and reduced the room to quiet. But only for an instant.

" It's the Jazz Band from old 147 ! " yelled the pilots and like a tumultuous waterfall they poured *en masse* through a doorway that was only wide enough for one at a time.

Whooping, shrieking and singing, the victors of some 400-odd combats with enemy airmen encircled the musicians from the enlisted men of 147 Squadron. The clinging clay mud of France lay ankle deep around them. Within a minute the dancing throng had with their hopping and skipping plowed it into an almost bottomless bog. Some one went down, dragging down with him the portly bass drummer. Upon this foundation human forms in the spotless uniforms of the American Air Service piled themselves until the entire Group lay prostrate in one huge pyramid of joyous aviators. It was later bitterly disputed as to who was and who was not at the very bottom of this historic monument erected that night under the starry skies of France to celebrate the extraordinary fact that we had lived through the war and were not to be shot at to-morrow.

It was the " *finis de la Guerre!* " It was the *finis d'aviation*. It was to us, perhaps unconsciously, the end of that intimate relationship that since the beginning of the war had cemented together brothers-in-arms into a closer fraternity than is known to any other friendship in the whole world. When again will that pyramid of entwined comrades — interlacing together in one mass boys from every State in our Union — when again will it be formed and bound together in mutual devotion?

THE END

OFFICIAL VICTORIES OF THE 94TH AERO SQUADRON

Date	Type of Plane	Region	Time	Alti-tude	Pilot	Confirmed by	Date
4-29-18	Albatros monoplace	Baussant	18 h 10'	2000 m.	Lieut. Rickenbacker Capt. Hall	French 8th Army	5- 3-18
5-17-18	Albatros	Richecourt	6 h 24'	4500 m.	Lieut. Rickenbacker	French 8th Army	5-27-18
5-22-18	Albatros monoplace	Flirey	9 h 12'	4500 m.	Lieut. Rickenbacker	French 8th Army	5-22-18
5-28-18	Albatros biplace	Bois Raté	9 h 35'	2500 m.	Lieut. Rickenbacker	French 8th Army	5-28-18
5-30-18	Albatros biplace	Jaulny	7 h 38'	4000 m.	Lieut. Rickenbacker	French 8th Army	5-30-18
9-14-18	Fokker	Villey Waville	8 h 15'	3000 m.	Lieut. Rickenbacker	G. O. No. 8	9-22-18
9-15-18	Fokker	Bois de War-ville					
9-25-18	Fokker	Billy	8 h 10'	4000 m.	Lieut. Rickenbacker	G. O. No. 6	9-17-18
9-25-18	Halberstadt	Forêt de Spin-court	8 h 40'	3000 m.	Lieut. Rickenbacker	G. O. No. 26	11-15-18
9-26-18	Fokker	Damvillers	8 h 50'	2000 m.	Lieut. Rickenbacker	G. O. No. 10	9-27-18
9-28-18	Balloon	Sivry-sur-Meuse	6 h 00'	1500 m.	Lieut. Rickenbacker	G. O. No. 10	9-27-18
10- 1-18	Balloon	Puxieux	6 h 00'	100 m.	Lieut. Rickenbacker	G. O. No. 12	9-30-18
10- 2-18	Fokker	Vilosnes	19 h 30'	On Ground	Capt. Rickenbacker	G. O. No. 14	10- 8-18
10- 2-18	Halberstadt	Montfaucon	17 h 40'	1000 m.	Capt. Rickenbacker	G. O. No. 14	10- 8-18
10- 3-18	L. V. G.	Danneveux	17 h 30'	600 m.	Capt. Rickenbacker Lieut. Chambers	G. O. No. 14	10- 8-18
10- 3-18	Rumpler	Cléry-le-Grand	17 h 07'	600 m.	Capt. Rickenbacker Lieut. Coolidge	G. O. No. 14	10- 8-18
10- 9-18	Balloon	Dun-sur-Meuse	16 h 40'	500 m.	Capt. Rickenbacker	G. O. No. 14	10- 8-18
10-10-18	Fokker	Cléry-le-Petit	17 h 52'	On Ground	Capt. Rickenbacker	G. O. No. 22	11- 2-18
10-10-18	Fokker	Cléry-le-Petit	15 h 52'	800 m.	Capt. Rickenbacker	G. O. No. 20	10-23-18
10-22-18	Fokker	Cléry-le-Petit	15 h 52'	600 m.	Capt. Rickenbacker	G. O. No. 21	10-27-18
			15 h 55'	1200 m.	Capt. Rickenbacker	G. O. No. 21	10-27-18

OFFICIAL VICTORIES OF THE 94TH AERO SQUADRON — *Continued*

Date	Type of Plane	Region	Time	Altitude	Pilot	Confirmed by	Date
10-23-18	Fokker	Petit-le-Grand	17 h 05'	600 m.	Capt. Rickenbacker	G. O. No. 21	10-27-18
10-27-18	Fokker	Carré Ferme Grand Pré	14 h 50'	2000 m.	Capt. Rickenbacker	G. O. No. 22	11- 2-18
10-27-18	Fokker	Bois-de-Money	15 h 05'	On Ground	Capt. Rickenbacker	G. O. No. 22	11- 2-18
10-30-18	Balloon	Remonville	16 h 40'	3000 m.	Capt. Rickenbacker	G. O. No. 22	11- 2-18
10-30-18	Fokker	St. Juvin	16 h 35'	200 m.	Capt. Rickenbacker	G. O. No. 22	11- 2-18
7- 7-18	Rumpler biplace	Bennes	9 h 50'	5000 m.	Lieut. Coolidge / Lieut. Garnsey	6th French Army	7-20-18
10- 2-18	Halberstadt	Bois-la-Ville	18 h 15'	60 m.	Lieut. Coolidge	G. O. No. 17	10-19-18
10- 3-18	Balloon	Cléry-le-Grand	16 h 37'	400 m.	Lieut. Coolidge	G. O. No. 14	10- 8-18
10- 3-18	Fokker	Dun-sur-Meuse	16 h 39'	200 m.	Lieut. Coolidge	G. O. No. 14	10- 8-18
10- 6-18	Balloon	St. Juvin	10 h 50'	600 m.	Lieut. Coolidge	G. O. No. 14	10- 8-18
10-10-18	Fokker	Doulcon	15 h 51'	600 m.	Lieut. Palmer	G. O. No. 20	10-23-18
10-13-18	Balloon	Andevanne	16 h 07'	400 m.	Capt. Coolidge	G. O. No. 20	10-23-18
9-26-19	Balloon	Nantillois	5 h 52'	800 m.	Lieut. Chambers	G. O. No. 17	10-19-18
9-29-18	Fokker	Cunel	17 h 20'	1700 m.	Lieut. Chambers / Lieut. Kaye	G. O. No. 13	10- 2-18
10- 2-18	Fokker	Vilosnes	17 h 40'	1000 m.	Lieut. Chambers	G. O. No. 14	10- 8-18
10-10-18	Fokker	Doulcon	15 h 48'	150 m.	Lieut. Chambers	G. O. No. 20	10-23-18
10-22-18	Two (2) Fokkers	Vilosnes-Bois-de-la-Côte Le-mont	16 h 00'	300 m.	Lieut. Chambers	G. O. No. 22	11- 2-18
8- 1-18	Enemy Plane	Bois-de-Dôle	10 h 05'	3000 m.	Lieut. Cook / Lieut. Cates	The French Army Oper. Order #73	8-11-18
9-26-18	Balloon	Grand-Ham	18 h 45'	75 m.	Lieut. Cook	G. O. No. 12	9-30-18
10- 3-18	Balloon	Grandpré	16 h 15'	On Ground	Lieut. Cook	G. O. No. 14	10- 8-18

OFFICIAL VICTORIES OF THE 94TH AERO SQUADRON — Continued

Date	Type of Plane	Region	Time	Altitude	Pilot	Confirmed by	Date
9-28-18	Balloon	Cléry-le-Petit	6 h 06'	On Ground	Lieut. Cook	G. O. No. 12	9-30-18
10-18-18	Halberstadt	Exermont	15 h 35'	800 m.	Lieut. Cook	G. O. No. 21	10-27-18
					Lieut. Kaye, Jr.	G. O. No. 21	10-27-18
					Lieut. Sherry	G. O. No. 23	11- 5-18
10-22-18	Balloon	Tially	5 h 55'	200 m.	Lieut. Cook	G. O. No. 21	
10-30-18	L. V. C.	Romagne	8 h 30'	800 m.	Lieut. Cook	G. O. No. 23	
4-14-18	Pfalz D-3	Toul	8 h 45'	800 m.	Lieut. Campbell	French 8th Army	4-14-18
5-18-18	Enemy biplace	Bonzée-en-Woevre	9 h 20'	5200 m.	Lieut. Campbell	Direction de 18 Aeronautique	5-18-18
5-19-18	Enemy biplace	Flirey	11 h 35'	4500 m.	Lieut. Campbell	French 8th Army	5-19-18
5-27-18	Enemy monoplace	Montsec	10 h 00'	3000 m.	Lieut. Campbell	French 8th Army	6- 9-18
6-31-18	Enemy biplace	Lirenville	8 h 05'	2500 m.	Lieut. Campbell	French 8th Army	5-31-18
6- 5-18	Rumpler	Mailly	10 h 20'	5000 m.	Lieut. Campbell	G. O. No. 10	9-27-18
					Lieut. Meissner		
5- 2-18	Albatros monoplace	Forêt de La Rappe	12 h 03'	4800 m.	Lieut. Meissner	French 8th Army	5- 2-18
5-30-18	Enemy monoplace	Thiaucourt	8 h 55'	4500 m.	Lieut. Meissner	French 8th Army	5-30-18
6-13-18	Hannover biplace	St. Mihiel	8 h 00'	4500 m.	Lieut. Meissner	French 8th Army	6-13-18
					Lieut. Winslow		
					Lieut. Taylor		
10- 5-18	Fokker	Bantheville	17 h 10'	400 m.	Lieut. Kaye	G. O. No. 17	10-19-18
10-29-18	Fokker	Landres St.	8 h 52'	1000 m.	Lieut. Kaye	G. O. No. 22	11- 2-18
10- 3-18	Balloon	Georges Grand Pré	16 h 15'	On Ground	Lieut. Palmer	G. O. No. 14	10- 8-18
					Lieut. Sparks		
					Lieut. Taylor		
10-31-18	Halberstadt	Forêt de Boult	9 h 05'	150 m.	Lieut. Palmer	G. O. No. 24	11- 7-18

OFFICIAL VICTORIES OF THE 94TH AERO SQUADRON — *Continued*

DATE	TYPE OF PLANE	REGION	TIME	ALTI-TUDE	PILOT	CONFIRMED BY	DATE
5– 3–18	Enemy monoplace	Amenencourt	10 h 40'	3500 m.	Capt. McK. Peterson	French 8th Army	5– 9–18
5–15–18	Two (2) E. A.	Thiaucourt	12 h 05'	5200 m.	Capt. McK. Peterson	French 8th Army	5–27–18
10– 5–18	Fokker	Romagne	15 h 50'	1500 m.	Lieut. Jeffers	G. O. No. 17	19–19–18
10–22–18	Fokker	Brieulles	15 h 45'	600 m.	Lieut. Jeffers	G. O. No. 21	10–27–18
4–14–18	Albatros D-5	Toul	8 h 45'	800 m.	Lieut. Winslow	French 8th Army	4–14–16
7–31–18	Fokker	Oulchy-le-Château	19 h 45'	3000 m.	Lieut. Cates	French 6th Army	
9–26–18	Fokker	Drillancourt	18 h 00'	600 m.	Lieut. Nutt	G. O. No. 12	9–30–18
9–27–18	Fokker	Montfaucon	17 h 45'	600 m.	Lieut. Scroggie	G. O. No. 21	10–27–18
11– 8–18	Balloon	Olley	10 h 05'	50 m.	Lieut. DeWitt	G. O. No. 26	11–15–18
11–10–18	Fokker	Mauecourt	10 h 50'	50 m.	Major Kirby	G. O. No. 26	11–15–18

J. D. DAVITT,
2nd. Lieut., Air Service, U. S. A.,
Operations Officer.

366

INDEX

Library of Congress Cataloging-in-Publication Data

Rickenbacker, Eddie, 1890-1973
Fighting the flying circus / by Edward V. Rickenbacker ; with maps and
a foreword by Laurence La Tourette Driggs.
p. cm. —(Wings of war)
Reprint. Originally published: New York : F.A. Stokes Co., 1919.
ISBN 0-8094-7954-0.— ISBN 0-8094-7955-9 (lib. bdg.)
1. Rickenbacker, Eddie, 1890-1973. 2. World War, 1914-1918—Aerial
operations, American. 3. World War, 1914-1918—Personal narratives,
American. 4. Fighter pilots—United States—Biography. 5. United
States. Army Air Forces—Biography. I. Title. II. Series.
D606.R3 1989   940.4'4973'092—de20   89-20261 CIP